D0866907

LUX·ET·LEX
BENJAMIN FRANKLIN
JOHN MARSHALL
·LIBRARY·OF·
·FRANKLIN & MARSHALL·
·COLLEGE·

Child Discourse

LANGUAGE, THOUGHT, AND CULTURE: *Advances in the Study of Cognition*

Under the Editorship of: E. A. HAMMEL

DEPARTMENT OF ANTHROPOLOGY
UNIVERSITY OF CALIFORNIA
BERKELEY

Michael Agar, Ripping and Running: A Formal Ethnography of Urban Heroin Addicts

Brent Berlin, Dennis E. Breedlove, and Peter H. Raven, Principles of Tzeltal Plant Classification: An Introduction to the Botanical Ethnography of a Mayan-Speaking People of Highland Chiapas

Mary Sanches and Ben Blount, Sociocultural Dimensions of Language Use

Daniel G. Bobrow and Allan Collins, Representation and Understanding: Studies in Cognitive Science

Domenico Parisi and Francesco Antinucci, Essentials of Grammar

Elizabeth Bates, Language and Context: The Acquisition of Pragmatics

Ben G. Blount and Mary Sanches, Sociocultural Dimensions of Language Change

Susan Ervin-Tripp and Claudia Mitchell-Kernan (Eds.), Child Discourse

In preparation

Eugene S. Hunn, Tzeltal Folk Zoology: The Classification of Discontinuities in Nature

James N. Schenkein (Ed.), Studies in the Organization of Conversational Interaction

Child Discourse

edited by

Susan Ervin-Tripp

Department of Psychology
University of California, Berkeley
Berkeley, California

Claudia Mitchell-Kernan

Department of Anthropology
University of California, Los Angeles
Los Angeles, California

Academic Press, Inc. NEW YORK SAN FRANCISCO LONDON 1977

A Subsidiary of Harcourt Brace Jovanovich, Publishers

Academic Press Rapid Manuscript Reproduction

ACADEMIC PRESS, INC.
111 Fifth Avenue, New York, New York 10003

United Kingdom Edition published by
ACADEMIC PRESS, INC. (LONDON) LTD.
24/28 Oval Road, London NW1

Library of Congress Cataloging in Publication Data

Main entry under title:

Child discourse.

(Language, thought, and culture)
Papers based on a symposium held at the meeting of the American Anthropological Association in Mexico City, Nov. 1974.
Bibliography: p.
Includes index.
1. Children–Language–Congresses. 2. Oral communication–Congresses. I. Ervin-Tripp, Susan Moore, Date II. Mitchell-Kernan, Claudia. III. American Anthropological Association.
LB1139.L3C436 372.6 77-2878
ISBN 0–12–241950–2

PRINTED IN THE UNITED STATES OF AMERICA

This book is lovingly dedicated
to two language-sensitive women:

Claudia Whiting Mitchell Tatum (in memory)
Marian Moore Ervin Woodard

Contents

List of Contributors *ix*

Preface *xi*

Introduction 1
Susan Ervin-Tripp and Claudia Mitchell-Kernan

Part I Speech Events

Play with Language and Speech 27
Catherine Garvey

"You Fruithead": A Sociolinguistic Approach to Children's Dispute Settlement 49
Donald Brenneis and Laura Lein

From Verbal Play to Talk Story: The Role of Routines in Speech Events among Hawaiian Children 67
Karen Ann Watson-Gegeo and Stephen T. Boggs

Semantic and Expressive Elaboration in Children's Narratives 91
Keith T. Kernan

Situated Instructions: Language Socialization of School Age Children 103
Jenny Cook-Gumperz

Part II Function and Act

Making It Last: Repetition in Children's Discourse 125
Elinor Ochs Keenan

"Oh Them Sheriff": A Pragmatic Analysis of Children's Responses to Questions 139
John Dore

Wait for Me, Roller Skate! 165
Susan Ervin-Tripp

Pragmatics of Directive Choice among Children 189
Claudia Mitchell-Kernan and Keith T. Kernan

Part III Social Meaning

Comprehension and Use of Social Rules in Pronoun Selection by Hungarian Children 211
Marida Hollos

Acquisition of an Aspect of Communicative Competence: Learning What It Means to Talk Like a Lady 225
Carole Edelsky

Bibliography 245

Index 259

List of Contributors

Numbers in parentheses indicate the pages on which authors' contributions begin.

Stephen T. Boggs (67), Department of Anthropology, University of Hawaii, 2424 Maile Way, Honolulu, Hawaii 96822

Donald Brenneis (49), Department of Anthropology, Pitzer College, Claremont, California 91711

Jenny Cook-Gumperz (103), Language Behavior Research Laboratory, 2220 Piedmont Avenue, University of California, Berkeley, Berkeley, California 94720

John Dore (139), Department of Psychology, The Rockefeller University, 1230 York Avenue, New York, New York 10021

Carole Edelsky (225), School of Education, Arizona University, Tempe, Arizona 85281

Susan Ervin-Tripp (1, 165), Department of Psychology, University of California, Berkeley, Berkeley, California 94720

Catherine Garvey (27), Department of Psychology, The Johns Hopkins University, Baltimore, Maryland 21218

Marida Hollos (211), Department of Anthropology, Brown University, Providence, Rhode Island 02912

Elinor Ochs Keenan (125), Department of Linguistics, University of Southern California, Los Angeles, California 90007

Keith T. Kernan (91, 189), Department of Psychiatry, University of California, Los Angeles, Los Angeles, California 90024

Laura Lein (49), Center for the Study of Public Policy, 123 Mt. Auburn Street, Cambridge, Massachusetts 02138

Claudia Mitchell-Kernan (1, 189), Department of Anthropology, University of California, Los Angeles, Los Angeles, California 90024

Karen Ann Watson-Gegeo (67), Culture Learning Institute, East-West Center, Honolulu, Hawaii 96822

Preface

The editors of this collection organized a symposium on child discourse at the annual meeting of the American Anthropological Association in Mexico City in November 1974. The lively discussion of the interrelations of the papers led the participants to conclude that a new field had emerged, which could be stimulated by the publication of the papers. Three other papers, one presented by Edelsky at the same meeting, and two by Dore and Garvey, were added to broaden the scope of methods and issues considered.

Most of the contributors to this volume owe their interest in the ethnography of speaking, or their current conceptualization of approaches to child sociolinguistics, to Dell Hymes or John Gumperz, both professors at the University of California, who together published another symposium as a 1964 issue of the American Anthropologist, entitled "The Ethnography of Communication." This was a benchmark for a new field. In that same year, Hymes published his large, careful compendium of the major work that he considered relevant to the new field, "Language in Culture and Society."

In Berkeley, the joining of this new perspective to issues of linguistic socialization occurred first in an informal seminar in which Hymes, Gumperz, Ervin-Tripp, Dan Slobin, and the Kernans participated. Eventually, joined by Jan Brukman and Brian Stross, the group produced a "Field Manual for Cross-Cultural Studies in the Acquisition of Communicative Competence," edited by Slobin. In this manual the authors presented known data and the issues, and suggested methods for the study of both linguistic and sociolinguistic development cross-culturally. The methods for studying sociolinguistic skills were not yet developed, however. While the four dissertations directly generated by the manual did not take sociolinguistic development of children as central themes, later work was strongly affected.

Brenneis entered graduate school with an interest in adult sociolinguistics, particularly in the area of dispute discourse. He came under the influence of the Kernans while at Harvard and as a participant in a seminar of Mitchell-Kernan's collaborated with Lein in a study of children's arguments. Keenan was a student of Hymes at Pennsylvania, and under his influence, when she heard the interaction of her own twins, extended her structural approach to adult discourse to examine child speech. The other participants were interested in children from the beginning. Lein worked with the Kernans while at Harvard and her early research focused on the socialization of a group of children of migrant farm workers. Hollos was trained in Berkeley in anthropology and was working on comparative studies of cognitive development, in relation to language.

Boggs had been working on comparative child socialization studies, by collecting verbal interaction data, and Watson had already been studying children's narratives when she took a seminar with Gumperz before her collaboration with Boggs. Cook-Gumperz had begun her work as a sociologist as a student of Basil Bernstein, her dissertation being a part of his large project on social differences in children's language.

Three of the participants come from backgrounds quite different from the comparative and anthropological training shared by the above group. Garvey and Dore are linguists, both have studied children's interaction through systematic observational sessions, and both have been strongly affected by work on the philosophy and linguistics of speech act theory, although Garvey began her experimental studies of children's interaction about the time of the Berkeley cross-cultural projects. She was thus the first to examine children's interactional discourse structure in detail. Edelsky became interested in sociolinguistics while an education student.

We are grateful for support of this work by the Center for Advanced Study in the Behavioral Sciences in Palo Alto, the Guggenheim Foundation, and the Center for Afro-American Studies at UCLA. We also wish to thank Jean Tremaine and Eleanor Singleton who provided bibliographic assistance, Karen Larsen and Marolyn Morford who collaborated in the preparation of the index, and Laghretta Bell who provided many secretarial support services during the preparation of the manuscript.

Introduction

SUSAN ERVIN-TRIPP AND CLAUDIA MITCHELL-KERNAN

In recent years a number of special disciplines have developed within the social sciences whose aim has been to stretch the boundaries of linguistic inquiry to include the study of language in its sociocultural context. The development of the ethnography of communication (Hymes 1962, 1964[a]; Gumperz and Hymes 1964, 1972), sociolinguistics (Labov 1972[d]), and conversational analysis (Schegloff 1968; Sudnow 1972; Turner 1974) constitute the starting point for this volume. In sharp contrast to the mainstream of American linguistic and sociological thinking in the 1960s, the new work shares some central themes:

1. *Natural conversation as a data source.* Linguists studying exotic languages have recorded ritual or folktale sequences, or speech elicited in interviews. Some contemporary linguistic theorists have argued that knowledge (linguistic competence) can be better assessed by judgments of presented sentences as to grammaticality, acceptability, presuppositions, or invariance of meaning. But introspection as a method renders inaccessible the study of child language, informal styles, and vernaculars in contact with standard languages.

As the concerns of linguists have reached beyond questions of grammaticality to issues of conveyed intent and semantic nuance, the limitations of the interview and introspective methods have become more apparent. First, the properties of the interview situation itself shape judgments and tend to skew data toward the most self-conscious style. Second, it has become clear that speakers are incapable of reporting out of context those aspects of language which are variant according to social or situational context. When major contextual variables are left uncontrolled, these contexts must be supplied from memory or imagination. Typically, the result is a lack of unanimity across speakers as to the interpretation and grammaticality of utterances.

Interest in the study of natural conversation is thus both theoretically and methodologically motivated. But the use of natural conversation as a data source raises new problems. What activities should be sampled, what settings, what participant groups? How large must samples be? These are old problems in the social sciences but new to linguistics, and as usual, knowing which contextual features to control requires that one guess the outcome of research before beginning.

2. *Sentences not the highest level of analysis.* Linguistic analysis has taken the sentence as the normal analytic unit. Except for anaphora and replies, grammatical rules appeared to be sentence-bounded. Current work on discourse structure has suggested many other highly systematic levels, such as moves, turns, exchanges, stories, conversations, and speech events. Structural features such as code switches, paralinguistic cues, or lexical markers can indicate the boundaries of such units. A new goal is to identify variable linguistic features that are systematic and interpretable by virtue of the properties of such discourse units, including their location within these units. Sentences which are paraphrases in one location in discourse are not in another, so adequate interpretation rules will depend on the discovery of these discourse determinants.

3. *Social context as relevant to linguistic rules.* Both the interpretation of what is said and rules for choosing among options depend on features of the social context such as setting and activity, and features of the speaker, addressee, and audience. These features came to linguists' attention when they affected structural contrast sets in place deixis (*here/there, come/go, take/bring,* etc.), personal pronouns, and inflectional politeness markers. It is now apparent that even knowing whether to interpret an utterance as a question or a command depends on social features extraneous to the linguistic context, in quite regular ways (Ervin-Tripp 1976[a]).

4. *Variability as a component of linguistic rules.* No textbook on English reports the finding of linguists that a speaker should omit the final consonant more often in "next" than in "mixed," to sound like a native speaker. A learner spontaneously deletes consonants in casual more than in formal speech, and before consonants more than before vowels. Variability of this type, however, is a systematic part of both phonology and grammar and appears to be related not only to linguistic context but also to social features such as sex, age, and setting (Cedergren and Sankoff 1974; Labov 1972[d]). The study of situated speech in a range of speakers made variability apparent. Its acceptance as a normal property of language renders features considered to be in free variation accessible to rigorous treatment and makes gradual language change amenable to study.

5. *Language functions as diverse.* The models of language central to linguistic analysis have focused upon the representational use of language. Modalities were seen as modifications of assertions, and negation, passivization, and interrogation were all seen as versions of these assertions.

Imperatives are an embarrassment to this approach. In contrast, natural conversations reveal that language is diverse in function, and that functions are not directly mapped by any structural features. In recognition of this lack of direct mapping, some linguists have proposed another level of performatives underlying each utterance, linked by an additional set of realization rules (Ross 1970; Sadock 1974).

Although some language functions are universal, the social emphasis on, and sanctions for different language functions, appear to vary culturally and developmentally. Potential differences arise in the formal structures learned or invented to accomplish these functions. A good example is the shift chronicled by Sankoff and Laberge (1973) and Sankoff and Brown (1976) for Tok Pisin. As its functions enlarged and the range of communicative tasks increased, pidgin speakers added new forms such as subordination markers, which made processing of complex sentences easier. Similarly, their Creole-speaking children shifted optional lexical categories, such as time adverbs, to make obligatory suffixes. In deliberate language planning, governments create such language features which accommodate to social functions. Halliday (1975) has proposed that in a parallel way, in language acquisition, enlarging functions change formal features.[1] So, he believes, changes of form to meet new functions occur spontaneously as children learn language or societies alter the functions of language.

Sociolinguistic Rules

"Sociolinguistic" is a term that has been used both to refer to differences in the linguistic structures of socially defined groups, and to those rules of speech that incorporate contextual features rather than purely linguistic or referential choices. These definitions are not completely unrelated. The social meaning of alternations of features may depend on the allusion they make to speakers who frequently use them. For example, the Kernans found shifts in pitch level and in the frequency of nonstandard forms in children role-playing adult men versus women.

A distinction can be made to parallel the paradigmatic and syntagmatic axes of grammatical analysis. **Alternation rules** are concerned with the selection of alternative events, acts, topics, and linguistic forms from the speakers' repertoire. These may be called rules of choice. The determinants of the choices, which can be categorical or variable, include both linguistic and social features. For instance, in the case of address terms, they may include rank and sex of addressee; in the case of requests, they include expected compliance; in the case of language shifting, inferred language knowledge of

1. There is surprisingly little evidence, despite its great interest both for child language and language change, of the functional source of language changes in children except in lexicon.

the audience, the topic, setting, and effect. These are **rules** rather than simply frequencies; when violations are remarkable, they change the interpretation, or can be judged funny or inappropriate.[2]

Co-occurrence rules concern the stylistic coherence of linguistic features. In language or style switching, we may find that a number of features shift together. The extent to which the features cohere is problematic; they could form a scale or simply a correlated set. Dozens of features have been identified in "baby talk," for example, but very little has been done in analyzing the relation of these features. An exception is Weeks's analysis (1970) of co-occurrences in child register shifts. For coherence in language shifting see Gumperz (1976); discussions of covariation appear in the studies of variability (e.g., Bailey and Shuy 1973).

Sequential rules refer to the framework of structural organization of interaction. According to their generality, they can be divided between **conversation rules** and **speech event rules**. General conversational rules have been studied extensively, especially by sociologists, who have examined adult recorded interaction for features common to a wide variety of speech events, including relaxed conversations among friends. The work on conversation has emphasized **focused interaction** (Goffman 1963) rather than the unfocused interaction which occurs often in children's play. Among the common exchanges and procedures are entering conversation (Schegloff 1968), leaving conversation (Schegloff and Sacks 1973), taking turns (Sacks, Schegloff, and Jefferson 1974; Duncan 1972, 1973), getting attention and changing the topic (Keenan and Schieffelin 1976), acknowledging moves (Keenan 1974[b]), handling digressions (Jefferson 1972), and querying (Garvey in press). Some speech events are tightly structured in constituent units, and some, such as court trials, have rigorous relevance constraints. It is not quite the case, however, that there are no constraints in relaxed conversation. Concurrent activity, ideational associations, and interpersonal intent can all account for progressions from one utterance to the next in relaxed conversation between intimates. While the grounds may vary, topic shifts still are accounted for, and even 3-year-olds may interpret them by searching for their motives.

Speech event rules are those which are genre-specific. The sequential structure of a ritual event and that of an intimate conversation may differ considerably. Sinclair and Coulthard (1975) studied structured events such as teacher-centered classrooms and medical interviews, in which a clear-cut task was central, information exchange or knowledge-testing was primary, and there

2. We are assuming that there are general features of behavior which are statistically frequent without being viewed as norms. For example, most people probably make false starts or pauses in speaking, but a speaker lacking these features might not be noticed. Small children may raise their pitch to babies or dolls, but not consider it aberrant to fail to do so, or to do so to other addressees.

was high role-differentiation. They found a constituent structure composed of acts, moves, exchanges, sequences, transactions, and lessons or interviews, which were successively embracing.

For each sequential unit, there may be a paradigmatic or alternation analysis turning on how that move is to be realized. Garvey's (1975) analysis of children's directives illustrated a sequential structure: (preparation) + (adjunct) + request + (clarification) + acknowledgment. Her analysis also illustrated a rich set of alternatives for adjuncts in the same article and for clarifications elsewhere (Garvey in press). The Ervin-Tripp chapter in this volume illustrates how the request unit can be elaborated or deleted in favor of the adjunct.

Sociologists such as Goffman and the ethnomethodologists have emphasized that interaction is not deterministic. Social categories may constrain what can properly occur or what is likely to occur, but cannot precisely identify what sequences or choices will be made. The rules we describe might be regarded as a resource speakers have to accomplish interactional goals and that listeners have to interpret intent and feeling. If interaction were totally predictable by a listener it would not communicate. Past experience in acting or observing others teaches children what has failed or succeeded in accomplishing goals and what is to be expected. Sequential regularities provide the child with clues as to a speaker's intention, by virtue of what normally occurs at a particular point. Thus, a reply immediately following an insult is interpreted against the context of the insult and is judged as a retort or an evasion (Mitchell-Kernan and Kernan 1975). Expected forms can become grounds for allusion in role-playing, joking, and sarcasm. When social features are ambiguous, they can be a basis for moves to occupy positions. In this volume, the Kernans discuss how children choose the directive forms of superiors to assert superiority.

The studies of Sinclair and Coulthard (1975) and of Gumperz and Herasimchuk (1972) reveal the contrast between a description of norms and an analysis of the strategies in an actual text. Many episodes in the text cannot be interpreted, except by reference to role norms and the rules for exchange types and moves, which are found in the Sinclair and Coulthard analysis. Yet in an actual event, the exchanges may not be assembled in the same way as the norms might suggest. Certainly it could be expected that children's construction of events may at first consist primarily of local routines and familiar exchanges, rather than hierarchically arranged units. There is a relation between constituent analysis of speech events, which highlights sequential rules and text structure and normative choice rules, and the analysis of conversational strategies, which presupposes knowledge of these norms by participants.

Perspectives in Child Sociolinguistics

Why should one study ethnography of communication with children? One reason is to cast a new perspective on the development of the child's linguistic apparatus. The child's language faculty is engaged only when the child needs to communicate. Language could not be learned if children did not, at the beginning, construe meanings from context. In this view, natural language learning has as a basic and necessary feature the dependence of the learner on communication. When this is absent, as in much experimental and classroom learning of languages, one enrolls the learner in problem-solving activity, which may have quite different properties than natural language learning.

The study of grammatical development has relied primarily on the collection of corpora of interaction. It was obvious that very young children could not be informants in the traditional linguistic sense, so that information about their grammatical features had to come from texts or tests. If it is the case that the development of formal structures is in part at the service of changes in communicative intent, then to study formal development without attention to function leaves change unmotivated.

The concern of most of the contributors to this volume, however, is not solely a deeper probe into the factors underlying the development of formal structures. Indeed, most of the authors are addressing a set of questions which reach beyond the development of linguistic competence. Basic linguistic competence is only one component of the knowledge that speaker-hearers must have in order to participate in a meaningful way in those settings in which speaking occurs. The chapters in this volume are all addressed in one way or another to questions that relate to what underlies peoples' ability to speak and understand one another in the real world. Each chapter probes some facet of what might be termed the child's acquisition of communicative competence (Hymes 1972[a]). The concept of communicative competence is meant to be broadly descriptive of the knowledge that underlies socially appropriate speech. It includes, in addition to grammatical knowledge, social knowledge, which acts as a constraint on the communicative process, and which shapes the way messages are realized in actual social interaction.

The chapters in this book have the common goal of describing and analyzing that knowledge—social and linguistic—that allows the child to use language to project socially appropriate identities and to engage in purposive social acts such as playing, teaching, persuading, and directing others, asking questions, narrating a story, and being a conversational partner.

Studies in the child's acquisition of communicative competence may begin in a number of ways. One common viewpoint is that children are merely learning the adult system, since they interact with adults and must therefore accommodate to them with increasing success. Thus, one can examine facets of the acquisition of the adult sociolinguistic system by children. Such a perspective encourages one to start by defining the adult rules and examining the gradual increase in complexity of the child's system as it approaches the system of adults.

As anthropologists, a number of the contributors to this volume have, in contrast, taken the view that they are studying features of the oral culture of the child. Many of the speech events in which children engage typically occur among children apart from adults, and they are explicitly taught, in many cases, by children. This is clearly the case in the insults described by Labov (1972c), and by Mitchell-Kernan and Kernan (1975), and in playing house (Speier 1969), and it is true of many games and tricks (Opie and Opie 1960).[3]

Regardless of the source of the form or content the child uses, the structural properties and complexity of speech events can be compared at different ages. One excellent way of discovering the child's constructive ability is to examine inventions. The following texts have a particular interest in that they are a written image of dialogue. They tell us what a 7-year-old abstracted as the core of argument structure. In some cases of inventive elaboration, the source is traditional, as in semantic transformations on nursery rhymes for humor. In some, the source is a partner's contribution, as in insult exchanges, or sound play. In this case, the core structure was the dialogue of arguments. The topic changes in the text were cued by objects seen while glancing about, and the fixed elements in the formal structure may come from the poetic tradition of repeated elements in a refrain. These examples of invention consist of a corpus of about fifty 4-page "Books of Fun Things" written by 7-year-old Catherine Tripp:

The structure of these items was the same across dozens of exemplars. The child began with the image, drawing the object at the center of the page. The language at first was formed around the object, with long words being squashed to fit. The first and third lines were the same in form in all poems, being *people think that* and *but that is not true,* an idea that may derive from poetry with

3. Labov (1964) and Stewart (1964) emphasized the peer group origin of children's phonology and syntax, but developmental studies in the child language literature rarely consider peer interaction as a major source of norms. Bilinguals develop deviant norms based on their own social network; so, too, it is not surprising to find that 5-year-olds will correct "threw" to "throwed" or that children as old as 9 may report that "brang" sounds better than "brought," while also observing that adults say "brought," and kids say "brang."

repeated lines, or song refrains. The content is a dialectic: an assertion of an opinion and its contrary, and, finally, an explanation of the paradox or a synthesis in which both are true. The synthesis is heard as a second voice, which is visually set off at the side like another person conversing. Poets report that emblem poems are popular with children. These are poems visually emulating the theme. While this child knew no emblem poems, she invented an emblem of dialogue.

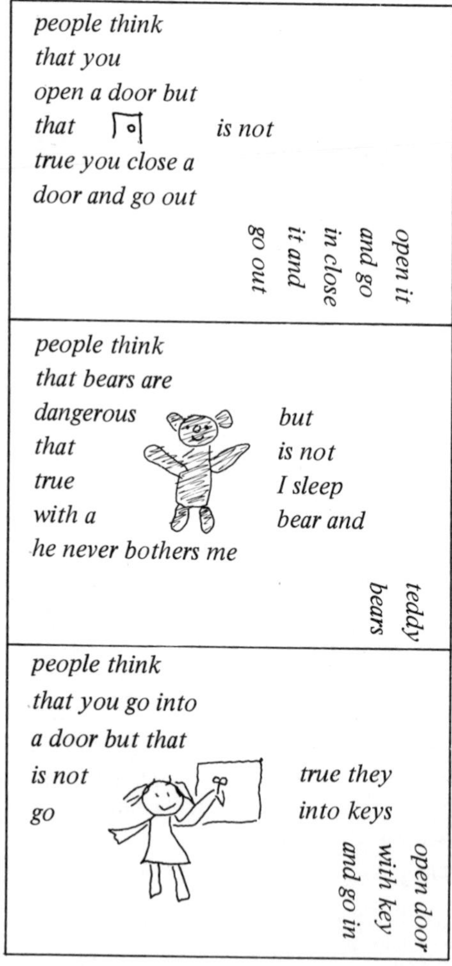

The child continued to create these poems until the semantic structure deteriorated. The first to weaken was the synthesis, which was replaced by a simple repetition of the first assertion, so that the semantics became ABA. The analysis of this development focuses on abstractable structural properties which can be compared to other performances.[4]

Several contributors to this volume have taken yet another perspective in studying language socialization (Cook-Gumperz, Keenan). These studies rest on the view that an interchange between parties has properties similar to a negotiation in which accommodations are made to make success possible. This work singles out and defines an additional range of sociolinguistic skills required for effective communication. From this perspective, adults and older children learn in interaction with young children, just as children learn from older partners. An example of one type of accommodation is the following:

SISTER: (9) *N, do you want to be Santa Claus?* [N (5), comes running] *Here's your toys. Now take them to the children in the basement.* (Ties arms of her nightgown, stuffs in her laundry.)

This child infrequently used a similar strategy of persuasion. She imbedded the act she wanted performed (in this case, delivery of her laundry to the basement) in a larger context of a pretend game. The imbedding was itself a sophisticated achievement of which the younger child would not have been capable. The larger game was framed in terms of the addressee's interests, so the enactment of the game accomplished the quite different purposes of both children.

The use of repetition (Keenan) to provide topic-comment sequences and to turn a previous message into shared knowledge exemplifies a convention negotiated by very young children in order to sustain dialogue. Keenan suggests that this particular organization of means not only reflects the limited cognitive and linguistic abilities of the children, but also their own cognizance of these limitations. The use of repetition to make explicit the connection between conversational turns suggests, as well, a kind of accommodation in which the child is anticipating the information needs of an interlocutor.

Gleason (1973) has claimed that there is a developmental change in the adaptation of speech to younger children. She points out that older speakers in her sample were somewhat better able to emulate baby's syntax than were 6-year-olds. Clearly the socialization cycle she described in adults and 8-year-olds involved considerable special knowledge, such as the young child's need to be warned of dangers, taught politeness, tutored or cued to convey new information. Even the

4. The manipulation of lexical ambiguity (*bears/teddy bears*) is a strategy commonly used by children in arguments and repartee. In the following exchange between two 8-year-olds, quick thinking permitted one child to deflect an insult by seizing the literal sense of a word and rejecting the metaphorical sense in which it was intended.

FAY: *Bobby say you're a sport, Karen.* (you're masculine)
KAREN: *I'm not a sport. I play games. A sport is a game and I'm not a game.* (Leventhal 1976)

4-year-olds studied by Shatz and Gelman (1973) tailored their instruction of 2-year-olds to what they believed the listeners knew about toys, and were sometimes able to state their assumptions explicitly. Ervin-Tripp and Miller (in press) say that there are multiple reasons for these accommodations, including conceptions of semantic simplicity, of appropriate types of speech acts and events, and of politeness. Except for certain conventions specifically relating to age and status, we can expect this process to have many similarities to other kinds of negotiated communication.

We do not know how early one can find forms of accommodation which do not rely wholly on feedback, but arise from preconceptions about the state of knowledge of the partner. One instance of such an early accommodation is the appearance in the speech of preschoolers of identifying information such as *she's my friend* or *that's my aunt,* instead of just a proper name, in an account to a person who cannot be assumed to know the person referred to. These instances are the first occurrences of the process of linking addressee and referent that Sacks (1972) has identified as normal to adult introductions or person reference. The function of such links is to provide some attachment for the new person to a category already known to the addressee.

Another context in which negotiation and accommodation can be seen is in contact between children who speak different languages. By 5, they can be seen teaching names, explaining actions and rules by gesture, and distinguishing information which is so complex as to require a translation (Fillmore 1976). How early such skills begin is not known. At the very least, as Shatz and Gelman have pointed out, these studies suggest that the emphasis on "egocentrism" has led to a serious underestimation of the capacity of young children to accommodate to listeners and, as Cook-Gumperz argues in this volume, to negotiate on-the-spot conventions which make the transaction work.

Finally, work on the child's communicative system can proceed by examining sociolinguistic features of speech that provide evidence of the child's knowledge of social roles and that reflect a conception of a social system, and the child's incorporation into it. This strategy can lead us to information about social development, particularly with respect to the learning of the social categories of the milieu and the rules for social roles.

It is possible to illustrate the relationship between roles and rules as follows. Alternations include selection of discourse types, such as stories, lectures, sermons, jokes, riddles and phone conversations. It is clear that understanding certain statuses, such as that of pupil, entails learning a discourse type, such as the lesson response types in the work of Sinclair and Coulthard (1975). Children's awareness of some discourse types begins very young. Especially obvious are ritualized openings and closings, which may be all a 2-year-old learns for some genres. A phone conversation may be: *Hi. Fine. Bye.* A similar primitive routine occurs in an 8-year-old's postcard: *I am fine. How are you? I hope you are fine.* A sophisticated 9-year-old says to a phone caller about his mother in the bathtub: *Mother is occupied.* Children's awareness of the discourse structures employed in roles other than those they normally enact themselves appears typically in role-playing games.

Selection rules may realize the role system in two ways. First, alternation rules themselves (for example, rules for address, pronoun selection, requests) are likely to include certain statuses as selection criteria. The child is likely to notice the difference and develop some notion of its basis. Second, the speaker's choices convey to the listener, or can convey, information about his or her own identity because of the repertoire employed. For example, several observers have noticed that if a shift to a new conversational episode begins with *now. . .* the speaker is usually in control of the situation and is likely to be of higher status. *That's right* as an acknowledgment spoken to someone who regards himself as the senior or superior of the speaker is taken as an inappropriate role-switch. Indeed, as the Kernans show in this volume, these formal contrasts can be the stuff of dominance disputes.

It is clear from the social differentiation in address terms, pronouns, and directives that children systematically must come to attend to the features of age and power and familiarity of addressees. We can assume, therefore, that for a child the "meaning" of an utterance is not a matter merely of ideational contrasts but an act of social interpretation which has more than a single source of interpretive knowledge as input. There is no way to study the acquisition of norms for sociolinguistic rules without at the same time learning about the child's socialization into the role system. The child's developing rules are not solely a function of her grammatical system, and her capacity for handling complexity, but also of her knowledge of social features. Some of these categories are codified lexically by children, and appear in the names they use in role-playing. *Big sister, it's time for dinner. Set the table. Get Baby.* Speier (1969) has vivid examples of such play. Social categories are also necessary in the alternation rules that select register. They may include: *"infant, man, adult, stranger, teacher, doctor, park, doctor's office."* Children's notions of the criteria for these categories may change: female medicos or those with thermometers are nurses; males with stethoscopes are doctors. The child's view of the criteria of life-cycle statuses changes with age. The discreteness of language and its amenability to formal statement make sociolinguistic rules a fruitful domain for the study of developing social processes.

In sum, it appears that the following perspectives are possible in examining children's sociolinguistic competence:

1. One can take as a starting point the adult system as far as we know it, and examine the development of understanding and use of these adult patterns.
2. One can examine children's discourse in a variety of contexts without

taking the adult system as a reference point but search for peer norms. An age comparative approach might show development of some features with age and decline of others. The complexity or other properties of inventiveness can be examined without regard to the source of the features generalized.

3. One can study the accommodation and negotiation between peers or between partners varying in age, to show how communication and socialization occur. From this perspective the experienced partner's accommodation is as revealing as the novice's.
4. One can examine sociolinguistic categories and rules in terms of their relation to social development.

Approaches to Data

Speech Events

The chapters in this volume illustrate a variety of ways to discover how children use language. One approach is to examine certain kinds of organized discourse as a starting point, including identifiable genres named in the culture. Play, arguments, narratives and teaching were chosen here for this purpose. They appear in all cultures and are sufficiently well bounded to make the analysis of their internal structure a definite task.

Play with language, as Garvey describes it, achieves its structure not by specific characteristic components, but rather by virtue of an identifiable "orientation" or stance that can bracket a long sequence of exchanges.[5] Garvey's chapter treats as play an apparently disparate set of performances, including singing, playing with sound features and voice qualities, semantic nonsense, and make-believe. Do all of these types of acts actually comprise a category, except by an adult term? One piece of evidence we can provide is that they do in fact occur in contiguity in texts.

Anne Carter (1974) reported the following sequence from a child at 1:3 in a play session:

> Called a rattle a *ball,* (laughed).
> Said *have that* [= take it] when had nothing to give.
> Said *hi* after period of play with peer, (laughed).
> Said *oh-oh* of own fall, not of object's fall.
> Babbled.
> Said *doggie* of each picture in a book, despite correction.

In a phone conversation between two 3:6-year-olds, Ervin-Tripp found the following sequence of moves:

5. Hymes (1972b) uses the term *"key"* to provide for the tone, manner, or spirit in which an act is done.

A: Makes funny noises.
B: Deliberately drops phone, giggles, while–
A: Giggles and sings.
B: Tells nonsense about animals, giggles, while–
A: Calls B *silly billy* and *funny bunny*.
B: Pretends to be a dog, barks, while–
A: Sings.
B: Says *bye*, then says *hi*, asserts he was kidding, tricking.
A: Fantasies wild trip, while–
B: Mixes up nursery rhymes.
A: Does nonsense sound play, then sings, while–
B: Tries to get the floor for a nursery rhyme joke.
A & B: Both participate in making funny endings for nursery rhymes, alternating turns.

These two samples suggest that Garvey is right that there is a general category of play. Babbling, sound play, singing, semantic nonsense, pragmatic play, and role-playing may all be similar to the child. One leads to another, and they are mixed in the same scenes. In partner's exchanges, whether simultaneous or alternating, one type is an appropriate reply to another type. Laughter, and perhaps the frivolous rather than 'sensical' relation between turns and sequences, identifies the whole event as play.

Play makes salient a dimension of variation between genres: the roles of partner and audience. The phone sequence above provides an example of a contrast between two types of turn-taking patterns, both typical of play. In the shared task of making funny endings for nursery rhymes, the initiator made a clear attempt to recover from interruption and demand the floor, and the two engaged in turn-taking. The turn-taking sequence, however, was preceded by another pattern, in which productions could be simultaneous, less focused partner attention was allowed, and only a sharing of key was needed. In this modality, each partner becomes a stimulus to the play of the other but neither requires proof of full attention. Discourse properties suggest three types of conversation from the standpoint of partner role: turn-taking (which requires acknowledgment as proof of focused engagement); monologues in which the speaker may play both roles and provide replies; and simultaneity. In the last two varieties, the other person acts as audience and hence stimulus, but not as turn-taking partner. Vygotsky (1962:136) showed that the social features and behavior of the audience affected children's speech even in the case of inner speech or monologues. Yet in earlier research, play lacking turn-taking alternation was called "egocentric" (Piaget 1955).

Garvey included full role-playing as a form of play. In its elaborated form with a phase of joint organization of parts and a phase of enactment (Speier

1969), the playing of reciprocal roles may not integrate easily with other types of play. That is a question to be studied.

As children engage in increasingly structured speech events the structure may constrain what elements can be combined. Brenneis and Lein, for example, show that in disputes playful semantic and prosodic contrasts built on the partner's immediately preceding turn are an important resource. Watson and Boggs also see specific play routines learned in early childhood as important components of the more highly developed narrative structures of later years. Garvey's chapter thus raises not only major research issues about play per se, but about the relation of play to other speech events.

Brenneis and Lein's chapter deals with a much more restricted and structured event, disputing. They deliberately elicited disputes under controlled conditions. Watson and Boggs, in contrast, dealt with naturally occurring events, but the results are similar. The chapter outlines the content and stylistic strategies, and the sequences of such strategies in a well-defined event with symmetrical roles. Disputes in the American groups required relatively strict turn-taking, whereas patterned overlaps occurred in Fijian children's disputes. The substance of the analysis is the relation across turns, as affected by the properties of the first move in a sequence. These relations are both semantic and stylistic, that is, involving surface structure or sound features. The children in the study did not use elaborate semantic strategies, such as we see in elaborate arguments or cross-examination, in which the opponent is led up to an entrapment many moves later. The maximum length of organization of such future planning appeared to be used in trickery, when a repeated routine is anticipated as the opponent's answer to a question (as in the folk song "No John No").

On the whole, the semantic strategies were immediate or local. Each strategy was based on an interpretation of the semantics of the opponent's turn, and the semantic transformation or routine being applied by the opponent in earlier moves in the sequence.[6]

A striking feature of the children's strategies noted by Brenneis and Lein was emulation of surface features, a feature of children's interaction also pointed out by Keenan in this volume, and by Gumperz and Herasimchuk (1972). These include imitation of rate, rhythm, and volume or intonation. Surface structure relations can provide major discourse tying, whether by repetition or by systematic contrasts. They can be used to constitute or to supplement

6. Garvey has pointed out that the older children in Brenneis and Lein's study were displaying sophisticated make-believe arguments, as she has observed in ritual play (Garvey 1974), and that they seemed to have in the **sequence** a structure analogous to the **round**, a repeatable exchange unit, in ritual play. (This note derives from comments circulated between the contributors to this volume.)

semantic strategies.[7] We do not know whether the age changes in the semantic structure of arguing is also related to changes in the degree and type of surface structure tying.[8] The Brenneis and Lein chapter and Boggs's comments give the first glimpse of what could prove to be cross-cultural universals in children's disputes.

The chapter on Hawaiian children's narratives by Watson and Boggs is a good example of the ethnography of communication. It describes the organization of a genre in use in actual cultural settings. The unique feature of the Hawaiian children's narratives is the joint production by several participants.

The narrative genre in many cultures takes the form of monologue, but in Hawaii it is regularly a dialogue. Turn-taking, universally an important basis for organizing talk in at least some speech events, can thus be seen to be culturally organized. Hawaiian children's turn-taking in the narrative genre is pivoted on allegations embedded in the narrative. These allegations form the basis for turn-taking and coparticipation because they can be examined for truth value and can be the basis for challenges.

The narrative in Hawaii is related to another speech event, "the contradicting routine," and shares its sequencing structure. One reason for the coparticipation feature of sequencing may be that the stories have goals other than entertainment. The stories have content that is selectively relevant to some member of the audience, and they serve the function of teasing, criticizing, or censuring that individual. Such a use of storytelling has also been observed among black Americans (Mitchell-Kernan 1971), West Indians, and West Africans (French and Kernan 1974).[9] It is obvious that such narratives obtain their properties from their situated use, and are peculiarly oral. Watson and Boggs explored other situational effects on storytelling, especially with respect to

7. Boggs has also found it possible to compare Brenneis and Lein's mainland disputing material to 55 examples of contradicting routines from Hawaiian children of comparable ages. He noted great similarity both of content and style. Incredible threats and allegations were common between parents and children, but did not occur between children except as a joke, primarily "because of the central importance of making supportable allegations." Bribes are absent, being in conflict with Hawaiian cultural values. The most common insults were sexual allegations or ridicule, including imitating and distorting, or mocking, and vocal insult symbols. He also found that the kind of structure of sequences described by Brenneis and Lein in role-playing situations which were initiated alternatively by assertions, imperatives, or insults tended also to have a larger pattern leading from one sequence type to the next on the list. "This constitutes a kind of dialectic process in disputing, and it is to this whole pattern that I have given the name '**the contradicting routine**'." (This note derives from comments circulated between the contributors to this volume.)

8. Boggs noted that there was a characteristic stylistic pattern associated with the contradicting routine he found. (This note derives from comments circulated between the contributors to this volume.)

9. Belize (West Indian) narratives so frequently are the vehicle for indirect comments about the audience that they sometimes begin with a disclaimer of relevance (French 1975).

turn-taking. This chapter deals, as well, with the development of pragmatic competence in children. The authors suggest that one source of skill in contrapuntal narratives is the teasing exchanges which occur in other speech events, and the challenges provided by interruptions by parents. As in many other kinds of narratives, Hawaiian talk-story includes dramatic or role-played imitated dialogue. How is this skill learned? Boggs mentions ridicule in disputing. In addition, role-playing with vocal mimicry occurs in early childhood play. Thus, there are varied sources for the components of narrative skill. But these sources remain to be explored systematically.

Kernan has examined the development with age of narrative structures, using as his base the proposed framework of Labov and Waletzky (1967). They had suggested that at the heart of every narrative was a set of temporally related events to which the narrative clauses might refer. But narratives can also expand this core of events to include introducers or abstractions, orienting information about time, place, and motive, evaluation (mediation in Watson's terms), and resolution (Watson 1972:78).

Kernan's corpus consisted primarily of personal experience narratives produced by black American girls between 7 and 14 years of age. He found a marked shift with age, especially between the 7-8-year-olds and the older girls in most of these structural components. Younger children are more likely to elaborate narrative details, but not tell the context, motives, or the point of the story. The older children more often mark the narrative with a summary, which abstracts its point, and they more often give contextual information and summarize the outcome.[10] The age related differences in the elaboration of particular narrative components is illustrative of developmental changes in the way children adapt their speech to the requirements of their addressees. The older children evidenced greater awareness that their own assumptions about such things as motives and humor might not be shared by a hearer and made these assumptions explicit.

If there are any universals in age change of elaboration, it will be important to find whether they arise from the difficulty of cognitively abstracting and summarizing, or the problem of anticipating the areas of ignorance of the listener. These issues recur in other comparisons of discourse across age in this volume.[11]

10. Watson's work on the structure of Hawaiian children's stories (1972[a], 1973) and her analysis in this volume corroborate Kernan's finding that abstracting and orienting tend to occur more with age. She also found there are important situational and cultural variations in the inclusion of the features in the Labov schema. (This note derives from comments circulated between the contributors to this volume.)

11. Hollos noted that the large differences Kernan found between the youngest and middle age groups in contrast to the minimal differences between the middle and oldest groups correspond to Piaget's conceptions of stages in cognitive development, where the period of 7-8 years is transitional between the preoperational and concrete operational stages. Her analysis in this volume corroborates Kernan's finding. (This note derives from comments circulated between the contributors of this volume.)

Children frequently undertake teaching of other children, both by word and example, when they have younger or novice participants in play. Jenny Cook-Gumperz created an experimental situation of construction by a blindfolded child under instruction by another, in order to compel the use of a vocal channel for more explicit instructions than would be normal in everyday practice. She sought to identify the negotiated instructions when obstacles were present, and to examine age changes and the relation to school norms.

Instructional style had two identifying features: choice of direct imperatives or of intonation cues marking either an instructional tone distinctly different from nondidactic passages, or a warning tone. Cook-Gumperz regards the meaning of these tonal patterns as "negotiated" in that the significance of the distinction can be inferred from their early contextual distribution on this particular occasion, and need have no further semantic marking in later occurrences.

Using the same paradigm as Kernan's for narrative analysis, Cook-Gumperz tested the structure as a formula for instructional sequencing. She found that abstracts were absent, that orientation was typically not lexicalized, and that complicating action frequently used pronominalized and hence contextually situated comments.

The 10-year-olds had two styles for correcting instructions that failed: To peers they used pronominal imperatives, to younger children lexicalized specifications.[12] The assumption underlying Cook-Gumperz's work was the view that the program of the school is to lexicalize what is presupposed or communicated by prosody or pronouns (cf. Bernstein 1971).[13] In contrast to Bernstein, who has argued that the use of contextualized speech has its origin in the class structure (1971), Cook-Gumperz advances the view that the use of contextualized speech develops as a natural part of the socialization process in the home where communication proceeds against shared background knowledge.

Cook-Gumperz conceives the interpretation of spoken language as depending on three basic orders of meaning: referential, conveyed, and situated. Each type of meaning is successively more contextually embedded with the interpretation of situated meaning being dependent on what has gone before in the discourse, including those semantic values that are continually negotiated within ongoing interaction. She provides evidence that the negotiated cues which were prosodic and situated were highly effective means of communication. The reliance of adults

12. Watson has commented on the implications of a two style system toward peers and for school or strangers. (This note derives from comments circulated between the contributors of this volume.)

13. Boggs (1972) has commented on the culture clash such a program provokes in Hawaii: "The teachers make every attempt to substitute instruction in a strictly verbal channel which is, moreover, often prosodically barren from the Hawaiian point of view. Thus Hawaiian adults complain about the excessive wordiness and aloofness (lack of prosody) of Caucasian speech." (This note derives from comments circulated between the contributors of this volume.)

on the verbalized semantic channel in similar situations may thus be a function of values and attitudes as much as the actual communicative demands of the situation. In Cook-Gumperz's work there were no ethnic or class differences, suggesting that children share the dominance of prosodic and contextual over lexical cues. This feature of children's speech, however, need not be interpreted as a stage in an inexorable, maturationally based march to lexical specificity. We also see some evidence of the situational—as opposed to cognitive—maturational factors, which might lead to lexical specification rather than other means of communicating. Moreover, while home and school values may affect differential mastery of the ability to utilize lexical selection and syntactic elaboration in communicating, situational factors no doubt shape the degree to which these skills are manifest in actual speech.

There has been a tendency in the literature to characterize contextual speech **(restricted code)** in terms of the features it lacks, rather than in terms of its unique characteristics. Cook-Gumperz's close analysis of all of the channels involved in conveying meaning, and her attention to situated meaning produced an expanded base for semantic interpretation and suggests that the semantic richness of contextual speech has been underestimated in many studies. The adequacy of the characterization of **elaborated code** as conveying specific, individualized meanings in contrast to the global, communalized meanings of **restricted code** is challenged by the concept of **negotiated meaning**, which would not seem dependent on any particular organization of means. If one took the text sentences in isolation, one would not understand how communication took place. Her work illustrates that mechanical counts of grammatical categories or even the interpretability of isolated utterances do not inform us about how communication occurs.

Speech Acts

In the previously mentioned studies, structural features of speech events were studied either in natural contexts or by elicitation varying in degree of artificiality. Another major area of research has been the abstraction of particular categories of moves, acts, or functions in interaction. These units can be analyzed from the standpoint of their event structure and their social distribution. Keenan's chapter on repetitions is a major critique. Its principle thesis is that investigators of natural interaction of children viewed as identical utterances which were superficially similar in one property—they repeated segments of the partner's speech. Keenan shows that repetitions vary enormously in function and play very important roles in child discourse. Her chapter brings into sharp focus a recurring problem in the analysis of speech, that is, the relation between form and function must be investigated systematically, rather than assumed.

Child language research has distinguished between elicited or instructed imitations–*Say what I say*–and spontaneous imitations, or what Keenan calls **repetitions**. She shows that children repeat for a range of reasons. Brenneis and Lein have pointed out that repetitions can link entries in disputes, and some of Keenan's examples also serve that function. Keenan shows that they have the fundamental property of acknowledgment, or **filling a turn**. Where topical continuity is at issue, they can acknowledge a new topic introduced by the partner. Probably a reason that repetition is used much more often in child discourse than in adult discourse is that it requires the minimum operation on the partner's speech.[14] But as Keenan points out, it is also frequent in adult talk. Corsaro (1975) found it was a major device of adults talking with children. Indeed, the expansions of child utterances characteristic of middle class, American adult speech to children can be viewed as a type of repetition. These expansions also appear to have a variety of pragmatic functions. In conflict with expectations, they do not seem to be the most effective training devices for grammatical and syntactic learning. The impact of expansions on development may not be narrowly linguistic but rather pragmatically facilitating.

Keenan's work is only in part a criticism of the older studies of imitation. Her question is not the same. The older studies were designed to discover the maximal grammatical competence of children, and whether imitation aided grammatical development. But even in terms of those questions, it is clear that the complexity of repetitions is likely to depend on their discourse function or intent.

More important, in terms of child discourse, is Keenan's observation that even 2-year-olds already have a rich variety of types of functions served by one conversational device. Scollon (1973) noted that repetitions had already appeared within the second year in attempts both to establish dialogue and to identify contrasts. The next question might be what other devices these children have to accomplish the same functions and how that repertoire changes.[15] It is not known whether all children employ repetition equally for these functions, whether particular adult interactional strategies affect child-generated repetitions, and what situational factors there may be in the use of repetition. It is known that repetitions peak in the third year and wide individual differences exist. The situation Keenan studied, like the Brenneis and Lein altercations,

14. In recent work on grammatical development, Italian researchers found children refused to imitate. So in some cultures it is censured.

15. Hollos commented that Piaget's work on cognitive development would not lead one to expect that children as young as Keenan's twins could engage in conversation. "At this first stage there is, strictly speaking, no conversation, since each child speaks only to himself, even when he seems to be addressing someone in particular" (Piaget 1955:72). Of particular interest is the fact that Keenan's children appeared to try to make their utterances comprehensible when one or the other was having difficulty understanding. (This note derives from comments circulated between the contributors of this volume.)

was centered on talk because of the absence of things. Topic-confirming, at least, might be less necessary in a different milieu.

Whereas Keenan's attention has been primarily focused on the development of conversational rules in children, especially those relating to the maintenance of discourse through acknowledgment of topic, Dore's work has been more concerned with interpersonal intentions or **speech acts**. His chapter, like Keenan's, contrasts two different ways of analyzing children's texts. Whereas Keenan has shown that a single surface feature realized many discourse functions, Dore has noted a mismatch between a surface category—"question type"—and speech acts. In contrasting the analyses, he shows that many replies to questions which are not grammatically matched are pragmatically appropriate. Dore's chapter addresses the question of defining pragmatic rules.

The coding of intention is not easy: Dore identifies other speaker utterances and hearer reactions as his major source, but he had videotapes which supplied contextual information as well. He found some important contextual relations of questions; many questions were employed for clarification, as Garvey (in press) has indicated. Others set the stage for directives, or were relevant to procedures to gain possession, or taking turns, which are major issues in nursery schools. It certainly is clear that his analysis is far more informative about conversational skills than assessment of grammatical appropriateness alone can be. Questions are a good focus for such analysis. They are highly frequent, require responses, and become a vehicle for a variety of intentions.

In the first table, Dore lists the categories of the larger coding frame he has been applying to nursery school interaction. This, like the more elaborate framework in use by Gordon Wells in Bristol, provides an elaborate taxonomy of speech acts. The contingencies between these acts are still being explored in these centers.

Ervin-Tripp's chapter is an exploration of evidence regarding one speech act, **directives**. This act has the special property that it requires work on the part of the addressee, so its form is sensitive to issues of social cost, face, and politeness. It is therefore a good locus for identifying social knowledge of children. The major problem in these acts, as in those discussed by Dore, is the mismatch between surface form and intention. This mismatch is systematic, involving the appearance of surface forms which look like questions or statements even when the intention is to direct. While there is considerable work currently in linguistics arguing for an elaborate interpretive process, this chapter suggests that many directives are socially motivated by factors that define the speech situation, with a reference point in social norms. The chapter further suggests a variety of techniques for studying the development of knowledge about the different ways requests can be realized and the social features of those alternatives.

There are examples in the chapter of elaborate requests by Turkish, Italian, and American children.[16] Hollos has recently addressed the issue of social differences in directive strategies, and found dramatic contrasts in the strategies of Norwegian and Hungarian children (1975[a]). If one examined the ages involved, it might still be the case that some common developmental changes are found, overlaid with social constraints.

Mitchell-Kernan and Kernan have examined directives used in role-playing and have noted that many of the social contrasts in directive form, especially in status, are reflected during dramatic play. They found there was less use of imperatives between equals, and more to subordinates than studies of adults have suggested. The differences in the distribution of imperatives between peers by children in contrast to adults appeared to be related to the functions directives served in peer group culture. An important new dimension is added by examining the underlying function of the directive forms. The Kernans found that children direct not only because an instrumental goal is important but because directing can be a vehicle for expressing social rank. The children's status strivings were expressed through directives with conventional social meanings. These meanings are immediately interpretable and affect the compliance of the hearers.

Ervin-Tripp (1976[a,b]) has argued that although it is possible to view the forms directives take as related to sincerity conditions underlying requests (Gordon and Lakoff 1971; Garvey 1975) the actual choice of directive type is socially motivated. Mitchell-Kernan and Kernan's analysis of the functions directives serve in peer interaction provides corroboration of the social meaning attached to particular directive types. Indeed, the use of directives in status manipulation cannot be understood apart from the conventional social meaning attached to the different types.

The chapter suggests the importance of moving away from an exclusive perspective that child language is solely a representation of stages in the progression from immaturity to maturity. As children enter into the period when they are incorporated into peer groups, it is likely that the interactional goals of

16. Boggs has commented that "All of these are cultures that positively value the individual's manipulation of others, and appear to train children positively to engage in such strategies. Hawaiians, like Ojibwa, do not. To them such manipulation among adults, as among children, is anathema." Boggs suggests that Hawaiian children cannot use an imperative to an adult, and do not use permission directives since they are too complex and formal. "To be verbose and explicit would be seen as importuning. Hawaiian children never repeat a request to an adult with increasing emphasis without risking a slap"; so any repetition includes a withdrawal of urgency. Typical forms he cites are "I like." "Go store?" "Go swim?" "I goin." The lack of explicitness about the actor in the questions makes them ambiguous with respect to their status as permission requests or question directives, Boggs interpreting them as the latter.

children's culture will shape the way they use language and that some of these goals will receive linguistic elaboration.

Social Meaning

Speech acts can be used as the core of a family of studies: on repertoire, comprehension of intent, the social features affecting alternations, recognition of social information in the choices of others, and appropriateness judgments. They can also be the organizing focus of metalinguistic tasks like reporting speech acts, producing them on instruction, correcting, or phrasing rules. Several of these methods are discussed in the Ervin-Tripp chapter, and the last two chapters in the book make systematic use of formal eliciting and judgment methods for testing social meaning.

Hollos used a role-playing task with predefined roles to elicit production of speech acts, but she found that many children had difficulty with the hypothetical situation. In addition, as Mitchell-Kernan and Kernan pointed out, role-playing can deviate systematically from natural behavior in the direction of stereotypy. But the stereotypes are a kind of knowledge too.

Subjective reaction tests can be used to obtain appropriateness judgments *(is it silly?)* or social category judgments *(who could be saying this? who could be the addressee?)* as in the Hollos chapter. These systematic methods make it possible to compare different age groups. Hollos has noted that just as in the areas of semantics and syntax, there is often a gap between performance in comprehension and in production. Thus, in the use of Hungarian pronouns with appropriate social selectors, there may be an experiential factor which results in a lag. Hollos argues that the child's interaction network influences the child's active pronominal contrasts. While farm children learned to understand social contrasts relatively rapidly, their ability to produce them was less than children in town who were exposed to more varied social relationships outside the family. If Hollos is correct in her view that an operational component accounts for the comprehension-production lag, this finding has implications for understanding the mutual interaction between social milieu, cognitive development, and linguistic development.

Edelsky has concentrated on the development of linguistic stereotypes, and has used a method of assigning social categories to speech features to assess developmental changes in stereotypy. This method is related to the technique used by Lambert (1960) and his colleagues who asked judges to rate on a variety of scales speakers (who in fact were the same voice) with different accents, and by Labov (1972[d]) who asked for social judgments about a variety of samples differing in particular features. These are all techniques applicable to children. Edelsky's task was very simple: identifying whether the utterance was spoken more often by men or women. Her most important finding is that there are two different categories of stereotyped features. One type develops relatively slowly, presumably on the basis of some induction from experience. Another type peaks by the sixth grade and declines later, possibly on the basis of explicit instruction, or clichés, which give way to more complex beliefs about situational diversity. Very little is known about the actual differences upon which any inductive learning might be based, so at this point the acquisition source is a matter of conjecture. Some of the differences—for instance, swearing by males—can also be found in preschool children's role-playing. In addition to Edelsky's relatively context-free method of assessing stereotypes, judgment tests may be developed which check the child's sensitivity to a combination of contextual determinants. For example, if a context is given such as a person dropping the spaghetti all over the floor, is *Damn it* judged less uniquely masculine? Edelsky reasons that it may be sensitivity to context which leads to a decrease in this stereotype, but in future work it might be possible to test contextual effects. Similarly, the Hollos method of studying appropriate addressees can be given context, if addressee age and status interact with other determinants, such as difficulty of task.

Studies in this book have included a gamut from ethnographic methods of exploring children's speech events in natural situations, through eliciting them, through testing them in increasingly specialized situations such as role-playing or making judgments. These methods explore different facets of children's knowledge and will all be needed to provide full information about sociolinguistic development.

Studies of children have routinely been seen as marginal to linguistics, psychology, and the other social sciences. They have been viewed as studies of imperfect participants, defective in that their knowledge is weak and their capacities immature. But knowledge of a social system changes throughout life. As individuals enter new statuses and participate in different groups, their capacity to shift strategies may increase. Our understanding of the repeated and continuing socialization of adults, as well as of culture change, is facilitated by the study of children. In addition, as work on children's discourse pushes back to the earliest stages of interaction, we expect to find through comparative studies those facets of human interaction which are fundamental and universal.

Part I

Speech Events

Play with Language and Speech[1]

CATHERINE GARVEY

Though many writers of stories and verse for children seem to know what children enjoy, students of language acquisition have very little information on spontaneous play with language. Collections of children's folk culture have tended to represent the more codified or institutionalized aspects of verbal play (Opie and Opie 1960). More recent observations of jump-rope rhymes and hand-clap games (e.g., Brady 1975; Eckhardt 1975), although providing instances of individual improvisation, focus primarily on those traditional forms of play that are transmitted from child to child in relatively constant form and that can be taught. Further, these collections and observations have most often dealt with the games of older, school-age children.

An exception is the chapter on the structure of play with contradicting routines and the stylized narrative speech events created by 5-7-year-old Hawaiian children (Watson and Boggs this volume). The storytelling performances they describe were a specialized dramatic form generated spontaneously (and often cooperatively) from components used in both playful and nonplayful conversational interactions.

In the period from 2 to 5, speech becomes fluent and social play, especially play with peers, becomes increasingly frequent and complex. As greater competence is achieved in language, speech, and social interaction, we should expect to see this mastery exhibited in playful deployment of these newly acquired abilities. The Russian writer of children's literature, Chukovsky (1963), considers this period as a high point in the discovery and enjoyment of language. The purpose of this chapter, then, is to point out some features of play with language in the preschool period, with special attention to interactive play with age-mates.

It is necessary first to state as precisely as possible what we mean by "play," since that term can be used to refer to a number of different concepts.

1. This chapter is a shortened and revised version of a paper presented to the Conference on The Biology of Play, Farnham, Surrey, June, 1975. Much of the research on which the chapter is based was supported by the National Institutes of Mental Health, Grant No. MH 23883-03.

It is now generally agreed that play cannot be defined in terms of specific behaviors, for almost any given behavior can be performed playfully or nonplayfully. Play is more usefully conceived as an orientation, a mode of experiencing. A play orientation can be adopted toward anything the child can do. Reynolds (1972) has called play "behavior in the simulative mode," stressing the important characteristic that playful behavior is uncoupled from the normal goals or consequences of the corresponding nonplayful action. Garvey (1974) characterized play as a "nonliteral" orientation to some resource or material, stressing not only the close relationships that hold between playful behavior and the nonplayful analogue, but also emphasizing the fact that play has intimate associations with systems of social meaning.

When a child plays, he must play with something. The playful orientation requires engagement with aspects of the physical, conceptual, or social world. Language provides resources at various levels of its structure (i.e., phonology, grammar, semantics), and in its pragmatic or functional aspects. Even the processes of speaking or of uttering sounds or noises offer potential resources for play. Halliday (1973) proposes that the imaginative model is among the various models of language held by the child. "Models" are the images of language use that are gradually distinguished and differentiated as the child's world expands.

From the practical point of view, the identification of play rests on the **principle of contrastivity**. Play contrasts not only with "work"; as any child knows, it also contrasts with "doing nothing." There are two situations in which it is difficult to say with confidence whether a child is playing. First, it is probably fruitless to ask the question if the behavior observed cannot be performed by that child in both playful and nonplayful ways. Running for protection to mother, for example, differs markedly from the gleeful, though possibly still unsteady, "escape run" of the toddler who has learned that he can start a game of chase by running away from mother. When he is just beginning to learn to walk, it may be impossible to draw the distinction between playful locomotion and nonplayful practice. The second situation in which identification of a playful orientation is difficult is when a child is alone. When no communication concerning the play orientation is required, the normally redundant marking of the state of play is often, though not always, reduced or absent. In a social situation, the message, "This is play" (Bateson 1956), is transmitted in various ways to coparticipants and is available to observers, as well.

In this chapter, then, we will examine types of play with language and speech, drawing primarily on a corpus of dyadic interactions of young children who were videotaped in an observation room furnished like a living room. Other sources will be cited, however, for data on solitary play or play at ages younger than those included in the corpus of dyadic interactions. In restricting the chapter to play, many phenomena of children's spontaneous speech that are potentially significant for the study of linguistic rule systems are excluded. Among these are overextensions of reduction transformations (e.g., *That chair doesn't fit you. Get a fitting chair for you to sit on.*), and noun formation processes (e.g., *Look! A sweep!* said on sighting a small broom).

SUBJECTS

Forty-eight dyads of same- and mixed-sex children drawn from five private nursery schools were observed for approximately 15 minutes each. Members of each dyad were previously acquainted and were from the same nursery class. All were from middle-class homes and spoke English as a first language. Twelve dyads were 2:10-3:3 years of age; 12 were 3:6-4:4; and 24 were 4:7-5:7. Data from an additional 40 dyads have recently been collected by Alicia Lieberman (1976). These dyads were all of same-sex composition and ranged in age from 3:0-3:8 years. Their members met for the first time in the observation room.

PROCEDURES

The previously acquainted children were brought in groups of three to our laboratory by their nursery school teacher. Two children were left in an observation room furnished with carpet, sofa, pictures, curtains, and a variety of objects including stuffed animals, small trucks, toy oven and dishes, telephones, dress-up clothes, and a wooden car big enough for two to ride on. The third child was occupied with discrimination tasks while the dyad was videotaped. At the end of the session, the composition of the dyad was changed. Thus each child was observed with two different partners. The 40 dyads of unacquainted children followed the same procedure with two exceptions: (a) children were brought to the laboratory by mothers or by a research assistant; and (b) each child was observed with only one partner.

DATA

Speech was transcribed and narrative accounts of the activity were prepared from the videotapes. "Utterances," defined as stretches of one child's speech bounded by the speech of the partner, or by a pause exceeding one second, were numbered. Both verbal and nonverbal behaviors have been subjected to various analyses with the objectives of (*a*) comparing the amount of social and nonsocial speech (Garvey and Hogan 1973); (*b*) describing subsystems of social speech such as requests for action (Garvey 1975); and (*c*) examining a variety of social play, the "ritual," which is highly repetitive and rhythmic (Garvey 1974).

PLAY WITH NOISES AND SOUNDS

The most primitive level at which verbal play is conducted is that of phonation, i.e., the actual process of emitting sounds. In the babbling stage, usually at its peak between 0:6 and 0:10, the child produces a great variety of sounds. These random noises, however, are probably not the immediate precursors of the vowels and consonants of language. Many disappear from the repertoire altogether, and others have little resemblance to the more organized units that later make up the phonological system that forms meaningful words. However, vocalizing continues in noncommunicative settings through the early periods of language acquisition. Recordings of solitary children of about 1 year (Eshleman n.d.) show long episodes of vocal modulation of a single vowel, with voice melodically rising and falling, varied with other sound effects such as quavering voice or sharp on-off glottal closures. Stable syllabic forms are also repeated at great length, with or without minor vocalic or consonantal modifications. When the child does begin to talk (production of the first intelligible word is usually reported at about 10 months to a year), then to learn to produce and to voluntarily control the contrast between making vocal noises and speaking, it is possible to identify episodes of verbal play with sound.

Repetitive, rhythmic vocalizations are associated with pleasurable states in the prelinguistic child, and infant-caretaker games very often include a vocal component (Stern 1974). The caretaker's "swelling" oooh-sound of mock threats and loomings, the popping noises and tongue clicking that enhance tickling, finger-walking, or jiggling are among the first models of vocal play the infant encounters. His own use of playful vocalizations continues as he learns to talk, and through the preschool period it becomes increasingly differentiated from other uses of speaking.

Syllable shapes and prosodic features such as intonation and stress provide raw material for early language play. Controlled variation in articulation such as rasping, constriction, devoicing, or nasalization are also favorite materials. Making noises can be enjoyed as an absorbing motor activity in itself, or can be used to provide special sound effects (e.g., motor noises). With strict temporal regulation vocal noises can provide rhythmic accompaniment for other motor play (e.g., humming or clicking the tongue while hopping or banging some object).

Vocalizations as accompaniments to motor activities move from hums, squeals, shrieks, and bellows to repetitive, often melodic strings of syllables.

Music to iron a fish by was provided by a boy (3:0). The syllables *dá ti; dá ti*[2] initiated the chant and were gradually varied in a loose singsong rhythm. A restricted inventory of vowels and consonants provided the main source of variation. The segmental base of the sequence was: *da ti di* (3*x*) *da* (3*x*) *do di da* (2*x*) *do di do di da do* (2*x*) *di do da di go bo di* (3*x*). His partner watched but did not join in this chant. But before the age of 3 sequences of nonsense syllables move to chants with recognizable word shapes and with fairly regular patterns of stress and pitch. In all these types of playful vocalizations the meaning of the words is secondary or nonexistent and it is the sound and rhythm alone that is enjoyed or that enhances the accompanying activity. An example is a chant produced by a 2:5-year-old upon completing a block-building project:

Now it's dőne un űn
Doñe un űn uñ.
(Johnson 1928)

Between the ages of 2 and 3 an important advance takes place. Conventionalized noises are learned and used to identify certain events and actions. These noises, each of which has a specialized meaning, appear to be an almost essential part of the particular event or action for the child who performs that action. However, insofar as they are conventional, the noises also serve to identify the meaning of what is happening for a playmate. Some of these noises are built from the sound units (phonemes) of the child's language, but others represent noises that do not occur in the formation of English words.

Examples of such action-identifying tags used by American children are: *ding-ling* (a telephone, of course), *ruff-ruff* (a dog barking), *tjap-tjap* or *njam-njam* (the sound of eating), *pow-pow* (explosions of a gun). *Beep-beep* is an automobile horn, and the racing engine could be written as *vroom-vroom* though that sound is much more complex, often involving either trilled velar [r] or trilled bilabial, nasalization, and lengthening of vowels. Reduplication of a syllable is the characteristic principle of formation for most of the tags. They are used to fill in or elaborate the context of pretending and always occur with the appropriate physical activity. Sometimes verbal

2. Some cited material will indicate stress only, distinguishing strong and weak or unstressed syllables. The symbol [´] directly over a vowel indicates strong stress and other levels are unmarked, e.g., [dá ti]. When it is necessary to indicate a stress level intermediate between strong and weak, the symbol [`] is written over the vowel. Other cited materials will indicate direction of pitch using, where relevant, the following symbols immediately before the point of change: [ˊ] high rising; [ˏ] low rising; [ˋ] high falling; [ˎ] low falling; [ˇ] falling-rising; [ˆ] rising-falling. In these examples only emphatic stress, i.e., extra-strong stress, is indicated, using the symbol [˝] over a vowel.

identification of a make-believe act is truly lexical rather than onomatopoetic. In one dyadic episode a girl (3:1) accompanied her broadly schematic actions of damaging and then repairing the stuffed snake by saying, *Cut, cut, cut, cut,* then, *Sew, sew, sew, sew.*

Distortion of normal articulation is another way in which vocal capabilities can be played with. "Talking funny" was engaged in by several dyads. For example, trying to speak with the lips held spread and rigid or talking in a squeaky or gruff voice was a source of amusement in itself and could be shared by a dyad. Just "talking funny" is somewhat different from the use of paralinguistic modifications to signal an adopted identity, e.g., infant, father, baby fish, in episodes of make-believe with role enactment. In the latter cases, which we will discuss in a later section, various aspects of speaking and of language are used to mark an assumed role and to express pretend attitudes, but are not themselves the major focus of play.

Solitary singing or humming frequently provides accompaniment to other activity. It can be related thematically to the concurrent nonverbal behavior as was the chant, *Now it's dône un ún.* But the song or chant can become a primary focus of attention, continuing beyond the action that was its immediate referential trigger. For example, a boy (2:10) began by picking up a small model of a dune buggy (named for him by an observer who then left the room). First the phrase *dunebuggy* was explored for its syllabic and segmental possibilities, then the stress and syllable pattern was adjusted *(dúnebùggy → dúne bú-ggý);* next the initial consonant was modified from stop to homoganic affricate *(dune → june)* and the first syllable was duplicated *(júne júne bú-ggý);* finally, to the four approximately equally stressed syllables was added a rhythmic contour with slight terminal pitch rise. Throughout the sequence the child walked about and casually examined a large wooden car and a stool with magnifying glass in the center. The chant itself had become the absorbing activity while the object that triggered it was virtually forgotten.

The preceding example and the one that follows utilize sound for play, but the sounds are more clearly linguistic elements and the intonational features are similar if not identical to the prosodic features of pitch and stress that are part of the phonological system of communicative speech. Thus these examples appear to be transitional between play with noises and sound, and play with features of the linguistic system.

Manipulation of the prosodic and segmental possibilities of word shape can be produced without melodic overlay. For almost 15 minutes a girl (3:0) engaged in taking apart, putting together, and varying the syllabic structure of the magic phrase, *Yesterday.* Most of the syllables were whispered as the child explored the room, handling various objects. Her speech was clearly noncommunicative and her companion paid no attention to the soliloquy. A brief excerpt of that speech shows primary and secondary stress only:

yéster yéster yèsterdáy
yésterdày yès tóo–
yéster diý yéster yèsterdáy–
yés tér yéster. . .

The last two examples were instances of the nonliteral (and nonsocial) exploitation of the sound properties of language for their own intrinsic interest. They exhibit a focus on the form and structure of speech, particularly on the phonological subsystems of syllable structure, stress, and pitch. In the dyads these kinds of sound play clearly contrasted with other instances of speech produced by the same child for various communicative purposes, and the sound play was generally ignored by the copresent peer. Further, the meaning properties of the phrases appear to have evaporated with repetition, much as in the process called **verbal satiation.**

Playing with sounds and noises appears to be primarily a private, solitary activity. Only one report of social play with nonsense syllables has appeared. Elinor Keenan (1974[b]) videotaped her twins (2:10) during the first hours of the morning when they were alone. She obtained a wide variety of joint, well synchronized, linguistic play activities (songs, poems, ritual insults), and several instances of sound play, which she defined as "utterances which cannot be referentially interpreted by an adult native speaker." Some of these employed possible English syllables, but many included sounds or processes that are not part of the English phonological system. Since our dyadic sessions contained no such **joint** sound play of this type, it may be that only children who are very well acquainted can produce structural verbal play like this excerpt from an episode created by Keenan's twins (stress was not indicated in her report):

CHILD 1	CHILD 2
1. *apshi: autshi:* (2x) *o:tshi: o:shabatsh*	
	2. *sha:shabatsh:*
3. *sho:babatsh*	
	4. *sho:babat shobabatsh* (laugh)
5. *sho:bababatsh*	6. *sho:batsh* (laugh)

The major processes are syllable reduplication, infixing and lengthening with a restricted vowel-consonant inventory. Basically, [a] ~ [o:], [a] ~ [a:], [o] ~ [o:], and [b], [sh], and [tsh] are repeated with [b] limited to medial position.

Play with the Linguistic System

The period from 2 to 3 is one of rapid linguistic achievement. Playful use of language at this time has been reported, though primarily for solitary children. One of the most detailed accounts is that by Ruth Weir (1962) who recorded the presleep monologues of her son, Anthony (2:10). These recordings revealed seemingly indefatigable practice of linguistic structures. Anthony experimented with the phonological properties of nonsense syllables and words (e.g., *Let Bobo bink. Bink ben bink. Blue kink.*), and with sentence patterns. He systematically substituted words of the same grammatical categories (e.g., *What color mop. What color glass.*), and built up and broke down sentences, thus isolating their components (e.g., *Stop it. Stop the ball,* and, *Anthony jump out again. Anthony jump.*). He exercised conversational exchanges, often asking and answering questions, congratulating or warning himself, and he practiced counting, listing, and naming. His paragraphs, defined by Weir as sequences of utterances chained by phonological, grammatical, or semantic links, often simultaneously show associational linking of elements at all of these three levels of language structure. A brief excerpt from a longer paragraph is:

That's office. That's office.	Sound play with the pronunciation
Look Sophie.	of That' [sɔfɪs] and [sɔfi] with
That Sophie.	substitution in sentence frame.
Come last night.	Breaking down a complete sentence.
Good boy.	Recall of recent event and
Go for glasses.	self-congratulations on keeping
Go for them.	hands off forbidden glasses.
Go to the top.	More systematic substitution in
Go throw . . . , etc.	frame. Rhyming phrase.

These voluntary performances have been called practice play, i.e., the repetition and variation of newly learned structures, and are believed to contribute to the child's developing mastery of his language.

It is likely that many children when they are alone conduct similar bouts of playful language exploration as a primary activity, but similar manipulations of linguistic forms can also be produced while the solitary child is busy with some other occupation. James Britton (1970) reports a performance, which he calls a "spiel," by Clare, a girl (2:2) who was drawing pictures. The monologue reflected her artistic activity, but it also suggests enjoyment of the sound properties of words beyond a simple running commentary on the picture:

Big eye. There's a eye–there's a eye–there's a eye–there's a little eye.
More big ones.
Draw a coat down.
Draw a ling-a-ling-a-ling.
Draw a little thing–little ear squeer big eye–little ear here–eye!
A little girl called Sinky and she's walking.

The buildups, repetition, substitution of words, alliteration (e.g., *a-ling-a-ling, a little*), rhyme (e.g., *ling-thing; ear-squeer-here*) are similar to Anthony's chains. In all these cases, the solitary speech differs on a number of dimensions from the child's speech produced in instrumental conversations as, for example, when he wishes to influence another person's actions. When alone, he experiments with the componential structure of sentences as well as with their prosodic possibilities. In fact, he takes apart and puts together playfully building blocks of sequences that he cannot, until several years later, consciously isolate or decompose (Holden and MacGinitie 1972).

In social peer interactions, the distinction between practice or exploration of linguistic abilities and play with language is somewhat clearer. First, each partner must know whether what the other has said requires a playful or nonplayful response, and thus the productions are likely to be redundantly marked if they are intended as playful. Second, the pressures of responsive social interaction do not seem to permit the lengthy and leisurely unfolding of private meaning associations, or privately intriguing sound variations such as Anthony and Clare pursued. Keenan's twins at 2:10 years did jointly produce, in alternating turns, sequences of nonsense syllables as well as intelligible phrases with rhymes and phonological variation that were very similar to Anthony's linguistic exercises. But in our dyads of schoolmates and of unacquainted children, playful exploitation of language resources was rarely shared until after the age of 3. And then the interactive play with language tended to be repetitive and predictably structured, that is, less like a stream of associations and more like a measured, alternating current. However, from 3:4 to 3:6 virtually all levels of language structure were used as a basis for social play.

From this point on we will examine the social play with language as conducted in the dyadic sessions. In that setting, of course, the children could be either socially engaged or could ignore each other altogether, and they often moved quickly from one state to the other. When not engaged, one or both children sometimes produced "private" speech that was somewhat similar to Anthony and to Clare's solitary performances. They sang fragments of songs, made up chants, explored word shapes, but indulged less in grammatical buildups, breakdowns, and substitutions than did Anthony Weir in his presleep monologuing. One girl (3:2) in a dyadic session after unsuccessfully trying to engage her partner in a conversation, conducted one with an imaginary Mr. Smugla, supplying both sides of the dialogue. It began:

–Smugla, Mr. Smugla I can't bring my daughter.
–Why? Why? Why? Why?
–She didn't have any dresses–or shirts or pants.
–Then I'll keep her in her pajamas.
–But she can't stay in them. . . .
[continued for four minutes]

It may be that the sheer presence of another child, no matter how uncooperative, leads another child toward forms of language play that are less "analytical" and more potentially interactive in form.

SOCIAL PLAY

Three types of social play will be distinguished: spontaneous rhyming and word play; play with fantasy and nonsense; and play with speech acts and discourse conventions. More than one type can be represented in a single episode, but the distinctions appear to reference some basically different uses of language resources for play.

Spontaneous Rhyming and Word Play

Spontaneous social word play arose most commonly from states of mutual attending and desultory conversation. It did not tend to arise in more mutually absorbing states such as pretending.

The most obvious type of word play is rhyme. Children's predilection for rhythm, rhyme, and alliteration is well known (Stern and Stern 1907). Only a few simple rhymes were constructed by the present sample of children. In this example, one child was responsible for the rhyme *high/sky*; the other repeated the leader's words and rhythm but concluded the sequence with a literal request for information:

M (4:1) (handles small ladder and pipe)	M (3:9) (watches)
1. *I need `this.*	
	2. *You need `that.*
3. *You go´ way up `high.*	
	4. *You go´ way up `high. Nobody can see.*
5. *You go´ high in the `sky. Nobody can see.*	
	6. *Nobody can´ see?*
	7. *Nobody can´ see?*
8. *ˎYeah.*	

A single word utterance provided a rhyming exchange for another young dyad: *sparky/darky*. However, only an older dyad produced a multiple exchange episode containing a sequence of rhymes and variations on word shape and prosodic features:

(both children simultaneously wander and handle various different objects, little direct gaze)

M (5:2)	F (5:4)
1. *And when Melanie and . . . and you will be in here you have to be ˋgrand ˋmother ˊgrand ˎmother. Right?*	
	2. *I'll have to be ˎgrand ˏmomma ˎgrand ˏmomma ˋgrand ˎmomma.* (in distorted voice)
3. *ˎGrand^mother ˎgrand^mother ˎgrand ˎmother.*	
	4. *ˎGrand^momma ˎgrand ˎmomma ˎgrand ˎmomma.*
5. *ˎGrand^mother ˎgrand ˎmother ˎgrand ˎmother.*	
	6. *ˎGrand^momma ˎgrand ˎmother ˎgrand ˎmomma.*
7. *‸Momma.*	
	8. *^Mommaˊ I . . . my ˎmommy ˎmomma.*
	9. *ˎMother ˎhumpf.*
10. *ˋHey.*	
	11. *ˋMother ˋmear* (laugh) *ˋmother ˋsmear.*
(laugh)	
	12. *I said ˋmother ˋsmear ˎmother ˎnear ˎmother ˎtear ˋmother ˋdear.* (laugh)
13. *ˋPeer.*	
	14. *ˋFear.*
15. *ˎPooper.*	
	16. *ˊWhat?*
17. *ˎPooper. Now ˋthat's a . . . ˋthat's a good ˎname.*	

The stress possibilities and the common lexical variants (e.g., *mother, momma, mommy*) were fairly well exhausted by this dyad. But the phonological properties of words appear to be more available for spontaneous play than their grammatical shape. A morphological process for forming diminutives, i.e., addition of (-i), to the last consonant of a monosyllable, e.g., *doggie,* or to a nonfinal consonant of a reduced polysyllabic stem, e.g., *Kathy,* and the formally similar process that means *having the quality of the noun,* (e.g., *fishy, rainy*) were the only grammatical operations the children played with. The first process, along with duplication of the word, is illustrated by the following exchange:

M (5:2) (inspects stuffed animals)	F (5:7) (busy with suitcase)
1. *`Teddy bear's^mine:*	
	2. *The `fishy´ is^mine.*
3. *No, the `snakey^snakey is ˬyours.*	

The second process was used as the basis for a sophisticated exchange of pure word play:

F (5:7) (wandering)	M (5:2) (moving ironing board)
1. *'Cause it's fishy too.* 2. *'Cause it has fishes.*	
	3. *And it's snakey too 'cause it has snakes and it's beary too because it has bears.*
4. *And it's . . . and it's hatty 'cause it has hats.*	

Play with Fantasy and Nonsense.

Nonsense verse, with or without rhyme, and nonsense stories add a dimension of meaning or meaning distortion as the resource for play. As soon as a child has learned how something is supposed to be, then turning it upside down or distorting it in some way becomes a source of fun. The most productive process for making nonsense at the word level in our corpus was the creation of proper names that are odd or impossible, and of meaningless common nouns.

Assignment of funny names to self, to partner, or to imaginary others reflects awareness of the importance of the normal name and address system. In nonplay exchanges, children were very insistent that they be called by their correct names. Several dyads engaged in serious discussions on the choice or the correct pronunciation of their proper names. There may be certain properties that make some types of play names especially amusing. Nonsense syllables, e.g., *dingba, poopaw*; nonname words, e.g., *Fool-around*; terms with scatological overtones, e.g., *Mrs. Poop*; and terms possibly intended as insulting, though also used of self, e.g., *silly face, My name's Dumbhead,* served as themes for social play among all groups except the youngest dyads. The following example represents at least two types:

F (5:7) F (5:1)
(Both children are using telephones to call friends)

1. *Mommy, mommy, I got new friends called Dool, Sol, Ta.*

2. *Dool, Sue, and Ta?*

(both laugh)

3. *Those are funny names, aren't they?*

4. *No, it's Poopoo, Daigi, and Dia . . . Diarrhea.*

(both laugh)

The manipulation of sense and nonsense is one of the components of many successful rhymes and stories written by adults for children, but children too can create nonsense. They not only use outrageous names, but also juxtapose improbable elements and invent unlikely events, retaining just enough sense of the real world to hold the fabrication together. In a number of cases the nonsense was produced as if it were serious sense and **was marked as play only by laughter after the performance.** With gestures and dramatic delivery, and a straight face, one boy (3:5) told another a story, about his Thanksgiving turkey, which was caught, patched up with a band aid, and cooked, whereupon it flew out the window. Both giggled happily after the narrative.

A girl pretended to write a letter with real paper and pencil. She produced the following poetic nonsense–which must have been her own unique creation–and that was heartily appreciated by her partner:

F (4:9)
(on the car, writing letter)

F (4:7)
(listening and drumming on stove)

1. *Dear Uncle Poop, I would like you to give me a roasted meat-ball, some chicken pox . . .*
2. *and some tools. Signed . . .*
3. *Mrs. Fingernail.* (smiles and looks up at partner)

4. *Toop poop.* (laughs)
Hey, are you Mrs. Fingernail?

5. *Yes, I'm Mrs. Fingernail.*
(in grand, dignified voice)

6. *Poop, Mrs. Fingernail.*
(giggles)

Manipulation of sense is often, except in intent, closely related to outright prevarication, and we must presume that when a child misnames or asserts an obvious untruth and marks it as playful that he has some awareness of the distinction between truth and falsehood. But several factors are involved here, factors that have to do with the use of language in context.

Play with Pragmatic Aspects of Language

Pragmatics has been defined as the study of linguistic acts and the contexts in which they are performed (Stalnaker 1970). Pragmatics subsumes such topics as logical and pragmatic presuppositions, the analysis of propositions, the structure of speech acts, and the rules for production and interpretation of linguistic acts that have been called **conversational postulates.** At a still higher level there is the organization of discourse, the ways in which conversations are opened, sustained, and terminated. The study of conversation also includes analysis of the mechanics of linguistic interaction, e.g., the distribution of speaker turns, and repair in case of errors or temporary breakdowns in exchanges. As we have seen, young children play with sound, with the structure of words, and with sense and nonsense. We might also expect that they would play with the rules that guide the normal use of language in its various social and cognitive functions.

An example of "misnaming" will illustrate the interrelation of the linguistic aspect of reference and the interactional aspect of language use. At the same time the following example highlights the distinction between a pleasant, but literal naming activity, and a play exchange based on the same linguistic resource, i.e., the relation of referent and word (or signifié-signifiant). I recently met a 2-year-old and her 5-year-old brother, David. Susie started to show me parts of her face, pointing to her eye, saying *Eye,* then her nose, saying *Nose,* and then her mouth. Her somewhat neglected brother, who had been watching, moved in and pointed to his forehead and said, quite dramatically, *Here's my mouth.* David and I laughed then, but Susie was not amused.

Distorting or violating the conventional match of word and referent is not only play with meaning, but at another level it is play with a rule of language use. The violation in this respect abrogates the convention that conversational partners will normally not attempt to mislead each other. According to Grice's

(1975) supermaxim, a speaker should try to make his contribution one that is true. Davison (1974) also reports instances of such play in a family setting. Sophie (3:2) found blatant misnaming of pictures and objects quite funny–if the interlocutor was her mother. With a stranger, however, she was less sure that this rule violation was intended as humorous and did not know how to respond to the mislabeling of a picture. Jean (2:0), her brother, also succeeded in playing with the convention with his mother, but was easily recalled to seriousness in cases when she did not go along with the joke. A still younger child (1:10) who was present did not recognize what Davison calls "nonserious" speech events.

Among the younger dyads "correct" labeling of objects was a favorite topic of conversation, as was the discussion of whether an object was "real" or a "toy." The older dyads, however, found outright prevarication and obvious misnaming a source of fun. For example, a boy (5:2) asked a girl (5:5) whom she would rather play with, Mary Ann or Lisa. She looked at him reflectively and replied, *Um. I think . . . um . . . Lisa, because she's a boy.* Then she giggled and her partner laughed and said, *No, she's a^gi::rl. You silly.*

The basic unit of human communication is the speech act, an intentional, verbally encoded social gesture directed by one person to another. It is likely that meaningful social acts are exchanged between child and caretaker before the development of the linguistic code (Bruner 1975). Thus, study of the developmental processes that lead to linguistic expression of interpersonal intentions is currently attracting a number of students of child language. The act potential of language is learned as the child learns to talk, and the structure of speech acts is still another resource for play. As with the other types of play, the nonplayful use of this resource contrasts with the playful use. That is, in order for a child to play with a threat or a promise, he must also be able to convey and respond to a threat or promise in a literal manner.

Speech acts rest on mutually shared beliefs that make performance of the act possible (Searle 1969). One means by which the structure of a speech act can be turned to a playful use is by willful and obvious violation of an underlying belief condition. Two belief conditions on the successful performance of a threat are that both speaker and addressee believe that the speaker is able to carry out an action inimical to the addressee, and that he intends to carry out that action. A conditional threat is one in which the execution of the threat is contingent on some specific behavior of the addressee. Successful conditional threats were frequently accomplished in our corpus. For example, *Please don't do that. If you do it, then I won't be your friend,* or *If you keep calling me Mother, then I will tell on you.* (The criterion for success of the act is that the addressee, whether compliant or not, realized on the basis of the speaker's utterance that a threat had been issued.)

Conditional threats can be defused in play by the speaker's "promising" to perform an inimical action when he obviously cannot, or will not carry it out, or by promising to perform an ostensibly inimical action that is actually not inimical (in both the speaker's and the addressee's opinion at that moment). This is a rather dangerous and delicate procedure, and misunderstandings do arise. An example will illustrate a playful use of a conditional threat and a nonconditional threat. The episode was marked not only by laughter, but also by explicit reference to the harmlessness of the action, i.e., *It won't hurt.* The actual throwing action was also restrained:

F (3:3)	F (3:8)
1. *If you throw that iron at me I'm gonna tell. If you're going to throw that at me, I'm gonna tell.*	
	2. *I'm going to throw something at you. Want me to throw this? It won't hurt.*
3. *Right. I know 'cause it's nice and furry, right?*	
	4. *Yeah.* (throws toy)
5. *That didn't hurt.*	
	6. *No that, that furry. See block.*
7. *Throw that at me. If you throw that iron at me, I'm gonna tell.* (laugh)	
	8. (laugh) *I did.*

Another episode from the same dyad illustrates the exchange of nonplay threats. In this example, one child withdrew her threat to tell her mommy by saying, *I don't want to tell.* She substituted for the threat a request for action, i.e., *Will you please stop that?*

F (3:3)	F (3:8)
	(hits at partner)
1. *I'm telling, when I get home to my mommy, I'm gonna tell.*	
	2. *I gonna hurt you.*
3. *Hm, stop it. I don't want to tell. Stop that, all right?* (crying) *Will you please stop that?*	

Play with requests for information in this corpus violated the conditions that the speaker does not know the "answer" and wants the information requested. Played requests for information were often ritualized, i.e., conducted with highly repetitive intonation and strict regulation of utterance and pause length. In the following example, it was clear that the boy knew the answers to his requests for information:

M (5:2) (picks up dress-up items)	F (5:7) (sits on car)
1. *What is this?*	
	2. *It's a party hat.*
3. *What is this?*	
	4. *Hat.*
5. *Funny. And what is this?*	
	6. *Dress.*
7. *Yuck.* 8. *And what is this?*	
	9. *Tie.*
10. *All yucky stuff.*	

Conversation incorporates speech acts, but represents a higher level of organization than the speech act. Insofar as we understand the structure of dialogues and the conventions that guide the sequencing of turns at speaking, as well as the content of those turns, we can examine children's use of these conventions in playful and nonplayful interactions. For example, techniques for opening conversations are relatively simple and well understood; these techniques, or **routines**, should be available for play at an early age.

Routines are predictable utterance sequences that serve a single or limited role, and are restricted to particular positions or specialized functions in respect to a conversation or interaction. A routine is highly conventionalized and is probably learned as a package. A familiar example is the summons-answer routine (Schegloff 1968). That routine was well controlled by all the age groups in our sample and was also used for play, as was the simple greeting. The latter was often ritualized, as when a younger dyad intoned the greeting, *Hi, bubba. Hi, mommy,* through ten exchanges. The routine was conducted repetitively for its own sake and its normal function as a greeting was forgotten.

As for play with the conventions that guide the sequencing of moves in conversation, we can mention two that appear to be quite productive as play material. One, stated in adult terms, in something like the following: If an assertion has been made and countered, introduce some support for the assertion or for the counter assertion. Children play with this convention by withholding support and by simply repeating, often at great length, the assertion-counterassertion exchange. In such episodes (as opposed to their more goal-oriented counterparts), there appears to be no real concern with convincing the partner or making a point. The conversation, instead of progressing, simply recycles, as in this example from one of the youngest dyads:

F (2:10)	M (3:0)
1. *That's your cowboy hat for when you go outside.*	
	2. *No, no it's not.*
3. *I bet it is.*	
	4. *No, it's not.*
5. *Yes it is.*	
	6. *No, it's not.*
7. *Yes it is.*	
	8. *No.*

All groups played this type of exchange and usually produced it in ritual form.

A second productive convention for play is one which has been called an invitation question. The convention, however, is probably not restricted to questions. It operates somewhat as follows: Respond to a question or assertion concerning your own state or experience as an invitation to contribute to the conversation. Thus, if a conversational partner says to you, *I heard that you had an unusual vacation,* or *Did you have a nice vacation?,* a simple *Yes* or *No* does not suffice to maintain interaction. As addressee, you have been invited to expand on the topic, e.g., *Yes, we spent a week in Portugal.* Some such convention appears to underlie play episodes in which one partner repeatedly questions and the other steadfastly refuses to elaborate, as in this example:

F (3:7)	M (3:7) (has just put on fireman's hat)
1. *Is that your fire hat?*	
	2. *Yeah.*
3. *Did you get it from school?*	
	4. *Nope.*
5. *From here?*	
	6. *Nope.*
7. *Where? In the car?*	
	8. *Um, no.*
9. *From you?*	
	10. *No.*
11. *From in the other room?*	
	12. *No. Yes.*

A nonplay or literal use of the same convention was, as we would expect, also possible for this same dyad, e.g., *You changed your mind?–Yes, I want to be the daddy.*

The fact that certain conventions are well known enough to serve as a basis for verbal play does not, of course, mean that children's nonplay conversations are in many or most respects well formed by adult standards. There are exchanges that impress us as strange or odd in some way. Future research will probably reveal that many of these are failures on the pragmatic level.

LANGUAGE IN THE SERVICE OF MAKE-BELIEVE

The preceding discussion of social play has focused on the resources of language and speech as the primary material of play. But language can also be used to support and enhance other types of play. One type of social play that relies heavily on communication is make-believe, and in our dyads verbal enactment of pretend identities was one of the major means of communication. In pretending to be a mother, child, father, baby fish, or fireman, children often modified their speech in form, manner of delivery, and even in content. We will present only a few examples of family role talk.

Shatz and Gelman (1973) observed the following characteristics in the speech of 4-year-olds to 2-year-olds as compared to their speech to peers or adults: more use of attention-getting devices; more simple direct request forms; shorter sentences; more concrete as opposed to abstract verbs. Gleason (1973) reported similar characteristics in the speech of 6- to 8-year-olds to younger children, as well as raised overall frequency, use of diminutives and terms of endearment, and an occasional "error" in baby-talk syntax, e.g., *That's ant* instead of *That ant*, or *That a ant.*

When our peer dyads played family, not only did one child shift to represent an adult, but the other child had to take the less favored baby role. Thus, we have the contrasting behaviors of talk-to-baby and baby-talk. Even among the youngest dyads, consistently differentiated marking of these roles was possible–at least for girls. Dyads composed of two boys tended to avoid these roles across the entire age range. Younger mixed-sex dyads assumed father-mother, or father-child roles, while older mixed-sex dyads preferred husband-wife roles.

Baby talk and talk-to-baby shared the feature of using third person pronouns and proper names in place of first and second person pronouns. A mother, while feeding baby, said, *That's for baby. It's not for mommy.* A baby announced of self, *Baby peed in her pants.* Both also committed the syntax error noted by Gleason, for example:

MOTHER (3:1)	BABY (3:1)
1. *Okay, put them on the table.* (cups)	
	2. *Where the table? Where table?*
3. *Here's table. There's that table. Put lunch there. Put your lunch there. That's table.* (gesturing to the wooden car)	

Baby talk was further marked by whining, crying, and imitations of babbling, e.g., [gu: gu:] and [ga: ga:], but the child in baby role spoke much less than did the mother. Mothers produced long strings of short, simple clauses, with frequent repetition of phrases, frequent interjection of *Baby* as term of address, and the sentence tag, *Okay?,* and some diminutive forms, e.g., *handsies, shoesies.* Overall frequency of pitch was higher than the child's nonrole-playing voice and as mother, the child often crooned as she attended to baby. The following example is typical of the pretend caretaking in the youngest dyads:

MOTHER (3:1) (showing baby a toy car)	BABY (3:1)
1. *Here's a little motor car. A little motor car. See that motor car? This is your motor car.*	
	(moves toward car)
2. *Your very own little motor car, okay?*	

Mothers were versatile, however, and if necessary could scold sternly as well as coax. And babies were not always compliant. One girl (3:0) called her father on the phone and after listening to him a moment, shouted, *My daddy, I don't want to, my daddy! No!,* then angrily threw down the phone. When boys played the role of father (to a girl's baby), they were stern, sometimes threatened the baby, and spanked it.

Our observations indicate that mother-baby role enactment is not only possible but fluent in the age range 2:10-3:3, and that one child can perform either role (these roles could be traded in the middle of a session). Comparison of these observations with Gleason's (1973) suggests that role-playing tends to elicit the adoption of age and status variants in speech at an earlier age than has been previously reported. Most important is the indication of the consistency in packaging prosodic, lexical, grammatical, and interactional features into the respective role enactments. Not one or two features co-occur, but a whole complex of modifications that reflect the children's concepts of appropriate baby and caretaker behavior.

CONCLUSION

There is little doubt that our growing understanding of discourse will provide a firmer basis for study of verbal play. The preceding overview was necessarily sketchy, but perhaps it has suggested a relatively neglected area for further research. A great deal is normally learned as language is learned. We have argued that many different aspects of language and language use become available for play as they are acquired, and that a closer look at play may help to reveal what has been learned as speech becomes fluent. The data of spontaneous interactions among peers furnish an important but as yet unexplored basis for investigation of communicative competence. Social play is built on shared resources. To play successfully requires that the partners communicate to each other that they are playing and what is being played. The signals are often subtle and differ from episode to episode, but can provide the observer with indications of whether a state of play is in force.

"You Fruithead": A Sociolinguistic Approach to Children's Dispute Settlement

DONALD BRENNEIS AND LAURA LEIN

INTRODUCTION

This chapter is an exploration of the structure and strategies of American children's arguments. The chapter has three central themes. First, arguments are speech events; an analysis of argumentative discourse reveals characteristic structural patterns in both content and style. We will consider the rules that underlie these patterns and that organize argumentative speech into socially meaningful episodes. Our second theme is the delineation of the kinds of speech skills required for children to speak effectively within the framework of these rules. Finally, we will discuss the range of argument–appropriate, alternative utterances available to children and the strategic choices evident in individual performances. Children display not only an understanding of discourse rules specific to argumentative speech events, but also the ability to use this knowledge for their own purposes.

In the spring of 1970 we participated in the seminar, "The Acquisition of Communicative Competence" given by Claudia Mitchell-Kernan at Harvard University. During the semester each participant in the seminar designed and executed a research project concerned with the ability of children to communicate. We were particularly interested in dispute behavior and conflict resolution. We wished to uncover the structures used by children as an illustration of the kinds of skills children must master in order to speak effectively.

Because Brenneis was acquainted with an elementary schoolteacher in western Massachusetts, we decided to work there. Data were collected in the first grade of the Marks Meadows School and the third and fourth grade classes of the Shutesbury Village School. The children we worked with were white, primarily middle-class children from the immediate area. The data were collected over a

3-day period during which children talked freely into the tape recorder and then performed role plays under our direction. The actual collection of dispute materials occurred during role-played events.

During each role-play session pairs of children were asked to perform one or more of the following role plays:

1. One of you will have the ball and will be playing with it on the playground, just having a good time. Then, the other one comes along and sees the ball. He really wants it, so he just walks over and takes it. Then you both act out what happens next.
2. One of you will have the pencil and you will sit here at the table writing with it. Then, the other one walks by and really wants that pencil, so he walks up and grabs it. Then you both act out just what happens after that.
3. Now, you both sit facing each other, but not touching each other, and have an argument about who is the strongest.
4. Now, I want you to sit facing each other, but not ever touching each other, and have an argument about who is the smartest.

Role plays one and two are substantially different from role plays three and four. In the first two role plays there is a concrete issue to be determined, i.e., who is to end up with the ball or pencil. The latter two role plays represent a much more straightforward display of verbal virtuosity.

Clearly, role plays are different from real-life situations. For instance, many children's arguments begin away from the immediate presence of adults. Children's disputes may end in tussles or grabbing matches which we did not allow. As we collected role plays and also watched the children in their regular, everyday activities, we realized that certain aspects of role plays are, in fact, not representative of spontaneous verbal exchanges. For instance, role plays last longer than most spontaneous disputes and the rules of argument are more rigidly adhered to. However, by-and-large, the techniques used in role-played disputes also occur in everyday interactions.

This chapter includes five sections. In the following section we will discuss the kind of content appropriate to dispute dialogue. The second section is a discussion of the stylistics of dispute. The third section is an analysis of the patterns by which content and style are organized. A detailed discussion of one role play is presented in the fourth section as an example of the tactics, stylistics, and sequences described in the previous sections. The fifth section presents some concluding remarks. The first two sections are essentially lists of relevant categories of content and style, and in the third section, we will consider the rules by which the use of these content and stylistic categories are bounded.

TACTICS AND CONTENT IN CHILDREN'S ARGUMENTS

We examined the content of 70 role plays in order to explore categories of content used in dispute exchanges. The frequency of certain content is one defining feature of a verbal dispute. We discovered these categories in several ways. Some kinds of content–such as threats and insults–were labeled as such by children. Such labeling might occur in the context of disputes, *Don't you threaten me.* Other categories represented logical contrast categories to those described by participants. Other categories of statements, although unspecified by participants, occurred with sufficient frequency to warrant categorization. In general, all categories of content could be specified in one of two ways: Argumentative statements might be statements about the opponent, things attached to him, his speech, or the relationship between the opponent and the speaker; other argumentative statements were concerned with preceding statements.

Most of our analysis categories had an "inverse," a kind of statement in some sense opposed to the initial category, but also used appropriately in disputes. For example, "bribes" as defined below may be considered an inverse of "threats." One is a promise of some valued good. The other is a promise of some evil or punishment. The use of inverses was seldom pointed out or discussed explicitly by combatants. Such statements often required an ironic or sarcastic tone of voice to be appropriate to the dispute. For example, a statement of agreement, the inverse of a statement of denial, would be delivered in such a tone of voice, *Sure you are* (stronger).

The categories of content listed below represent much of the content format of disputes. In our role plays these categories accounted for virtually all statements made.

The first group of content categories includes those statements concerned with explicit statements about the opponent:

1.	**Threats:**	Promise of personal harm to the opponent, those attached to him, or in general.
	Examples:	*I'll kill you.* *I'm going to tell the teacher on you.* *The building will fall down if you do that.*
1′.	**Bribes:**	Promise of personal profit to the opponent (often delivered ironically).
	Examples:	*I'll give you a dollar if you can.* *I'll give it right back to you.*
2.	**Insults:**	Name-calling, or ascription of negative value to opponent or things attached to him.
	Examples:	*You dummy.* *Your shirt is filthy.* *You're too fat to be strong.*

2′. **Praise:** Ascription of positive value to opponent or those attached to him (often delivered ironically).
Examples: *You are smart.*
You sure look pretty today.

3. **Command:** Order or outright demand.
Examples: *Give it back.*
Don't say that.

3′. **Moral persuasion:** Statements of reasoned argument.
Examples: *I had it first.*
It's my brother's.

4. **Negating or contradictory assertion:** A statement in direct contradiction to a preceding assertion, without being a simple statement of a negative (which would be classified as a denial).
Example: JULIE: *I'm the strongest.*
JOHN: *I'm the strongest.* (Negating assertion)

4′. **Simple assertion:** Statement of fact/opinion (something of a catchall category).
Examples: *That's my shirt you're wearing.*
I'm so strong I can lift you up.

[**Note:** "Simple assertion" is a relatively loose category, but is important to dispute. These statements may be "just talking." But they represent the interlude, the change of pace, or variation in content. One kind of assertion particularly frequent in dispute is a statement of comparison, such as *I got my math done before you did,* **and** *I'm stronger than you are.*]

The second group of categories represents statements about or reactions to previous statements:

5. **Denial:** Use of negative.
Examples: *No, you can't.*
Unh-unh.

5′. **Affirmative:** Use of "yes" or other explicitly affirmative term (often delivered ironically).
Examples: *Yes.*
Yes, I want it.

6. **Supportive assertion:** Statements presenting evidence in support of an argument.
   Examples: *(It's mine) Because I bought it.*
   (I'm stronger) Because I'm bigger than you.

6′. **Demand for evidence:** Request for proof or evidence from opponent.
   Examples: *Prove it.*
   How do you know?
   I bet you can't.

7. **Nonword vocal signals.**
   Examples: *Nyeeh-nyeeh.*
   Aaaargh.

A number of kinds of expertise are necessary in order to use these content categories appropriately in the context of a dispute. First of all, the disputant must possess sufficient knowledge of his world and society to understand what kinds of statements are suitable. For instance, a threat of *I'll tell the baby on you* is not in the nature of a threat as is *I'll tell the teacher on you.* [Mitchell-Kernan and Kernan's (1975) discussion of the misapplication of situationally specific insults by young children stresses the importance of the acquisition of such cultural knowledge for communicative competence.]

STYLISTIC TACTICS IN CHILDREN'S ARGUMENTS

We will use the phrase "stylistic tactics" to refer strictly to those suprasegmental elements of speech which, apart from content, determine the mood or tone of a verbal exchange and in so doing define the nature of the speech event. Paraphrasing Kenneth Burke, Hymes (1974:106) suggests that style is the "arousal and accomplishment of expectations." Appropriate and characteristic stylistic conventions mark an event as an argument and enable an audience to anticipate the structure of ensuing exchanges. Even without hearing the words, most listeners can tell what sort of speech event is occurring by noticing such gross stylistic variables as pitch, volume, and speed.

In analyzing our corpus of 70 arguments, we isolated four types of stylistic features used both idiosyncratically by speakers to emphasize particular utterances, and as more elaborate interactional tactics: volume, speed, stress, and intonation. Volume was coded on a continuum from very soft to very loud; speed was similarly coded on a continuum from slow to very rapid. Stress was coded as an element when it was used markedly to emphasize particular words or utterances; exaggerated intonational contours used for emphasis were similarly noted. Our recognition and coding of these elements in the transcripts depended partly on our intuition in determining what were ordinary, unmarked uses of the variables and what constituted salient cases.

Volume

Volume is seen as a virtue by many children. Three patterns of volume-based sequences were found. Least common was inversion (loud-soft-loud-soft). More common was imitation; a loud utterance would be responded to by an equally loud one. Most common, by far, however, was escalation. The reply is louder, and the third utterance is even louder. Through such a sequence, and volume sequences average 10 turns or more, a general crescendo effect is evident. Reaching an absolute fortissimo, louder than which neither disputant can go, signals the end of a sequence and time for a new tactic. A finalization rule for such sequences is that volume increases to fff and stops. Volume escalation is the single most popular stylistic strategy with younger children.

Speed

Markedly slow speed is most common in idiosyncratic usages where drawing out particularly significant utterances gives them great emphasis. Response to this in kind is relatively rare. Imitations lasted, at most, two turns. However, reciprocal acceleration often develops in short utterance arguments. In one outstanding, but not singular passage, the two opponents, arguing about who was stronger, built up an alternating chorus of *me's*, becoming faster and faster as well as louder and louder, and ending when their outbursts were simultaneous. A finalization rule for speed sequences is that acceleration continues until the utterances are simultaneous. Following such simultaneity children initiate a new sequence based on another semantic or stylistic program. We believe that such termination is linked to the strict turn-alternation followed by the children; simultaneous utterances violate this rule. Acceleration was the most common stylistic gambit among the older children but very rare among the younger.

Stress

Stress is a particularly complex issue. It is used idiosyncratically for emphasis. The sequential use of stress depends upon the development of rhythmical patterns. Responses in such sequences must not only be in the appropriate rhythm but novel in content; this contrasts with volume and speed where either the content or the style changes, but not both. The following is a first grade example:

GEORGE: *Little girly.*
SUE: *Little boyey.*
GEORGE: *Little girly.*
SUE: *Little boyey.*

George's *little girly* is a repeated trochee with particularly marked accents. Sue felt constrained to respond not only with a semantically suitable item but one cast in trochaic pattern as well, although phonologically the neologism *little boyey* emerges as more of a diphthong. This fourth-grade interchange further demonstrates rhythmical patterning:

BOB: *You're skinny.*
TOM: *You're slimmy.*
BOB: *You're scrawny.*
TOM: *You're . . . I don't know.*
BOB: *You're weakling.*
TOM: *You're the slimmiest kid in the whole world.*
BOB: *You're the weaklingest. . . .*
TOM: *You're baloney* (etc.).

Several points are interesting in this. First, the ordinary, conversational prosodic pattern of the first five utterances would stress the second syllable, e.g., *you're skinny*; Bob and Tom, however, place considerable stress on the first syllables, creating a dactylic pattern. The dactyl *you're skinny* requires a dactylic response. Tom comes up with the neologism *you're slimmy,* which fits rhythm. After another exchange, in which Tom cannot produce the proper response, Bob also appears to have overreached his potential, when he uses the noun weakling as an adjective. Tom does not feel it necessary to respond in rhythmic kind to this, and escalates with the superlative slimmiest. Bob tries out *weaklingest* but stops in mid-utterance, realizing that it didn't work out too well.

Intonation

Speakers often use exaggerated contours to emphasize what they are saying. Occasionally, as in the previous example, there are instances of imitation, but intonational contours are most commonly marked in idiosyncratic usage.

PATTERNS OF CONTENT AND STYLE IN CHILDREN'S ARGUMENTS

In this section we will discuss the ways in which content and style are organized into argumentative sequences. First, we will define and discuss an analytical unit of discourse, the **sequence**. Second, we will describe various structural patterns of sequences. Finally, we will explore the significance of the argumentative sequence as a paradigm for continuing the analysis of a dispute situation.

A sequence is part of an argument built around one kind of content category and, possibly, its inverse, or around one stylistic program. Each sequence begins with a statement different in content and/or style from those immediately preceding it in the argument. Sequences consist of at least two turns, i.e., of an exchange of utterances. In the arguments we have analyzed it is evident that the children respect each other's turn-time; a child will not begin his own turn until it is clear that his opponent has completed his. Preliminary data from a similar study of Hindi-speaking children in Fiji where children frequently break into each other's turns suggests that this strict alternation of turns in the United States is culturally specific, learned etiquette.

Another important aspect of the argumentative sequence is that it often results in one child winning and one losing. New sequences are initiated when one child is unable to respond strongly, rapidly and appropriately to another's utterance; hesitant and faltering responses mark the loser of a particular sequence.

Argumentative sequences are structured in one of the three basic patterns as in the following illustrations:

Repetition

Two successive statements in an argumentative sequence may be repetitive. For example, at its simplest, such an argument may look like this:

JACK: *I have an apple.*
ROB: *Well, I have a peach.*
JACK: *I have an apple.*
ROB: *Well, I have a peach.*

Escalation

Successive statements are each stronger, more imaginative or longer versions of preceding statements. Each statement expands on the previous utterance by increasing its power:

DAVE: *I'll bust your brain out.*
JIM: *I'll tear yours out first.*
DAVE: *I'll knock your teeth down your throat.*
JIM: *I'll punch your head off.*

Inversion

Successive statements may be drawn in turn from a category and its inverse, or, in some cases, from a category and one other category which represents a denial or negation:

DAVE: *I am, you dumb-dumb.*
LARRY: *I'm not no dumb-dumb, dodo.*
DAVE: *Yes, you are.*

LARRY: *No, I'm not.*
DAVE: *Yes, you are.*
LARRY: *No, I'm not.*

This is an example of inversion between affirmative and denial statements. The following example is a sequence based on the alternation between assertion and negating or contradictory assertion:

ROSE: *That's my ball.*
LINDA: *That's my ball.*
ROSE: *That's mine.*
LINDA: *That's mine.*

These argumentative sequences are the building blocks of dispute between children. The construction of each argumentative sequence demands the appropriate deployment of sequential rules by each party to the argument. It also demands the appropriate combination of content and style. Breakdown in the structure by inappropriate usage by one of the disputants is usually followed by the beginning of a new sequence.

Understanding the structural pattern of a particular sequence also enables a child to anticipate his opponent's response and to vary his own turn to trick the opponent, as in this example, from an argument about who is smarter:

ANN: *I am.*
JOHN: *I am.*
ANN: *I am.*
JOHN: *I am.*
ANN: *You are dumb.*
JOHN: *I am.*

Embedded arguments are a special kind of sequence. They are subarguments concerned with one particular issue, embedded in the framework of an argument about another contention altogether. Such embedded arguments can determine the outcome of the whole argument; and they are often the terminal sequences of arguments. The winner of the embedded argument may win all, even if the point he wins has no relation to the ostensible focus of the argument. A detailed example of embedded argument is provided in the sample analysis in Section 4.

In examining 22 sample arguments, certain recurring patterns were evident at the beginning of the arguments. Fifteen began with either an assertion or a comparative assertion:

I'm stronger.
My ball.
I got my math done before you did.
That's mine.
Bet I'm stronger than you.

Three began with an imperative: *Give me that ball.* Four began with insults:

You're a weakling.
You're dumb.
I am, you dumb-dumb.
You're skinny.

These beginnings constrained the structure of the rest of the argumentative sequence. Let's take the insults first. Two of the insults were answered with similar insult, and it is notable that the arguments continued with such exchanges, sometimes creating an argument of escalation. For those arguments where the initial result was answered by a negation, the pattern of insult negation continued throughout the argument segment:

ARG. 1

AMY: *I am, you dumb-dumb.*
SUSAN: *I'm not no dumb-dumb.*
AMY: *Yes, you are.*
SUSAN: *No, I'm not.*
AMY: *I say you are.*
SUSAN: *I say I'm not.*

ARG. 2

JACK: *You're a weakling.*
BRUCE: *No, I'm not.*
JACK: *Yes, you are.*
BRUCE: *No.*
JACK: *I'm stronger than you.*
BRUCE: *No, you aren't.*
JACK: *Yes, I am.*
BRUCE: *Nooo, sir.*

This suggests that insults usually initiate one of two kinds of exchanges for this group of children: (*a*) repetitive or escalated insults; (*b*) inversion between the original insults and denials. It also suggests that the original exchange is in some sense a model for the rest of the argument.

The three arguments which began with an imperative all have certain characteristics in common. Each time the imperative is followed by a negative response:

JIMMY: *Hey, give me back my ball.*
JOEY: *Can't have it.*
JIMMY: *I'm going to tell Mr. Barnes. . . .*
JOEY: *Go ahead.*

JIMMY: *". . . if you don't give me it."*
JOEY: *You're not going to get it.*
JIMMY: *You're going to get it.*
JOEY: *Go ahead.*

This becomes most evident in an argument where the ball changes hands several times:

JIMMY: *Give me that ball, you little. . . .*
JOEY: *No.*
JIMMY: *Give me that ball.* (Jimmy grabs ball.)
JOEY: *You give me that ball back.*
JIMMY: *No.*
JOEY: *You give me it. Give me that ball.* (Joey grabs ball.)
JIMMY: *Give it.*
JOEY: *No.*
JIMMY: *Yes, I got it first.*
JOEY: *I got the ball.*
JIMMY: *Give me it.*
JOEY: *No, I got it.*
JIMMY: *Yes.*
JOEY: *No.*

Next we come to those arguments that begin with a simple assertion. There are more variations in this pattern than with either of the other two patterns. The most obvious and most frequent response was to answer with a similar assertion:

ARG. 1

JIMMY: *I'm the strongest.*
JOEY: *Me, I am.*
JIMMY: *No, me.*
JOEY: *Me.*
JIMMY: *Me.*
JOEY: *It's me.*
JIMMY: *Me.*

ARG. 2

JIMMY: *I can lift everything in the whole wide world.*
JOEY: *I'm stronger in stuff like that.*
JIMMY: *I can lift everything in the whole universe.*
JOEY: *I can lift everything in the whole wide world.*

One assertion calls out another assertion, either identical or in an escalating mode.

The next most common type of response to an assertion is an attempt to negate that assertion, using a negative phrase or a negating assertion:

ARG. 1

JIMMY: *Bet I'm stronger than you.*
JOEY: *You aren't.*
JIMMY: *Bet I am.*
JOEY: *Bet you aren't.*

ARG. 2

JIMMY: *I'm stronger.*
JOEY: *No, I am.*
JIMMY: *I am.*
JOEY: *No, I am.*

And last of all, an assertion can be answered by moral persuasion, an argument that constitutes a morally powerful defense against the assertion:

ARG. 1

JIMMY: *My ball.*
JOEY: *I want that ball. I had it first.*

ARG. 2

JIMMY: *I'm stronger.*
JOEY: *Well, I already claimed it.*

This analysis suggests response patterns in the role-playing situation, such as those in the diagram below:

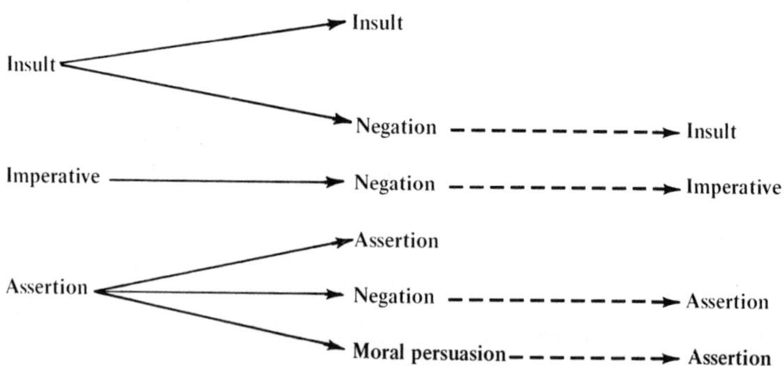

This is not to say that children's arguments are completely predetermined once the first remarks are hazarded. Rather, one remark indicates what the next remark will probably be, because the arguments are constrained by structural rules.

The use of stylistic strategies in arguments was more difficult to analyze systematically. First, semantic continuity is the organizing rule for argumentative sequences. Exchanges within a given sequence must be linked by a common subject or theme; failure to respond with a semantically related utterance terminates a sequence. Stylistic elements, however, can be used idiosyncratically; the challenge of a particularly loud outburst, for example, need not be taken up by one's opponent. Stylistic continuity and regularity are less important than the semantic links. However, in our analysis of 70 arguments, we did find some significant patterns of stylistic sequences.

Content and style seem to be reciprocally redundant. Arguments characterized by short, repetitive content exchanges are much more elaborated stylistically than are more semantically complex arguments. We distinguished two general types of utterance; short, i.e., single word, phrase, or simple subject-verb sentence turns; and more grammatically elaborate, long utterances. Arguments tended to be consistently either short utterance or long utterance throughout their course. Idiosyncratic uses of stylistic elements which did not engender a response were more common in long utterance arguments. Stylistic sequences developed more frequently in short utterance arguments. In such arguments semantic continuity was maintained through simple repetition; argumentative elaboration and strategies depended upon stylistic features.

Once the opponent responded in kind to a stylistic gambit, sequences were more predictable. While it was easier for us to derive rules for how content sequences began than for their termination, finalization rules could be determined for stylistic sequences. It proved impossible to predict when a stylistic sequence would begin, but some prediction is possible of how, once begun, they will end. The same three types of dynamics obtained as in content strategies:

REPETITION (imitation)

JAMES: *I can climb higher than you.*
MIKE: *No you can't.*
JAMES: *Un huh.*
MIKE: *Nooo sirrr* (drawn out)
JAMES: *Unnn-hunhhhh* (drawn out)
MIKE: *Nosir* (quickly).
JAMES: *Unhuh* (quickly).
MIKE: *Cannot. Can't, can't, can't, can't.*
JAMES: *I can, I can, I can, I can.*
MIKE: *No you can't.*
JAMES: *Un-huh.*
MIKE: *Nooo youuu caan't* (drawn out)
JAMES *Unnnnn-hunhhh* (drawn out)

Several things are evident in this example. Content is definitely secondary to stylistic variation. Second, James is making stylistically proper responses by being aware of and cleverly imitating the other's style.

In those arguments where imitation occurred, it continued throughout the course of the argument. Inversion was less common than repetition in stylistic sequences. Escalation along one stylistic dimension was the most frequent strategy. Escalation was discussed in detail in the analysis of individual elements.

THE MAGIC MAN ARGUMENT

In Table 1 we present a lengthy role play between two first grade children on the topic of who is strongest. In this argument a number of sequences are developed.

TABLE 1

Analysis of the Magic Man Argument

Speaker	Transcript	Content tactic	Content pattern	Style tactic	Comments
		SEQUENCE 1			
Joey	*All right. I can lift up this school. What can you lift up?*	Assertion Demand/evidence			
Ann	*I can lift up our whole fámily. I bet you can't lift that up with one finger.*	Assertion Neg. Assertion	Escalation		
Joey	*I can lift the whole wórld up with one finger.*	Assertion	Escalation		
Ann	*Well, I can lift up the whole universe. So why don't you just be quiet about thât?*	Assertion Command	Escalation	Increased speed	The injection of new stylistic elements and Joey's weak response signal the likely beginning of a new sequence.
Joey	*Yeah–you too. I can. . .*	Break		Increased loudness	
		SEQUENCE 2			
Ann	*I bet you wouldn't dare go near the sún.*	Neg. Assertion			
Joey	*I can pick up everything, catch the world, catch the sun, catch Jupiter, catch everything, and with one finger.*	Assertion	Escalation	Repeating rhythm	
Ann	*Even if yóu touched the sun, you'd burn up.*	Neg. Assertion	Inversion		
Joey	*If I'd touch the world, then the world'd touch the sun.*	Assertion	Inversion		
Ann	*Then everybody'd burn up on the world.*	Neg. Assertion	Inversion		
Joey	*So what?*	Neg. Assertion			This response breaks the rhythm and signals the likely beginning of a new sequence.

TABLE 1–Continued

Speaker	Transcript	Content tactic	Content pattern	Style tactic	Comments
Ann	*I'd throw you up on the world and yóu'd burn up too.*	Threat			
		SEQUENCE 3			
Joey	*Nó, I'd be fine. I'm a mágic man.*	Assertion Assertion			
Ann	*Oh, you're not a magic man. Whynsha be quiet about that? You don't even have a magic hat or a magic book like all magic men have.*	Neg. Assertion Command Neg. Assertion	Inversion	Intonation	
Joey	*Yes, I do. You never saw it before you came over.*	Assertion Neg. Assertion	Inversion		
Ann	*I sneaked over to your house yesterday and I sneaked through your whole house and closets and everything and I couldn't find that magic hat.*	Assertion Neg. Assertion	Inversion		
		SEQUENCE 4			
Joey	*Well, I gave it to my friend.*	Assertion			This beginning to a new sequence is marked only by the introduction of a new content theme.
Ann	*Well, that means yóu're not a magic man anymore.*	Neg. Assertion	Inversion		
Joey	*No. I gave it to my friend to protect them cause I knew you were coming over.*	Neg. Assertion	Inversion		
Ann	*Oh, you did not.*	Neg. Assertion	Inversion	Increased speed	
Joey	*Because you called my mother up and my mother said you were coming over.*	Assertion			Here again, a break in the pattern of the argument signals the likely beginning of a new sequence.
Ann	*Yeah, but I didn't say when.*	Neg. Assertion			
		SEQUENCE 5			
Joey	*Ah, she knows. She's magic too. My whole family's magic.*	Assertion Assertion Assertion			
Ann	*Ah, now I couldn't find your whole family's magic hats.*	Neg. Assertion	Inversion		
Joey	*I gave them to my, to my friend.*	Assertion	Inversion		
Ann	*And I went over to your friend's.*	Neg. Assertion	Inversion	Increased volume	
Joey	*So what?*	Neg. Assertion		Increased volume Intonation	Again, here, a break in pattern leads to the beginning of a new sequence.

TABLE 1–Continued

Speaker	Transcript	Content tactic	Content pattern	Style tactic	Comments
Ann	*I checked his whole house through. That means you're just telling lies. You're not magic.*	Assertion Insult Neg. Assertion			
		SEQUENCE 6			
Joey	*All right. If you want to say that, I can lift up everybody in the whole world.*	Assertion		Intonation Drawn out	
Ann	*You cannót.*	Neg. Assertion	Inversion	Stress	
Joey	*Yes, on my finger. They could stand on each others' heads.*	Assertion	Inversion		
Ann	*Your finger'd break.*	Neg. Assertion	Inversion		
Joey	*No it wouldn't.*	Neg. Assertion		Intonation	Break in pattern leads to a new sequence.
		SEQUENCE 7			
Ann	*I could lift up a boulder with óne tóenail.*	Assertion			
Joey	*I could lift up a boulder with nóthing.*	Assertion	Escalation		
	Laughter				
Ann	*How could you lift it up with nothing? It would come down and smash your head open.*	Neg. Assertion	Inversion		
Joey	*I could lift it up with a little téeny whíttle píece of dírt . . . with my finger under it.*	Assertion	Inversion	Rhythm	
Ann	*You are crazy today. Now you aren't magic and you don't have any friend that's keeping your magic hat either.*	Neg. Assertion	Inversion	Increased speed	
Joey	*So yóu júst bé qúiet.*	Command		Marked accent	This break in pattern ends the dispute.

CONCLUSION

Many researchers have begun to document the structure of different kinds of speech events and to infer the kinds of skills necessary for participation in such events. For instance, Abrahams (1970) discusses the oral tradition of blacks in northern urban centers. Labov (1972[c]) discusses the structure of "the dozens" and the skills necessary for successful participation. Other authors (Ervin-Tripp 1973; Bernstein 1971; Hymes 1974) have documented the different variables to be accounted for in describing and analyzing speech events.

In this chapter we have begun to take a close look at the structure of one kind of speech event and the inferred skills and abilities necessary for participation in that event. This is a tentative first step in the analysis of elements that define appropriate speech usage in the context of an event. We believe that continued work with this kind of analysis will lead to several kinds of findings. The meaning of speech in the context of specific kinds of events is related to a combination of content, style, and sequencing or pattern of the speech itself. Detailed analysis of speech should lead to the identification and description of the elements that are appropriate to speech events. Through this we will begin to understand how these different aspects of speech are used and interpreted and how they define speech events. While this chapter has been concerned with structural rules and strategies in argument discourse, it also suggests some of the features important in rules of identification of a speech event as an "argument" (cf. Labov 1972[c]:123).

Analysis of speech and its meaning and interpretation lead to an understanding of the skills necessary to appropriate speech. We learn not only how speech is used and interpreted, but what the complex of skills necessary for making and interpreting appropriate speech are.

Such research has particular relevance to problems in education. Since speech is a participatory event, the quality and quantity of speech bv one participant are affected by the speech of other participants. Also, the speech of any one participant is affected by his interpretation of the speech event and his analysis of what is appropriate to it. Thus, children's speech, in the classroom, under test situations, playing with friends, is related both to the speech addressed to the child or spoken in his hearing to other children, and to his interpretation of the kind of event signaled by that kind of speech. As we understand what elements of speech lead to the definition of a speech event, we may be able to restructure the events in which children participate in school to allow them to increase the rate and quality of their participation.

From Verbal Play to Talk Story: The Role of Routines in Speech Events among Hawaiian Children

KAREN ANN WATSON-GEGEO AND STEPHEN T. BOGGS

NT (NĀPUA TEAM)

(Kona and Keahi, girls, 6.5, Noela, boy, 7, and W., Watson) (numbers refer to lines in transcript)

KO 112: *[An da de- . . . an da devil, dey get knife, you know* (warningly).
KE 113: *[An he-he get . . . down den–if you] stayed a-walk da beach, he go stab you,*
114: *[You go die from you* (rapid, affectively detached).
N 115: *[I go all night, I like go some* (voice trails off).
W 116: *Mmm* (to Ke, very low).
KE 117: *Den he go_____you, he going_____.*
KO 118: *'Keh, you go, you going die . . . Noela.* (Gloss: 'All right, if you go, you are going to die'.)
KE 119: *Den he really_____.*
KO 120: *I not lie.*
121: *[I telling da truth–*
N 122: *[Mmm* (vague).
KO 123: *[Somebody else lyin* (innocent, slightly accusatory).
KE 124: *[He go kill somebody else.*
125: *So he get –dey wen eat guys, yeah?*

(Note: Overlaps are indicated by [.)

KO 126: *[Yeah, da guys–*
KE 127: *[Dey–dey–*
KO 128: *[–Dey–*
KE 129: *[–chop em up–*
KO 132: *[–devil–*
KE 133: *[–fight for da kine, and dey suck da blood* (voice constricted, loudness cut–gives impression of shock, disgust, understatement).
134: *Dey suck da blood* (very softly).
KO 135: *Dey wen | eat | all | da | bones, boy* (measured, gives impression of forcing out the consonants; severe, very tense in body and face).
KE 136: *Yeah.*
KO 137: *Dey eat da na'au* (intestines) *an evryting.* (Watson 1975)

In the shadow of the Ko'olau mountains of windward Oahu, two Hawaiian girls are telling a story to a few friends. Within sight are the caves and beaches which the narrators will incorporate in the plot, as together they weave an explanatory tale of spirits and devils. The excerpt is from one of many sessions on the lanai of an elementary school in a Hawaiian homestead neighborhood, where Watson was studying the speech acts of children for 10 months in 1970-71. All 55 of the sample children were members of Nāpua Team, an ungraded class of 5- to 7-year-olds, and were speakers of Hawaiian English, a local variety of language undergoing rapid decreolization towards Standard English. Tape recordings of stories, conversations, joking and teasing, argument, recitation, and other speech events were made on the school grounds, but without a teacher present.

During the 10 months of the study the children of Nāpua Team, 26 of whom told stories, jointly produced 150 narratives. Analysis indicated that the stories were long and complex. Thus the 102 stories told during the last 5 months averaged 148 words (mean), which compares favorably with stories told by 5-year-olds of superior intelligence from professional families in New Haven recorded by Ames. The mean of the latter was 93, 63 for boys and 124 for girls (Ames 1966; Watson 1972). All but one of the 102 stories was extended, i.e., contained clauses in addition to those reporting the essential action (Labov et al. 1968). They averaged 10.8 narrative clauses and 12.4 nonnarrative clauses per story. Two-thirds or more of a sample of 30 stories contained initial orientation, later description, summarizing, and formal closings, while half contained interpretation (Watson 1972).

The rhetorical skill of the narrators was particularly striking. To attract and hold audience attention they used dramatization–acting out the behavior of individual characters–and implicated passersby in the story, thus drawing them into the audience. One girl, for example, went from an audience of two or three to 12 while inventing a story that lasted for almost 40 min. Yet it was not individual skill alone that made such a performance possible, for members of her audience indicated, by knowing looks, that they recognized the gestures and what they were intended to symbolize.

In this chapter we discuss some of the factors that may have enabled the children of Nāpua Team to perform in such a complex manner. So far as we can tell from studies of children from similar background, the ability to tell such stories does not depend upon extensive practice. Rather, our evidence suggests that the children made use of a variety of verbal routines that were familiar to them from other contexts in order to construct their performances in the Nāpua Team group. Evidence of this can be found by comparing the sexual teasing that they engage in elsewhere with the sexual narratives that evolved in the group, the pattern of verbal disputing as it relates to the contrapuntal structure of the narratives, and the forms of dramatization used in the narratives with similar forms of adolescent and adult behavior. We examine each of these lines of evidence in turn, following a description of the sources of the data referred to, and our reason for believing that the children lack extensive practice with storytelling under natural conditions.

Evidence cited in the final section of the chapter indicates to us that knowledge of verbal routines is not sufficient in itself to organize such complex performances in a group of children at this age. Therefore, we conclude with a discussion of some of the situational and contextual factors that may have been additionally responsible for the narrative performances that occurred in the Nāpua Team group.

Data Sources

As mentioned previously Watson's data were collected from Nāpua Team, a group of part-Hawaiian children living in a suburban community in Hawaii. ("Part-Hawaiian" is a cultural category including many, but not necessarily all, who have some Polynesian ancestry.) Various speech events, including conversation, joking, recitation, arguing, and singing were tape recorded before a self-selected peer audience. Watson made no attempt to control the size, composition, or the responses of the audience. Initially, children who wished to hear their voices on tape had been presented with the eliciting frame, "Tell us a story." Subsequently, they frequently asked to hear the recording of their voices after telling a story. No attempt was made to control the content or style of their speech. Soon the eliciting frame became unnecessary. The children quickly learned how to work the recorder and took charge of the recording sessions. Often Watson's attention was elsewhere, not on the performers. Of the tapes made over the school year, a total of 8 hr of recorded talk from 14 sessions have been examined for this chapter. These data include the active participation of 45 children, though all 55 participated as performers or audience at some time during the year.

Data from other sources include recordings made by mothers of three 5-year-olds of their children in everyday interactions at home. The mothers were discouraged from attempting to elicit speech, and instead encouraged to turn on the recorder whenever the 5-year-old seemed to be most loquacious. In all, 16 children were included in these recordings. They ranged from infants of less than 1 yr to 8-year-olds, with one entry of a 13-year-old girl. A total of 7.5 hr of tape were obtained, a minimum of 1 hour from one family. In each case the mother was asked to identify the participants and provide a rough transcription.[1]

In a second, briefer study, recordings were made in a kindergarten classroom of an experimental school. Ten children were recorded as they talked in the doll corner, during juice time, and at lunch. They were recorded without their knowledge. Though teachers and others were present, the children generally disregarded them except in a few cases (which have been omitted from the analysis). Total recording time was 1.25 hr.[2]

These recordings contain only three narratives told by children under 8 years of age, all of them personal experiences told to other children. They are rich, however, in a great variety of verbal routines: disputing, teasing, dramatic play, play with words, jingles, and speech accompanying eating, dressing, manipulation of objects, and caring for younger children (Boggs 1974). The paucity of narratives is regarded as indicative of the children's actual experience with this form.

Participant observation since 1966 by Boggs in a wide range of settings has not produced any evidence that children tell stories to one another or to adult members of their families at this age. In any case, their practice in storytelling is clearly more limited than their participation in other routines.

STORIES BASED UPON SEXUAL TEASING

In this section, we present and discuss the evidence to indicate that sex narratives in the Nāpua Team group may have evolved from a pattern of sexual teasing that the children already engaged in. It is also noted that this pattern of teasing has its sources in adolescent and adult behavior.

1. Training of the mothers was carried out by Richard Day, assisted by Violet Mays and Boggs. During the home recordings, no outsider or researcher was present. A Sony 110 with internal microphone was used for the recordings. The research was supported by the Kamehameha Early Education Project (KEEP), a research and development effort of the Kamehameha Schools towards improving methods of educating Hawaiian children.

2. These recordings were made by Violet Mays, as part of the Kamehameha Early Education Project. A major purpose of the two studies was to determine how much the children shifted in their use of Hawaiian English between home and school when not specifically doing school work.

The most prominent of the narratives told in the group in terms of number and length concerned lovemaking and its consequences: marriage, pregnancy, and childbirth. Such stories were initiated by the following tale told by Kekoa on Keaka, who was present and listening.[3]

NT

Once upon a time dey was a girl name . . . Ke-aka.
She was married to Aggie.
And . . . she was big (pregnant).
She had a baby.
She had a . . . twin boy an girl.
And da boy name was Pono.
Yeah. S-she marry Po- Pono.
Uh, then she had boys, two boys and two girls.
An then . . . the mother Keaka count all her baby.
She counted op to ten. (counts)
She said, "Aw my gosh! I din know I had ten babies."
Here. Finish now.

(Note: participation and comments by audience deleted.)

If pregnancy and childbirth did not directly connote "sex," they were at least emotionally loaded topics for Nāpua children. Though Keaka had laughed and accepted Kekoa's story with good humor, she insisted on telling the next story at the expense of Kekoa. This story, referred to in the introduction, became the prototype for the more than 80 stories about love and sex to be told over the next several months. Its explicitness was a marked departure from Kekoa's discreet rendition. The following are excerpts from the story:

NT

Once uponna time da name–her name was Ke-koa.
She had one baby and one boy.
Dere name was Kekoa a-an Pono.
Kekoa and Pono had beeg kee-kee (kiss-kiss).
An afta Kekoa would take a bad way home and all kine stuff.

An afta Kekoa say, "Come on honey, let's go to da show."
An afta he-he say, "OK, let's go, let's go."
She was walking jus like one egg.
An afta Kekoa and Pono wen walk away to da show,
and den kiss in dere, OK.

3. The children have been given pseudonyms to protect their identity. All data from Nāpua Team are labeled NT. For convenience, all girls' names in this set begin with "K" and boys' names begin with other letters.

Pono say, "OK, come on Kekoa. Get on your back!
Come on, Kekoa, get on your back."
Said, "Get on na back, I-I wen found you some pua (flowers, babies, sweethearts, love) *heya.*
"Come on, Ke-ko-a. Give me dat pen-cil befo I cwack em on your head."

"Oh bruddah, he seek (sick) *man," say Kekoa.*

—

*An she say, "**Oh-h-h** let me take a bath wit you."*

Keaka's story required nearly 40 min. to complete. A tribute must be given to Keaka's mastery of rhetoric and performance: she built her audience by spontaneously weaving passersby into the story as characters; she paid attention to inputs from the audience and was sensitive to her effect on audience response; and she dramatized the story by acting out the roles and behavior of characters both paralinguistically and physically. In fact, there was no other child in the group who could match Keaka's performance. Yet clearly the Nāpua audience understood and appreciated the meaning of her words and actions even where the researcher did not understand.

What, then, were the sources for the content and form of these sex stories that were so well understood by the children?

In recordings made in other settings there are a number of examples of teasing involving allegations such as "X loves Y" or the following:

1: *You get peepee.*
2: *Kulei like you' skinny* (=penis), *ae?*

Sex-linked taunts and insults like these are exchanged:

1: *Come ova hi' and pus* (push) *dis **head*** (=penis)!
2: *Teu yo' madda you go show* (=have intercourse).
1: *I touch yo' oko-ole* (=butt)!
2: *An eat your ow'd **butt**!*

The children of Nāpua Team engaged in similar exchanges. The following exchange illustrates the close connection between such sexual teasing and narratives based upon them:

NT

KAPUA: *Once uponna time Kekoa love Lopaka.*
And uh, an um, Kaleo (laughs and tries to fight off Kaleo who is beating and pulling at her).
KONA: *Kaleo!*
KAPUA: *Uh don't. Keaka love . . . Keaka love. . . .*

KONA:	(undecipherable)
KAPUA:	*Keaka love uh–Maleko. And den Pono love . . .* (laughter).
?:	*Tell em, Kapua.*
KAPUA:	*Um-um. And Keaka love Pono.*
KALEO:	*Kapua honey-honey bun.* (Pun: "honey-honey"=sexual intercourse).
KEKOA:	*An Kaleo love–*
KAPUA:	*And da honey-honey bun.* (Retaliation through mimic) *And dere–* (laughs)
KEKOA:	*Kaleo loves–Kaleo loves–Kaleo loves–*
	[material omitted]
KAPUA:	*Kekoa. An Kekoa wen behind da . . .* ——— *an she make utu-utu* (sexual intercourse) *with ummm, no wait, um Maleko. OK, I pau, dat's di end.*
KALEO:	*My turn.* (Claiming right to retaliate)

Other types of insults are frequently exchanged by part-Hawaiian children, but they did not enter into the narratives told in the Nāpua Team group. The reasons for this difference add to our understanding of the function of sexual teasing in the production of narratives.

For one thing, insults, which refer to attributes, do not lend themselves to narratives as well as sexual teasing, which refers to acts, since narratives consist of a series of events (acts). For instance, insults such as the following two examples would require a great deal of imagination to turn into events:

NT

KEAHI: *You get ukus* (=nits) *in your hair.*

—

MALO: *You know him, hah? He don' know* (how to) *talk.*
He talk Japani.

Of course it is not impossible to base stories upon attributes. Black children only a few years older base teasing stories upon physical characteristics, poverty, and hunger. Hence there may be a cultural factor involved here as well. It seems easier for Hawaiians to take the idea of two people loving each other and formulate episodes for a story. At any rate, there were no examples of successful stories based upon nonsexual insults in any of the data. Insults instead were simply exchanged, as in the following example in which a group of Nāpua boys and girls are looking at a picture from Hawaiian mythology. The picture shows a boy whose legs can stretch magically so that he can reach to the top of a cliff (the stretching motif is a common Polynesian motif in folklore and mythology, Kirtley 1971).

NT

KEIKI: *Oh, you stupid, yeah?*
KEALOHA: *No, da opposite.*
KEHI: *I not gon have beeg legs.*
KEALOHA: *When you grow op, gon have beeg legs.*
KEKOA: *Yeh, when you grow all-l-l da way up to dere, you going to have beeg legs.*
HALE: *Yeah, an when you get married you gon be–* (obscured)
KEHI: *I n'gon have beeg leg–*
KEKOA: *An un-uh _____, you gon have beeg legs like your mommy* (laughs).
KEHI: *Shut op.* (Argument follows: "like you," 'beeg ears, beeg mout'," etc.)

Another reason why sexual teasing may have lent itself to narrative development is that it generated great interest and excitement—so great that serious arguments and fights followed serious teasing (Watson 1972). It was thus good material for attracting and holding audience attention under the conditions of severe competition as will be discussed. But storytelling has an advantage over teasing. The "as if" or make-believe aspect of storytelling provides the narrator with certain protections. The make-believe aura, as well as its stance of reporting, remove some of the directness of allegations, since the narrator claims that he or she is not responsible for them. By their tone of voice narrators of Nāpua Team clearly took this stance both in sex stories and in the more fantastical events of folktales (for evidence see Watson 1975).

Finally, given the expectation that stories would be told, and the discovery that "getting it on tape" was a good way to retaliate for insults, the invention of sex narratives seems to be an understandable development, with sexual teasing providing the materials. In the final section we discuss the role of such retaliation in the evolution of turn-taking within the group.

In considering its origins in experience it should be noted that sexual teasing is not limited to children. As described in the section on dramatization, Bernstein points to its central importance in a group of part-Hawaiian adolescents. Children frequently observe not only adolescents but also adults engaged in sexual teasing (Boggs field notes). Beyond this, parents engage their children in such teasing, as in the following recording made at home:

(1 is a boy 5 years old. 1's brother, 4 years old, has just teased mother by threatening to call up grandmother)

MO: *You call gramma your* ***neck.***
1: *Ne^{j}k.*
MO: ***You'*** *neck.*
1: ***Your*** *neck.*

MO:	***Skinny!***	Gloss: 'Shrimp' (also=penis)
1:	***Skinny.***	
MO:	***You! Skin-ny!***	
1:	*Bwa-a!*	Emphatic form of 'Boy', 1's name. Gloss: 'I'm Boy.'
MO:	*Bwa-a skinny* repeats with taunting intonation).	Gloss: 'You're Boy, but you are still skinny.'

On another occasion, in the midst of a wrestling match with her three sons and daughter, this mother, with great hilarity, calls them ugly, Dracula, and "puka" (=vagina), among other things. She also threatens to *twist you guys' head like the snake.* "Head" carries the added connotation of penis.

The Contradicting Routine and the Contrapuntal Structure of Narratives

Further evidence of the influence of verbal routines upon narrative performance in the Nāpua Team group can be inferred from a comparison of familiar disputing routines with the contrapuntal structure manifested by all types of narratives. As Watson has demonstrated elsewhere (1975), both joking conversation and folklore narratives in Nāpua Team exhibit a contrapuntal structure: that is, a joint performance in which two or more speakers alternate rhythmically to produce the event (Reisman 1970). Sexual joking and teasing is obviously a joint performance, the speakers alternating in their allegations and counterallegations, as illustrated previously. Folk and personal experience narratives were likewise joint performances, however, the several speakers mutually developing the plot and commentary. Significantly, they often supported, challenged, or competed with one another (see Watson 1975 for supporting data).

Underlying this contrapuntal structure, we suggest, is a form of exchange that Boggs has labeled the **contradicting** routine on the basis of its most ubiquitous component: the outright contradiction of another speaker. The routine begins with one speaker making an assertion (claim or allegation), which the second speaker contradicts with a denial or counterassertion, as in the following two instances:

(1 is a boy 12, 2 and 3 are his brothers, aged 6 and 7)
(Looking at snapshots)

1: *'As my aunty da aunty like drink.*
Da ***lika*** *one.*
2,3: *Not! [Aunty Lani.*
1: *[Am–] ow no-ot!* (continues)

All of the relevant exchanges are included in the following. It is presented in full because it constitutes the longest contradicting routine recorded for 4- and 5-year-olds. Sequences are also indicated to facilitate comparison with Brenneis and Lein's chapter (this volume). The girls, sisters, are addressing a 7-year-old friend.

(Speaker 1 is 5 years, speaker 2 is her 4-year-old sister.
They are addressing a 7-year-old friend.
Mo is the younger girls' mother.)

SEQ. 1	
1: . . . *Momma, How [o'd–*	1 starts to ask mother how old they all are.
2: *[Five.*	Claims age.
1: *Her fo'.*	Contradicts 2, correcting her.
2: *No, I **five.***	Contradicts, repeats claim.
SEQ. 2	
1: ***I** five.*	Contradicts, argues (see following for rationale).
2: ***I** five.*	Contradicts, returning argument by repeating it.
SEQ. 3	
1: *I'm five.* (fast)	Repeats argument. Note intonational shift.
2: T^{ry} *ask **Mommy.***	Suggests appeal to mother.
1: (silence)	Ignores.
2: T^{r}*a'k **Mommy!***	Repeats suggestion, increased emphasis, escalating.
SEQ. 4	
2: *'ai Mommy sai' me* ^{y}*an **you-u fi-ive!***	Argues, quoting authority. Note intonational shift.
1: *'m 'm* (mouth closed)	Contradicts. Note inversion of 2's intonational pattern.
2: *Da **Mommy**, Mommy sai' me* ^{y}*an you **five.***	Repeats argument, but note change of stress on /me/ and other changes that de-escalate. She may also have started over.
SEQ. 5	
(1 appeals to mother for confirmation of brother's age. Mother does not respond.)	
2: *Mo'i* (Mommy) *me an **her** wouldn't **ea-eat!***	Attempts to gain mother's attention with report.
MO: (silence)	Ignores.

SEQ. 6

2: *Five.*	Repeats her claim.
1: *Her not* ***five.*** *Her not in kindəgarten.*	Contradicts 2, offers allegation as argument.

SEQ. 7

2: *Mommy, I go ᵗschoo'?*	Appeals to mother for evidence.
1: *Da* ***man****–Mommy sai'–*	Starts to argue, quoting authority.
2: *No, wha' my mathə say–me an her is [fi-ive!*	Argues, quotes authority.

SEQ. 8

1: *[æ-æ you bu' liaə!*	Acting as if contradicted, 1 dismisses, insults 2.
2: ***You*** *cry I put dis . . . inside ə you' eye.*	Threatens trial by ordeal.

SEQ. 9

2: *Blinked you' eye.*	Claims victory.
1: *You blinked* ***your*** *eye.*	Counterclaim.

The response to the contradiction may be simply a repetition of the initial assertation (as in Sequence 1 above) or a supporting argument, allegation, or appeal to authority (as in Sequences 3 and 6 above), with or without a further denial. At any point a challenge may replace the contradiction. This may take the form of an explicit statement objecting to the initial assertion or a subsequent one, or a question implying that the speaker doesn't know what he is talking about, as in the exchange between Ahi and Palani following. At some point, usually later, but sometimes near the start, one speaker will insult the other. The reply to an insult is a counterinsult (as in the instances cited in the previous section), a threat, or suggestion of a trial (as in Sequence 8 before). The insult is often "Lia!" which carries the connotation of not knowing what you are talking about, and not necessarily that you are attempting to deceive. Thus the issue of knowing is involved in several ways in the contradicting routine.

The routine is found in recordings from each of the families and the KEEP kindergarten, where it was observed daily by Boggs. It likewise appears in the interaction of the children of Nāpua Team. In the following instance it is used twice:

NT

(Kealoha, 7; Nakau and Hale, 6; Kapua, 5)

KE: *Kapua love . . . tough Kona.*	Sexual allegation
'Ey, don't (as Ka hits her).	
I–	

N:	(to Ka) *[I no] like you do dat to my cousin.*	Reproves Ka, also making a threat on basis of kinship, to defend Ke.
KA:	*Dat ain't yer cousin.*	Contradicts N.
N:	*It is.*	Contradicts Ka.
KE:	*OK, I sorry.* (undecipherable)	Apology to Ka for allegation.
	I sorry, Kapua. I not sorry fo real, but–	Retracts apology, thus contradicting.
KA:	*What?! You no sorry!*	Challenges Ke.
KE:	*Hey!* (pushing Ka off as Ka attacks)	
KA:	*You no sorry fo real? Get–I'm gonna burn your eyes out.* (Goes behind Ke and puts hands over her eyes, presses hard, until Ke cries out.	Repeats challenge. Threatens. Note similarity to trial by ordeal in previous example.

In another instance, contradicting is part of word play as Kaleo attempts to insult Kapua:

NT
(Ka=Kapua, 5; Kl=Kaleo, 6.5, Ko=Kona, 6.5)

KA:	(telling a sex story) *Dey make hug-hug* (sounds like "hag-hag").	
KL:	*What's "hug-how?"* (defiant)	Mimic, pun, challenging Kapua.
KA:	*Hug-hug!*	Contradicts, corrects Kl.
	D'you know what is "hug-hug?"	Challenges Kl on lack of knowledge.
KL:	*What's "hug-how?"*	Repeats challenge to indicate not knowledge, but literal pronunciation is the issue.
KA:	*I neva say "kow-kow."* (all laugh)	Pun, contradicting Kl, challenging Kl's own pronunciation, correcting.
KL:	*I say, "how-how." What's "how-how?"*	Defensively Kl mimics Ka's ploy, ridiculing her.
KA:	*I neva say–*	Starts to contradict Kl.
KO:	*Hug-hug.* (undecipherable)	Corrects Kl, mediating.
KL:	(to KA) *Talk, talk.*	Surrenders, ordering Ka to resume.

As in this example, the contradicting routine often leads to interruptions in storytelling. At times, such interruptions appear to be triggered by a member of the audience interpreting a narrator's statement as a claim to know. One example of such interpretation occurs in the following:

NT
(Ahi and Palani, 6)

A:	*You know ova deh? My dad was walkin op da mountin (æ ?).*	Formal opening phrase, orientation, request for confirmation.
P:	*[Who!*	Challenge (P knows who).
A:	*He saw one mountin lion. A followin him climb op da mountin, eh? He seen one [mountin–*	Continues story.
P:	*[Who] climb da mountin!?*	Repeats challenge, more explicitly.
A:	*My fa'er, he cotchin one mountin lion.*	Answers, alleges fact.
P:	*[Oh, cannot.*	Contradicts A.
A:	*[Yes he] [did! I betchu dolla.*	Contradicts P, suggests trial by wager (note overlapping indicating anticipation).
P:	*[He cannot.* (interaction ends)	Contradicts A.

The effects of the contradicting routine on storytelling extend beyond interrupting, for they may lead to rebuttal. This can be seen in the exchange quoted at the outset of the chapter. Noela, as a member of the audience, contradicted the storytellers by claiming that he would walk about in the allegedly dangerous park at night, notwithstanding their warnings. It is important to note that his contradiction is not based on a disbelief in devils or similar dangers, for even older boys share such beliefs (Boggs in press 1977). Rather, Noela is challenging Kona's implied claim to know of the existence of devils and spirits at the park. Evidence for this interpretation is in Kona's reply in Lines 120-1: *I not lie. I telling da truth.* She recognizes that her knowledge has been challenged. She goes on in Line 123 to archly return the accusation, saying: *Somebody else lyin,* that is, Noela himself. All of this is an instance of the contradicting routine, which has partly interrupted the story. But Kona simultaneously offers a rebuttal to this impugning of her knowledge, beginning at Line 118: *'Keh, you go, you going die . . . Noela.* The allegations supporting this assertion in Lines 125-37 contribute directly to the story. In this instance, the contradicting routine contributes directly to the narrative.

The use of narrative to support oneself appears in the home tapes. On one of the very few recorded there was the following:

(1 is a girl 5, 2 is her 4-year-old sister)

2: (mentions boy, Kalae, in school)

1: *Kalae in my* **class.** *How you know who he was? He was–his name Kalae?*

2: *Caused I kno'! Cause da+a dr time I tae'um* **me.** *'N he have his own water and den he was–down'tairs with* **us**–*Kalae. An Kalae was doin* (gesture) *hɛ? An de'guy was Debu* (Devil). *An nen–an Robert came –came ovə deə, heɛ? "zae-aep! Robert?"* (rising intonation) *No was –no was–dats da toy one.*

(Gloss: 'Cause one time I ask him myself. And Kalae had his own water and was downstairs with us (i.e., in our area–classes are on different floors). And Kalae was doing (something), hɛ? And the guy was the Devil. (Someone) went "zap!" (kill by disintegration) "Robert?" (i.e., "Robert! Where are you?") It (the gun) wasn't (a real one), it was a toy one.')

Finally, conarration provides a solution to the problem of contradiction during story performance. As noted, conarration, consisting of supporting or competing assertions relating to the story, is a key feature of the contrapuntal structure. Instead of contradicting or competing by telling a different story, or engaging in some other routine, a second speaker can join in the storytelling, surreptitiously competing, as it were, by adding his or her own knowledge (or guesses, as is often the case with children). Again this is illustrated in Lines 125-37 of the story at the beginning of this chapter. Viewed in this way storytelling takes on the characteristics of a transaction. The first storyteller accepts the contributions of the second as a way of minimizing outright contradiction, while simultaneously gaining support. Moreover, when the two storytellers are good friends (as in the case of Kona and Keahi), the transaction becomes a mutual reconfirmation of their relationship. That they recognized their collaboration is indicated by the following:

NT

KE: (to Ko) *You know da story me and you just 'old, da same–da otha one, on Sea Life Pa'k in da night time?*

KO: *Talk about em.*

KE: *Me and you, 'keh? 'keh?*

It may also become an additional claim to the validity of their knowledge, in that Kona and Keahi most often presented their stories as if they had both witnessed the events together.

Turning to the ultimate source of the routine, we note again, as in the case of sexual teasing, that parents use it with young children. In the following instance the parent initiates the routine. This was observed in one of the other families where recordings were made, and often by Boggs (field notes).

(1 is a boy, 5, 2 and 3 are his brothers, aged 4 and 3. Mother has been questioning them and they are responding warily.)

MO: *Play? Flowa? Whe'+you+guys+^{w}go+pick+up+all+da+flowers+o'de'?* (fast)
2: *In schoo'* (wary)
MO: *No-ot!*
2: *Yeah!*
MO: *['ae'i* (Daddy) *downstɛiz?*
1: *[Yeah] jest+'ch[ool.*
3: *[Not 'ida njan.* (Mother's gloss: 'Daddy not downstairs.')
2: *No-ot.*
MO: *Shua-a.* [A few lines later mother admits her attempt to deceive them.]

The mother twice tries to provoke the children into contradicting her, and then proceeds to contradict them. The atmosphere of most of these is one of suspicion mixed with laughter. This one is exceptional, probably because the children have been punished before for going to the wrong place. But it clearly illustrates induction of children into the routine by an adult, which is typical.

Children associate this form of teasing by an adult with having fun, and frequently initiated it with Boggs and Watson. The following is from Watson's data:

NT

(Kaleo, 6, and Watson)

KA: (to Watson) *Talk.*
W: *What do you want me to tell you?*
KA: *Someting.*
W: *Someting.* [Note: This is one way of initiating the game, but Ka does not respond at this point, probably because she wants to hear W talk.]
KA: *Go.*
W: *'Keh . . . I'll tell you something. I'll tell you a secret.*
KA: *'Keh, tell.*
W: (whispering) *Kaleo's pretty.*
KA: *Go, tell.*
W: *Kaleo looks very pretty today, that's the secret.*

KA: *Not. Dat's not da secret.* (a simple contradiction, not a game at this point)
W: *Yes it is.*
KA: *Not.*
W: *OK I'll tell you another secret.*
KA: *What!*
W: (whispering) *I love Kaleo.*
KA: *Not!*
W: *Yes!*
KA: *Not.* (the game begins)
W: *Yes.*
KA: *Not.* (Repeated 3 times, Ka's voice dropping in pitch with each repetition until the fourth time, when W laughs.)

Dramatization Routines and Mime

A final example of the influence of familiar routines upon narrative performance in the Nāpua Team group can be seen by examining the common forms of dramatization that occurred in storytelling. Some of these routines have obvious sources in adolescent and adult behavior observed by the children. Dramatization not only calls upon or mimics such behavior, it is a common characteristic of many verbal routines. That is, the attributes and behavior of target characters who are the focus of a verbal routine are often mimicked or enacted. Simple dramatizations may include hand, body, head, or face movements and expressions which emphasize, illustrate, or aid interpretation of the content of what is said. Some dramatizations with complex combinations of movement are like skits and may carry a related but independent message from the content of speech. For example, to insult another, a child may strut about with hips wiggling or with backside stuck out. Two very popular kinds of dramatization routine are those which imply clumsiness and/or stupidity, and those which connote sexual behavior ranging in degree from flirtation to sexual intercourse, depending on the subtleties of body angle and gestures. Although dramatization is most often used as illustration or commentary on what is said, it may also be used to imply something altogether different from, or contradictory to, the spoken message, and thus as a nonverbal source of humor of insult. Finally, on occasion dramatization approaches mime by standing alone without any speech.

The most frequently used dramatic technique among the children is quoted dialogue. Many examples of the application of quoted speech to insults, stories, and other verbal routines appear in excerpts throughout this chapter. Quoting the words of a character is a means of avoiding direct claims of knowledge in certain cases. For example, if a story character or someone known to the narrator can be quoted as claiming that a particular fact is the case, then the narrator avoids making a claim to that knowledge himself, and thereby may also avoid contradiction or assault from the audience. Similarly, in insults and teasing, to show that the targeted child has afflicted the insult on himself by something he said (whether actual or pretended), is again to avoid or attempt to avoid direct conflict. Furthermore, quoted speech lends intimacy, immediacy, and realism to events.

In storytelling as well as in joking, children nearly always dramatize by voice intonation and imitation of speech. This means that they will imitate dialect accents, alter their voices to indicate age, sex, and personality of a character, or distort their speech to insult a target child or group. Watson found that storytellers used intonation and imitation of speech in 60% of the narratives she collected, and body movements in about 20% of the stories (1972:186).

Where do mime and other dramatization routines come from? The family is one obvious source. Children act out family roles in many of their stories, and may assign such roles as auntie, grandfather, or cousin to members of the audience during narration. One example of dramatization from Nāpua Team that seems clearly derived from home experience is Keaka's enactment of a scene between a father and mother:

NT

KE: *And afta, na mamma, "You let go I not your mommy!"*
(She gives a childlike scream)
Mommy said, "I did wash one head off before I d-i-e."
("Die" is sobbed)
Pono say, "Don' die before I get down dere!"
(Pono is ironic in tone, matter-of-fact, masculine)
Afta she n get da ambalance, you know, an afta she said—and Kekoa was dead. . . .

A number of these miniscenes—each a self-contained skit—may be woven together to form a single plot of interrelated events and situations.

A second source of dramatization is experience in playing house, playing hospital, store, and school. These experiences may come at home, in the neighborhood, or even in class (e.g., the doll corner). The dialogue from such dramatic play enters into some of the stories told in the Nāpua group, as it does into many personal experience narratives told to Boggs (in press).

But there are other sources of dramatization routines, too. Consider the following very stylized enactment, again by Keaka:

NT

KEAKA: *An afta Kekoa say, "Come on honey, 'et's go to da show."* ("o" sounds like "eu," mouth rounded, very affected tone, high pitch. She is sashaying around, mike in hand, wiggling her hips.)

KEKOA: *You finish.*
KEAKA: *Uh-uh, I not! An afta he-he-she say, "OK yes* (let's) *go."*
She was walkin jus like one egg (laughs).
(Keaka walks disjointedly with wrists bent sharply and fingers limp, staggering forward with bent legs)
KEKOA: ***You*** *walk one like egg.* (Note Kekoa's syntactical error due to excitement)

Keaka's audience immediately exchanged knowing glances and laughed with hilarity. As Watson noted earlier, this particular routine may well be "transmitted by adolescents, especially girls" (1972:190). Bernstein (1969 and personal communication) describes a similar dramatization which accompanies sexual humor and storytelling among adolescent girls. When leaders of the group's social hierarchy broke sexual "kapus" established by the group, order was restored by the presentation of an impromptu skit:

> . . . body posture and voice are changed. The instigator will bend her knees slightly and stick out her rear end. Hands are often limp and loose wristed. When someone in this state walks they resemble a duck. . . . The voice ranges from that of a drunk to that of a young child, depending on the actor. It gives the impression that the actor is not in control of himself and therefore cannot be held responsible for his actions . . . (Bernstein 1969:12-13).

A similar performance has been observed among 4- and 5-year-old boys (Boggs: field notes).

In certain instances dramatic techniques appear to be borrowed from professional entertainers. For example:

NT

(Hele, 6; several boys and girls, 5-7)

H: (seated, he takes the mike, looks thoughtful) *Umm. . . .*
?: *One up–[on a–*
H: *[Once uponna] time dis was Ow'd Mudda Goose.*
(gives half-laugh, throws head back, tone masculine:)
Mudda Goose laid da big ffat egg.
(Words spaced, almost spat out, suggests obscenity)
ALL: (laughter)
H: (Smiles broadly, tips chair back against the wall, eyes the group candidly, tips head, says slyly:) *Pretty good story, yeah?*
ALL: (hearty laughter)
MANY: (excitedly) *[Now one–once–Funny story.* (etc.)

Hele also displays a very sensual style when dancing rock and roll to songs, which he and his friends have learned from listening to the radio, and his playful behavior towards other children is often very flirtatious. It is likely that he is imitating the style of *mahu* entertainers.

Of course, all of the children have many opportunities to observe various kinds of entertainers at luaus, so that few of them do not imitate such performances at one time or another. But they also pick up routines from many other sources, including television. For instance, 6- to 11-year-old boys enjoy imitating the aggressive, gravel voice of Johnny Baran, a cigar-chomping local wrestler who is popular in the islands (Boggs: field notes). More recently the characters of the television program "Hawaii Five-O" are important models for behavior. Below are some cases of borrowing regular closing lines from certain television programs to terminate stories:

NT

KEAKA: *Das da whole story, so bye, boys and girls, bye!*

–

KEAKA: *An it's five to nine, an gonna have da late news now.*

–

PONO: *So everybody, hele on* (=move on)!

Pono's "hele on" is from a popular song, and the phrase is used by entertainers as well as generally among friends in the Hawaiian community as a sort of goodbye, similar to the American youth culture's "keep on truckin'."

The Development of a Group Norm

While the children in Nāpua Team were prepared to interact with one another by means of the routines described above, and could thus use them to construct narratives, knowledge of the routines was not sufficient to organize their interaction. Instead, as discussed below, the circumstances provided by recording in a group typically produced a jumble of routines, and not the long and complex narratives that emerged. Situational and contextual factors in the group must have been partly responsible for these performances. In this section we discuss such of these factors as we can discern. While admittedly tentative and incomplete, we hope that this analysis may stimulate others to experiment further with the goal of isolating those factors we may have missed. It is of some importance to do so, since the ability of children to perform verbally and cognitively in such a complex manner at this age is not generally appreciated, particularly by those who teach part-Hawaiian children.

One important factor promoting storytelling in a group is the presence of an interested adult. Previous studies of part-Hawaiian children, in particular, have shown that cues of receptivity by an adult stimulate verbal productivity by children (Boggs 1972; Gallimore et al. 1974). Children in the study by Boggs, for example, told 76 stories as individuals to him responding to such cues on his part. But adult interest is not sufficient to produce narratives when recording with a group of children. Instead, what repeatedly happens is that the child who is first offered the microphone often seems to have nothing to say even though he or she was at first eager for the chance to record. But as soon as another child begins to talk, nearly everybody in the group tries to talk at once. The verbal routines that occur in this burst of talk, taken in the order of approximate frequency, include greetings, shouts, and obscenities (one or two words); verbal play (including nonsense words, entertainment routines, singing, etc., variable in length); personal insults and threats (phrases several words or longer); questions about the recorder or the adult; and very occasionally a personal experience narrative directed to the adult rather than to the other children. Challenges from members of the group are answered by verbal and nonverbal responses directed to the challenger. It is pandemonium, and the larger the group the greater the tangle of voices.

The first and overriding problem in recording performances in a group, therefore, is to organize turns. Extensive experimentation by Boggs and others at KEEP, plus Watson's experience, indicate that an adult's attempts to control turn-taking in such a setting are absolutely futile. And the reasons are clear enough. With each individual, or pair, choosing a different routine, there is only overlapping. For some reason, the Nāpua Team group developed a norm of its own that allocated turns. We can only speculate in retrospect as to how this occurred. We think it important that control of performance in the group rested with the children, since this facilitated collaboration, which would solve the problem of allocating turns to some degree. But we do not know the whole story.

First, there is evidence that a concept of turn-taking did develop in the group. Requests for speaking rights abound in the recordings, for example, *I like talk,* or *my turn,* as well as complaints that *she wanted one turn,* or *he have moa dan one* [turn]. There are many cases of urging one child to turn over the microphone to another. Sometimes the arguments led to insults, physical struggles for possession of the microphone, and physical combat. Nevertheless, recognition of a right to a turn evolved, as evidenced by the following remarks:

NT

KA: (to another girl) *You neva have one chance* (=turn).

—

The following is the begining of the story quoted at the start of this chapter:

KO 1:	*Only one ti-. . .*	Ko claims the right to speak using formal opening for a story.
KE 2:	*I did, I did, okeh now.*	Ke, distracted, didn't realize that Ko was starting. Now urges her to talk. Gloss: 'I already told a story, it's your turn.'

Recognition of turn-taking was carried to its logical extreme by Kekoa, who early in the storytelling sessions made a list of children on whom she was going to tell stories. In some cases the name of a child was put on the list in order to retaliate for an insult, and in other cases a child was added to it because he or she had talked earlier. Kekoa rigorously followed the list over several storytelling sessions, referring to it whenever she was given a turn to talk. She used the list as a threat to those talking about her:

NT

KE: *We put your name down dea, you know. I go talk about you. Afta Kina comes Pono, den Kaipo.*

There is some evidence from two other studies that turns are allocated by peer norms when older children control the exchange. Chong (1969) observed such a norm among members of an older group when their teacher turned control of discussion over to them after having defended individuals from verbal attack by the others. Boggs observed more instances of conarration among 10- to 12-year-old boys under comparable conditions of peer control than when an adult attempted to control the event. In this study, approximately 18 boys were recorded during four 3-day camping trips for a total of about 15 hr. Careful attention was given to the occasions on which narratives were told. On just five occasions boys became conarrators, contributing elements of a single story. In all of these the adult present limited his participation to that appropriate for a peer: he took no turn speaking, or he limited himself to requesting information, making interested comments, or narrated himself. On no occasion did he attempt to assign turns or exercise a veto over any topic or routine. On those occasions when he did so a very different phenomenon appeared. There were no instances of successful conarration. Attempts to conarrate broke down when two or more speakers competed to say the same words, or mocked one anothers' words. Unfortunately, adult control was not the only difference on these occasions. Conarration occurred all five times in a small, organized group, whereas attempts by the adult to control the event occurred twice in a larger, unorganized group and twice in a small, organized one. In view of the small number of occasions, we cannot be sure that the differences are not due to chance. Further experimentation with groups variously constituted is needed.

Children were in control of the recording sessions in the Nāpua Team group. Except in circumstances of physical emergency, Watson consciously avoided attempting to control the children's behavior. She did not defend speakers or attempt to shape the nature of stories told, or any other speech event that the children wanted to engage in. She was nonjudgmental about what the children said and did. That she was perceived as a friend rather than an authoritarian adult is indicated by numerous exchanges like the following:

NT
(Kaleo, 6)

KA: *You neva come.*
W: *No, I didn't come for a long time because I had–*
KA: *How come?*
W: *'Cause I was behind in my school work so I couldn't come.*
KA: *Why?*

This interrogation continued for several more exchanges. Children do not importune parents this way (Boggs 1974). They do talk this way with friendly outsiders and relatives who treat them as favorites (Boggs: field notes). This role was undoubtedly important in stimulating the children to talk to her.

Summary and Conclusions

Recordings of a group of 55 part-Hawaiian children 5 to 7 years of age, who were interacting under particular circumstances, contain 150 narratives. Comparison with 5-year-old children from professional families in New Haven indicate that the Hawaiian children's stories were long (Ames 1966). They were also complex, both structurally and rhetorically. In nearly 9 hr of recordings of 26 children of similar age and part-Hawaiian backgrounds, who were interacting with parents, siblings, and peers under natural circumstances at home and in kindergarten, there were only three narratives, but a great variety of other verbal routines. These findings suggested that the children were able to construct such long and complex narratives in the particular circumstances of the group interaction by making use of verbal routines learned and practiced elsewhere. A comparison of some of these routines with characteristics of the stories told in the group suggests the following interpretations.

An established set of routines for sexual teasing provided a potential for story plot, and content, and a subject with high audience interest, while the circumstances of recording in the group provided a new opportunity for making insults more permanent by recording them and playing them back. At the same time, storytelling had an advantage over the usual teasing–which could lead to physical conflict–because of its make-believe quality and stance of objective reporting. Consequently, stories about sex, marriage, and childbirth told about other members of the group were the most frequent told in the group, whereas they were quite rare in stories told by individual children to Boggs.

Watson has demonstrated (1975) that both sexual joking in the group and personal experience narratives containing folklore materials involving devils, ghosts, etc., have an intrinsic contrapuntal structure, that is, they are joint performances by two or more speakers. In this chapter we have traced this structure to the influence of an established routine for disputing. The contradicting routine, as it is termed here, is learned in teasing interaction with parents, but is used by children in disputing with one another. Because of this experience any claim to know, or any allegation that can be perceived as a claim to know, is likely to elicit a contradicting routine. Because of this listeners may interrupt a storyteller. But they may also join in and support the storyteller, while also contributing parts of the plot or some of the allegations. Either way, the routine may lead the storyteller to anticipatory defenses, thus elaborating the story, or to acceptance of the contributions of a conarrator. In this manner, narratives that had nothing to do with sexual teasing came to share the same contrapuntal structure the latter had.

Finally, common rhetorical devices can be traced to established verbal and nonverbal routines. Thus, stories are usually enacted with extensive use of gestures, bodily actions, and quoted speech. Sources of the behavior include the observed role behavior of family members and other adults, which children rehearse while playing house, store, hospital, and school. They also incorporate specific stylized gestures (e.g., walking like a duck) that appear to be learned from older children and adolescents, who use such gestures to symbolize clumsiness and/or sexual humor. Routines are also freely borrowed from professional entertainers, who are observed at luaus, on TV, and heard on the radio.

But despite knowledge of these routines, children at this age rarely tell stories to one another in the absence of an adult audience, to judge from the recordings made at home and in the kindergarten. Particular circumstances of the group, therefore, had to be partly responsible for the long and complex stories told there. Certain of these, such as the advantage of making insults more permanent, have been suggested above. Others more general in their effects have been suggested. There is evidence, for one thing, that a concept of turn-taking developed in the group. This was crucial. For although an adult alone stimulates children in a group to attempt reports or narratives, adult attention by itself also produces a jumble of verbal routines that precludes complex performances of any duration. We are not certain as to why a norm of turn-taking evolved in this group. But one factor was probably that control of performance in the group rested strictly with the children. Other influences may have been historical, such as one girl's list for organizing chances to retaliate. There is evidence from other studies that older children organize their own turns when they control the interaction. Adult attempts to control turn-taking in group recording sessions, on the other hand, are futile, apparently because they interfere with the natural development of collaboration outlined above.

Considering our findings in a developmental perspective, it should be noted, although we are not able to present the evidence in this chapter, that adolescents and adults engage in much more sophisticated narratives and sexual joking than young children do under natural circumstances, i.e., the home and kindergarten recordings.[4] Yet, under the particular circumstances of the group recording sessions, they were able to approximate the performances of persons many years older. This view of what may have happened suggests an interesting possibility: that children acquire the basic structure of some verbal routines and have the ability to perform them some years before they regularly have an opportunity to practice them or demonstrate their ability to others.

4. Bernstein (1969) has documented joking routines in one group of part-Hawaiian adolescents.

Semantic and Expressive Elaboration in Children's Narratives

KEITH T. KERNAN

In this chapter, I shall deal with some aspects of the narratives of black American girls.[1] Specifically, I shall deal with some verbal techniques and some structural relationships between clauses that serve two general functions: that of **semantic elaboration**; and that of **expressive elaboration**. By semantic elaboration I mean elements of the narratives—and structural relationships between clauses in the narratives—that do not serve to relate the temporally sequenced events that constitute the narrative proper, but serve to provide information that is necessary to the desired semantic interpretation of the narrative, or serve to organize the semantic elements of the narrative in a particular way. By expressive elaboration, I mean elements of the narratives that serve to make the narratives interesting to, and appreciated by, the audience.

The data were collected from residents of a black, lower economic class, urban West Coast community. The community itself is separated from the large urban community of which it is a part by the light industry, and banks of railroad tracks that form its boundaries. The language spoken is black American English, as identified and described by Labov (1972[a]), Mitchell-Kernan (1971), and others. As such, it is variable in its structure and in the speech styles, acts, and events it employs; ranging, dependent on variables such as speaker, setting, topic, and so forth, from Standard English to an extreme form of black American English. It is somewhat marked, due to the recent emigration from the rural South of many of its members, by what Mitchell-Kernan (1971) has identified as "country forms." These are not common enough, however, to make the

1. The data upon which this chapter is based come from a study of the development of sociolinguistic skills conducted by Claudia Mitchell-Kernan and myself in 1973 and 1974. I wish to thank Claudia for her many helpful comments. The research was supported by the National Institute of Mental Health, grant number RO 1 MH24340-01.

language or speech patterns different in any significant way from those urban black speech communities discussed in the recent literature.

The 18 narratives I will discuss here are narratives of personal experience as told by girls to black female interviewers whom the girls knew well. There are six narratives from each of the three age groups in our sample: second and third graders (7-8 years old); fifth and sixth graders (10-11 years old); and eighth and ninth graders (13-14 years old). The narratives are mostly in response to prompting questions by the interviewer, although a few in the oldest age group occurred spontaneously in conversations among peers. The interviewers attempted to ask eliciting questions which fit into the ongoing verbal interaction. For example, when one of the older girls stated that she was late for an appointment because she had been kept after school, she was asked "what happened" and produced a narrative detailing the events that led to her detention. Others were produced in response to a few general questions, similar to those used by Labov and his coworkers, which we found were particularly effective in eliciting narratives: questions such as *Were you ever in a fight?* and *Were you ever really frightened?* Whenever possible, however, we tried to use questions that fit the context of the ongoing interaction. The narratives range in length from a few clauses to over 100 clauses. Those I will deal with here were selected from a middle range of length, and vary from 7 clauses to 31 clauses. Because these narratives were selected so as to avoid the very short and very long, they do not represent (as far as I can tell) the average length of the narratives produced by the various age groups. Of the 18 narratives used in this study, the narratives of the youngest group averaged 16 clauses, those of the middle group, 11 clauses, and those of the oldest group, 18 clauses.

Labov and Waletzky (1967) define a narrative as a method of recapitulating past experience by matching a verbal sequence of two or more clauses to the sequence of events that (it is inferred) actually occurred. A narrative, then, is only one means of verbally recapitulating past experience. It is one that frequently occurs in the speech community studied, however, and this definition provides a means of delimiting the data to be studied and compared. This study, then, examines the style of children's performances of one of the speech events existent in the repertoire of the speech community; a speech event that is one of the possible ways of accomplishing the function of recapitulating past events.

Labov (1972[b]), expanding upon the work of Labov and Waletzky (1967), posits six elements, or sections, in the overall structure of well-formed, extended narratives. These are, in usual order of occurrence:

1. Abstract
2. Orientation
3. Complicating action

4. Evaluation
5. Result or Resolution
6. Coda

Many, in fact most, of the narratives collected by Labov and his coworkers, as well as those narratives discussed here, do not contain all of these elements. After all, a speech event qualifies as a narrative if it consists of as few as two clauses in the complicating action, or narrative proper, section of the narrative. Some narratives, however, do contain all six elements and may be referred to as "extended narratives." An extended narrative, however, is not necessarily a better narrative in terms of appreciation by an audience of peers, and, in that sense at least, is not necessarily a narrative that exhibits a better form than narratives that do not contain all six elements. The sections are simply analytical categories, developed by Labov and accepted here, that permit analysis and discussion. They are neither units labeled by the informants themselves or units necessary to the success of the narrative itself.

"Abstracts" are clauses at the beginning of the narrative that summarize the entire story or the result of the story. Examples are:

1. *We almost drowned in L.A.*
2. *I was in a fight with this boy–his name is Jimmy Jones–in the classroom and outside too.*
3. *First time I ever got scared is when–when you know, that them two mens got killed down there.*

Narratives also sometimes begin with what may be called an "introducer," that is, some relatively stylized way of indicating that what follows is a narrative and, among other things, is not subject to the rules of sequencing that apply to dialogue or conversation. Some examples of introducers are:

1. *I remember one time when I was 6 years old.*
2. *Well see, this what happen.*
3. *Girl, let me tell you.*

Abstracts and introducers both serve the structural function of marking what is to follow as a narrative. Abstracts, by definition, also perform the semantic function of presenting in the form of a general statement what will be specified in the narrative to follow. They may be, therefore, considered to be a subtype of introducer. Even introducers that are not, strictly speaking, an abstract of what is to follow, may perform a semantic function as in Clause 1, which provides some orientation information, as well as introduces the narrative.

The youngest group in the sample only once used either an abstract or an introducer to begin their narratives; the middle group five times; and the oldest group four times. This type of distribution with a large difference between the narratives of the 7- to 8-year-old children and 10- to 11-year-old children, and a negligible difference between the narratives of the 10- to 11- and 13- to 14-year-old children, is repeated for other aspects of narrative form and should be noted.

A complicating factor that makes the figures regarding the use of abstracts and introducers quite tentative is the fact that some of the narratives were elicited with standard questions, others with situated questions, while still others occurred spontaneously. Those that occurred spontaneously or in response to situated questions were often preceded by dialogue that may have been considered by the narrator to serve as a sufficient abstract or introducer. In those cases where the narrative was in response to either a situated or standard elicitation question, the question itself may have been considered to be a sufficient abstract or introducer. There does not appear to be any significant difference by age group in terms of whether the narratives under consideration here were preceded by dialogue, a situated question, or a standard question, however. Yet, the two older age groups used abstracts or introducers more frequently than did the youngest age group.

The second element or section of narrative structure is that which fulfills the function of "orientation," that is, clauses that provide some information as to time, place, persons, and their activity or situation. In addition, orientation clauses may provide background information such as knowledge that characters in the story may or may not have, mood of characters, or other information that is necessary to understanding the narrative. Viewed in this way, orientation clauses have a semantic function.

As can be seen from the examples of abstracts and introducers, clauses may have more than one structural function. *I remember one time when I was 6 years old* is both an introducer and an orientation clause, for example. If we include clauses that serve these sorts of double functions, then every one of the 18 narratives exhibits one or more orientation clauses before the first narrative clause occurs. All the children feel it necessary to provide some sort of background information before they relate the actual events that comprise the core of their narratives. The mean percentage of orientation clauses for each group as compared to the total number of clauses in the narratives for that group is 11% for the youngest group, 27% for the middle group, and 22% for the oldest group. Of these, the youngest group devoted only 3% of the total clauses to background information and conditions, while the middle group devotes 20% of the total clauses, and the older group 17% to that specific function. In terms of percentage of orientation clauses devoted to background information and to conditions necessary to understand the action that follows the figures are youngest, 27%; middle, 69%; and oldest, 71%. Not only do the two older age groups devote a greater proportion of their narratives to orientation, a greater proportion of that orientation is devoted to such background information as mood and motivation. The younger children are more concerned with identification of specifics such as time, place, and characters. Even in the identification of characters, the children in the two older age groups differ significantly from the children in the younger group. Approximately 25% of the orientation clauses in the narratives of the youngest group identify characters only by name, even though the listener may not be familiar with those characters. Another 25% of the orientation clauses of the youngest group identify the characters by name, plus identifying characteristic or status (often a kinship term), or by identifying characteristic or status alone. Characters are never identified by name alone by the middle group, and only once by the older group. These two groups identify characters by name plus status, or characteristics, or by status or characteristics alone in 26% and 25% of their orientation clauses. In raw totals, the middle and older groups each mention status or characteristics twice as often as the younger children.

Those clauses that comprise the complicating action and result sections of the narrative constitute the narrative proper. That is, they relate the events that occurred in the sequence in which those events occurred. They are, by definition, semantic or referential in function, and their quantity depends upon the number of isolatable events that actually occurred and are to be related. Since the narratives under consideration were selected on the basis of their medium length, the number of clauses devoted to complicating action and result are a function of the percentage of clauses devoted to other sections of the narratives, and need not be considered further here in terms of quantity of such clauses by age. The semantic interrelatedness of clauses, which will be discussed later, will include consideration of those clauses that occur in the complicating action and result sections of the narratives, however.

Labov defines the function of the evaluation clauses of the narratives he discusses as making the narratives appreciated and considered by the audience to have been worth the telling. As Labov (1972[b]) puts it, every good narrator is continually warding off the question *So what?* in regard to his narrative performance. Labov and Waletzky (1967) originally posited an evaluation section that consisted of a clustering of evaluation clauses near the end of the narrative. As Labov (1972[b]) points out, however, evaluation clauses may occur at any point in the narrative. Such is the case with the narratives under consideration here. Evaluation clauses may occur at any point in the narratives and they are not clustered at any particular point. Moreover, as Watson (1973) has pointed out, the evaluation function, as defined and applied by Labov, actually includes a number of isolatable narrative techniques, ranging from a direct statement by the narrator concerning his attitude toward the related events, to such aspects of the internal syntactic structure of clauses as the use of modals. These are not only widely divergent narrative techniques, but also serve a variety of more specific functions. At any rate, evaluation clauses fulfill an expressive rather than a semantic function. Some expressive techniques used by the children in the narratives being considered here will be discussed later.

"Codas" constitute the final section in the Labov and Waletzky framework of overall narrative structure. Codas are structural in function and serve to signal the end of the narrative. Examples are:

1. *I just sat there playing with my compass, that's all.*
2. *And they still letting her play no matter what they say.*
3. *And that's all.*

Narratives may also end with a direct statement of the moral or main point of the narrative. Examples are:

1. *I felt sorry. I shouldn't did that in the first place.*
2. *That's how they get killed. By going in other people's business.*

Usually, however, narratives simply end with the last clause of the complicating action or result sections of the narratives. These sections, then, are the principle elements of overall narrative structure.

There are narrative techniques utilized by the children that may appear anywhere in this overall structure. These techniques are defined in terms of the semantic interrelatedness that exists between certain of the independent clauses of the narrative. They include the exact repetition of clauses, the paraphrase of a preceding clause with no new semantic information necessary to the interpretation of the narrative, the restatement of a semantic notion with added detail, the specifics of a preceding abstract clause, an abstract of preceding specifics, and the use of certain lexical items which indicate the type of relationship that exists between two clauses expressing independent semantic notions. The functions of particular occurrences of these techniques are both variable and difficult to interpret. Moreover, as seems to be the case for most speech acts, the function of any occurrence of these clauses may be multiple and hierarchical (Hymes 1962). The repetition with some added detail of an orientation clause, for example, may itself function as an orientation clause in that it adds some semantic detail, which the speaker considers necessary for the proper interpretation of what follows, or it may be intended to serve an expressive function, and to increase the listener's appreciation of the narrative and of the narrator's storytelling ability. Since this is the case, and since the purpose of this examination of the semantic interrelatedness of clauses is to determine the semantic structuring used by the narrators, no exhaustive analysis of the extrasemantic functions of these techniques will be attempted. The clear and obvious structural functions of the repetitions, etc., such as picking up the story line after interruptions, will be discussed, however.

Clauses may be repeated exactly or with minor modifications such as change of tense. Repetitions for all three age groups are relatively rare. The percentage of repetitions in terms of total clauses for the three age groups are: youngest, 7%; middle, 6%; and oldest, 4%. Usually, the repetitions serve to pick up the story line following an interruption from the audience, or a digression or elaboration of some point by the narrator. They therefore indicate something of the narrator's notion of "well-formedness" of the narrative in terms of the sequencing of clauses. When repetitions serve this structural function, they are necessarily separated from the clause they repeat by the interruption or digression.

In the following example, the line *He got mad at her,* is repeated twice and follows both an interruption and digression:

1. *O yeah, my little cousin, he 2 years old.*
2. *His sister 6.*
3. *He got mad at her.*
4. *'Cause she wouldn't give him no soda.*
5. *He got real mad at her.* (added detail)
6. *An look at her like she was retarded.*
7. *An then start beating her up.*
   AUDIENCE: *A little 2-year-old boy?*
8. *Uh-huh, it's her little brother.*
9. *He got mad at her.*

In one instance, each in the middle and older age group, an exact repetition of an earlier clause with intervening clauses between them seems to serve the function–in the first occurrence–of an abstract of what follows. The intervening clauses then give the specifics and are followed by the repetition of the initiating clause which then serves as a summing up of the specifics. The following example is from the middle group:

1. *I was so scared.*
2. *'Cause, you know, I saw when they took the dead men out of the car.*
3. *An all one side of his face was all smashed up.*
4. *An slob was running out of his mouth.*
5. *An I got so scared.*

In a few cases, a repetition immediately follows the clause it repeats. The function of such repetitions is unclear but may, in some cases at least, serve to emphasize the clause.

Clauses may be restated in such a way that some detail or more specific information is added to the original clause. For example:

1. *When they have fights, they have invitations.*
2. *They invite people to their fights on a hill.*

1. *An she took off her shoe.*
2. *An start chasing Larry around.*
3. *She took off her clog.*
4. *An start chasing Larry around the yard teacher.*

In the latter example, Clause 3 adds detail to Clause 1 in that it specifies the **type** of shoe. Clause 4 adds detail to Clause 2 in that it specifies **where** Larry was being chased. The youngest group devotes 9% of the total clauses to specifying details in this way; the middle group, 12%; and the oldest group, 9%.

Another technique that is similar in that it utilizes clauses which add detail, is that of following a general statement with a clause, or clauses, that give the specifics of the general statement. For example:

1. *And then we had some fun. Me and Kathy and them.*
2. *We was playing* Down Down Baby, Down by the Roller Coaster (chanting)
3. *And we start playing* Junior.
4. *And then we came to the park.*
5. *And we start playing on the slides and running up and down.*

Here the general statement, *We had some fun,* is followed by the specifics. Such specifications of more general statements constitute 5% of the clauses in the narratives in the youngest group, 3% in the middle group, and 4% in the oldest group.

Relationships of specificity and generality between clauses may also go from the more specific to the more general. That is, the specific occurrences may precede the more general or more inclusive clause. This did not occur in the narratives of the youngest group, however, and occurred only once in the middle group's narratives, and twice in the narratives of the oldest group.

One other method of restating a clause occurred in 10% of the clauses of the oldest group, but not at all in the narratives of the middle and youngest groups. This is the use of **paraphrase**. Paraphrase is the restatement of a particular semantic notion with **no** additional, more detailed, or more general information added. When paraphrase occurs as evaluation, it may appear as an exaggeration of a previous clause. It is clear, however, that the narrator intends no new semantic information but is exaggerating for the sake of dramatic effect, as in the following:

1. *An girl, you know, half of the cake was gone.*
2. *I was so mad I almost cried, girl.*
3. *I say "Mama, I told you Tommy was gonna eat all that cake,"*
4. *I mean, Tommy had him a big, giant piece, girl.*
5. *That cake was gone.*

Here the narrator does not intend to convey, by Clause 5, that the cake was entirely eaten. She is exaggerating for effect and the audience knows that.

With the exception of the use of paraphrase, there is no impressive difference across age groups in the frequency of use of the techniques discussed above. That is, all three age groups devote similar percentages of the total clauses in their narratives to repetition, detail, and specific and general statements. There is, however, an interesting difference by age in the distribution of these techniques in the narratives themselves. Children of different ages utilize these techniques to elaborate and expand different sections of the narratives. For the youngest age group, 57% of these techniques occur as narrative clauses and 35% as evaluation clauses, and only 8% occur as the orientation sections of the narratives. For the middle group, on the other hand, 60% occur as orientation clauses, 27% as evaluation clauses, and only 13% as narrative clauses. For the oldest group, 46% occur as orientation clauses, 45% as evaluation clauses, and 9% as narrative clauses. The two older groups devote much higher percentages of these techniques to orientation, and much lower percentages to narrative clauses than does the younger group. The older children seem to be more interested in elaborating the background information necessary to a proper interpretation and understanding of the narrative than do the younger children. The higher percentage of these techniques in the narrative clauses of the younger children may indicate greater concern on their part that the narrative events themselves be more clearly understood. Such an interpretation, however, does **not** imply that the narrative sections of the younger children's stories were better organized, since their use of the techniques often follows what appears to be digressions that are not relevant to the story line, and are, at times, uninterpretable.

This study has not been concerned with the internal syntactic structure of clauses. However, there is an interesting syntactic feature of many of the clauses that deserves mention in that it signals the type of semantic interrelatedness that exists between adjacent clauses. A variety of kinds of semantic relationships may exist between clauses of course, but two occur frequently in the narratives and are easily identifiable in that they are marked by the conjunctions *and, then,* and *and then* on the one hand; and by *so, so then,* and *and so then* on the other hand. Clauses introduced by *and, then,* and *and then,* indicate a relationship with the preceding clause that is either independent, or temporal, or both. That is, although the events related by the adjacent clauses did presumably occur and did occur in a certain order, the occurrence of one does not imply or depend upon the occurrence of the other. They are separate and independent events that may be related temporally but are perfectly understandable in and of themselves. Clauses, on the other hand, that are introduced by *so, so then,* and *and so then,* depend, for their proper interpretation, on the existence of the preceding clause or clauses. They are dependent in the sense that the preceding clause must be stated in order that the following clause may be understood. The preceding clause serves as orientation (even though it may also be a narrative clause) for what follows. Table 1 presents the percentage of total clauses introduced by these lexemes for the three age groups. There is a steady decrease from younger to older children in the use of *and, then,* and *and then.* The oldest children use *so, so then,* and *and so then,* with much greater relative frequency than do either the youngest or middle children. Both these distributions contrast with the usually larger gap between youngest and middle children as compared to the difference between middle and oldest children.

TABLE I

	Youngest (%)	Middle (%)	Oldest (%)
And, then, and then	55	42	28
So, and so, and so then	6	6	20

Up to this point, I have been concerned primarily with presenting the results of an analysis of the distribution of certain elements and relationships of semanticity. Narratives, however, are concerned with more than making sense. They are also concerned with being appreciated, being amusing, being considered well done, and so on. That is to say, some elements of most narratives are devoted to fulfilling the "expression function." This is similar to Labov's evaluation function, but there is a major difference. Labov (1972[b]) includes, as elements which serve the evaluation function, all departures from what he terms "basic narrative syntax." These syntactic departures are categorized as intensifiers, comparators, correlatives, and explicatives. Labov has not convincingly demonstrated, however, that any of these categories (with the exception of intensifiers), nor any of the specific syntactic structures that are subsumed by the categories, are in a one-to-one relationship with the evaluation function, and, therefore, in each instance of occurrence, fulfills that function. Labov recognizes that explicatives do not always serve the evaluation function, and that some of the syntactic features he discusses have a purely referential function (1972[b]). That is, they are concerned with semanticity. He further states that the examples he gives illustrate, but do not prove, the association between syntactic complexity and evaluation, and promises to offer such proof later in the chapter, but, it appears to me, does not. Yet, to the extent that his work deals with the development of the evaluation function with age, it is based entirely on the use by the narrators of these four types of internal syntax of clauses. I shall not deal with the syntax of clauses here. Rather, I shall deal with clauses that indicate in some way the feelings of the narrator toward the events he is relating and that are used to attempt to convey that feeling to the audience. Labov (1972[b]) terms such clauses "large-scale, external mechanisms of evaluation" and deals with them briefly. I shall also discuss the use of quotation and the use of lexical items for intensification or emphasis.

Clauses that serve the expressive function by indicating the attitude of the narrator toward events in the narrative may simply state such feelings; for example, *I was so scared.* They may imply the attitude or feelings through a report of what happened, for example, *I had nightmares three nights straight.* Finally, they may be a quote that implies the attitude, for example, *I said, I'm getting out of here.* Labov and Waletzky speak of the degree of embedding of these means of indicating attitude, ranging, in the examples I have given, from least to most embedded in the narrative.

The youngest group performs the expressive function in these ways in 19% of the total clauses, the middle group 26%, and the oldest group 31%. The youngest group performs the function primarily by implying emotional state through a report of action or what happened: 78% of their expressive clauses are of this type; 22% of their expressive clauses simply state the attitudes, and the youngest group never implied attitude through the use of quotation. Corresponding percentages for the middle group are 18% stated attitude, 58% implied in action, and 24% implied in quotations. For the oldest group, 29% are stated; 45% implied in action, and 26% implied in quotations.

The children in our sample, then, utilize these three methods of fulfilling the expressive function in narratives with greater frequency with increasing age. There is a slightly greater difference in the frequency of usage between the youngest and middle groups than between the middle and oldest groups. In terms of the manner in which attitude is indicated, however, the younger children are much more likely to imply the attitude in the action of the story and are much less likely to use the device of quotation.

Finally, I would like to consider some elements of narrative that serve expressive function and which may be termed **emphasis**. There are a number of devices for accomplishing emphasis in narrative, among them are stress, marked intonation, gestures, and sounds such as slaps and finger snapping. Here I shall consider only the use of lexical items.

Lexical items that emphasize include words such as the following:

1. *I got* ***real*** *mad.*
2. *She cussed out* ***three*** *teachers.*
3. *I mean, Tommy had him a* ***big, giant*** *piece.*
4. *And* ***girl,*** *you know,* ***half*** *of the cake was gone.*

The youngest group uses lexical emphasis in 7% of all clauses, the middle group 8%, and the oldest group 15%.

The narrative performances by each of the three age groups may be characterized by the degree to which they exhibit the various devices of semantic and expressive elaboration, and, in some instances, by the nature of the semantic information that is elaborated.

The youngest children devote most of their narratives to the narrative section proper. They are less concerned with preparing the audience for what will follow through the use of abstracts or introducers. Their narratives differ significantly from those of the older groups, not only in the use of abstracts and introducers, but also in the use of orientation clauses. The younger children devote a smaller proportion of their narratives to background information necessary to the proper semantic interpretation of the narratives. Not only is less background information provided, but it differs in kind from the information supplied by the two older groups. Younger children supply names, places, and dates, but do not elaborate character, motivation, and circumstance. As a result, their narratives are more difficult to interpret and often seem to lack a point. The orientation information supplied by the older children is more likely to be designed to render actions that occur later in the narrative understandable to the audience. Concerning those techniques that repeat, detail, give specifics, or provide a general statement of the semanticity of some previously occurring clause or clauses, the younger children, again, devote most of the semantic elaboration to the narrative proper, while the two older groups devote most of their semantic elaboration to the orientation sections of the narratives. In terms of the elaboration of the expressive function, the younger children more often imply attitude toward events in the narrative by utilizing descriptions of events, than do the two older groups. Finally, there is a differential use of lexical items to indicate the semantic interrelatedness of adjacent clauses by age. The clauses of the youngest children are more likely to be experientially independent or related only temporally, while those of the oldest children are more likely to be related in such a way that the semantic interpretation of a particular clause depends upon the existence of the clause that immediately precedes it.

There is an interesting and common element to these somewhat diverse observations. The younger the child, the more likely it will be that the understanding and appreciation of the narrative by the audience will be based upon the narrative events themselves. The older the child, the more likely it will be that a proper understanding and appreciation of the narrative will be assured through the use of contextual and extranarrative elaboration. The younger children seem to assume that the communication of the events themselves will result in the same understanding and appreciation on the part of the audience that they themselves have. The older children, on the other hand, realize that the interpretation and appreciation of the narrative events will depend, at least in part, upon knowledge that is external to the narrative events themselves.

Situated Instructions: Language Socialization of School Age Children[1]

JENNY COOK-GUMPERZ

"A bad danger. Yes I see. How very upsetting," said the Chief Rabbit, looking anything but upset.
Watership Down

LANGUAGE LEARNING AS SOCIAL EXPERIENCE

Ambiguity is endemic to human spoken communication systems. The possibility of communicating in several different modalities simultaneously makes agreement on the meaning of messages an open set of possibilities. Conventional usage and ritual govern and constrain some of these possibilities, but others remain open for negotiation on the occasion of each social encounter.

From this perspective we will be considering how children learn the social uses of language, given that their experience of language in action presents a model of imperfect communication. We shall be asking how the child reveals understanding of the social possibilities of language through the strategies adopted to achieve the various goals and activities of communication.

In terms of early language development we assume that language acquisition intrinsically entails an acquisition of knowledge of social processes. Both the strategies for acquiring syntactic knowledge, and the child's development of semantic categories, depend upon an awareness of social relationships, and these strategies continue to structure social reality for the child (Clark 1973; Nelson

1. This paper was written while the author was on postdoctoral funding by NICHD. Data for this paper was collected while the author was with the SCIS Project at the Lawrence Hall of Science, University of California, Berkeley, and was funded by National Science Foundation.

1974; Ryan 1974; Slobin 1973[a]). A recent study of children's prior and early postlinguistic communication has shown that even during the beginnings of the mastering of syntax, the child's linguistic development seems to be interdependent with the acquisition of social usage and notions of appropriateness (Bates 1976[a]). Bates's work shows in detail how the development of prelinguistic communicative intents and shared communicative assumptions form a basis for the presuppositions by which the child interprets the performative use of utterances. While this work considers, in some detail, the cognitive consequences of the social usage of language, it does not consider the interactive consequences of language acquisition. An interactive approach requires us to consider not only the child's communicative intent, but also the child's success at achieving the conduct of interaction as a sequence of meaningful exchanges. We can consider meaning in this context to be construed as "making sense," that is, that meanings are concerned not only with perceivable content or with the ability to construct interpretable messages, but more especially with the resolution of a sequence of social actions between two or more participants, such that the exchange of talk and action **demonstrates** some appearance of a satisfactory outcome, a happy resolution.

Grice's distinction between language use as an **indicative** force, to influence the hearer's belief or feeling about the speaker's intent; and as an **imperative** force, where the speaker's intent influences the actions of the hearer, forms a good starting point for a study of the social actions of language. It has been suggested by several researchers that children learn this universal distinction between the indicative-imperative mode very early in the acquisition of language (Bates 1976[a]; Halliday 1973; Keenan 1974[b]). From an interactive perspective, we could refine this conceptual distinction by discriminating several properties of language use. Firstly, language is used to direct present ongoing activities—language, as it were, imbedded in a stream of action. Secondly, language is used to recollect past or plan future projects. Finally, language shapes the grounds for its own understanding in use through enabling comments to be made that retrospectively change the interpretation of past actions and so change the course of ongoing interaction. We suggest that the growth of these three social uses of language extends beyond early language learning, as a continuous language socialization experience, through childhood.

Theoretically, what we are suggesting is that in viewing language as an interactive social experience, we should focus not upon the child's intent to communicate per se, but **upon the child's interpretive ability, demonstrated in the way that meaning gets accomplished in social settings.**

In a previous paper (Cook-Gumperz 1975) it was suggested that the interpretive features which adults background, such as kinesic gestures, physical features of setting, prosodic information, all provide information that enters equally into the child's interpretation of the ongoing communicative event.

The child judges the social intent or effect of the verbal message, equally by its **situated** character, the manner and physical setting in which it is performed, as much as by the semantic-syntactic form of the message. We suggest that the possibility of **foregrounding** the semantic-syntactic channel, as the **dominant** and **socially** recognized[2] carrier of meaning, is a particular communicative skill which develops gradually after the initial acquisition of some semantic-syntactic competency. This sociolinguistic skill, to foreground a part of the meaning components of the message, involves the ability to state (in so many words) the purposes of the verbal activity itself, so that this can govern the future course of the action and its outcomes, such that there will be a gradual dominance of the channel of **lexicalized intent** over other sources of interpretive information.

Two Types of Ambiguity

The argument for this position is as follows: the child grows into a communicative system which is governed largely by the social-ecological constraints of the maternal caretaker's activities. **Shared communicative assumptions** and understandings arise naturally out of the regularities and rituals of necessary practices of early child rearing. The development of particular features of the mother-child communication system can be described from an ethological perspective (Blurton-Jones 1972). It is into this system of shared understandings that the child's intent to communicate develops and the takeoff into language takes place. Recent studies show how the child builds upon the assumed, shared understandings and previously developed meanings to convey the communicative intents through the early limited syntactic-semantic language systems (Bates 1976[a]; Bruner 1975; Sugarman 1973). These recent studies suggest how plausible it is to consider the child as beginning to use language within a framework of presupposed knowledge in which the surface, syntactic mapping realized as the verbalized forms are seen as only a part of the total message communicated by both child and adult participants. Further, it has been indicated that the child learns early to distinguish and to mark linguistically the known or shared component of meaning from the new or novel components (Bates 1976[a]; Halliday 1973; Keenan 1974[b]).

In the communication system of the home, the child develops the ability to communicate and interpret meaning within a system where there is an already assumed basis of shared knowledge. On occasions of miscommunication or difficulty, the speaker, or listener's need to disambiguate messages relies upon

2. What we mean by a socially recognized carrier of meaning can be illustrated by our epigram, in this case the statement by the Chief Rabbit that he regarded the information as upsetting, would be treated as a fact in the interaction, although absence of the "look" of being upset would be noted and backgrounded for possible retrospective reinterpretation.

the good faith of the partner who will wait for the purpose of the interaction to become clear, or use background knowledge to resolve what appears to be contradictory to the main theme or tone of the interaction. These judgments of good intent take into account not only the semantic-syntactic message, but the prosodic-kinesic accompaniment of the spoken message. Because speaker's meanings always index more than can be said, ambiguity is always possible in spoken communications.

However, outside of the home situation, the child will encounter a second type of ambiguity in communicative situations. The thrust of school-based communicative experience is to teach the child to recognize and develop strategies for dealing with this ambiguity. The very vagueness that is necessary to everyday communication, which signals the shared assumptions and expectations of the interlocutors, becomes a problem in school situations because communication does not proceed against a background of tacit shared agreements.[3]

Teachers themselves often rely, even with young children, on the established, everyday interpretive ability of participants to fill in the necessary detail to make a communication meaningful or to make a message an adequate guide to action (Cicourel et al. 1974; Gumperz 1972). The formal language socialization of school requires the child to avoid such ambiguity of messages that comes from assuming a tacit understanding of communicative conventions or negotiated meanings. The child must learn to realize what of the speaker's assumed communicative knowledge must be expressed explicitly in any particular situation. Thus, the second ambiguity of school communication stems from a failure to lexicalize and to make available unknown assumptions as new information for any social encounter. School language socialization provides children with experiences of how to interact with unknown others, in new contexts or situations, and thus to make their communication less dependent on contextually based, tacit knowledge. We suggest that the goal of teaching literacy to children is to teach them how to disimbed verbalized conversations from a stream of action which realizes a part of the meaning of the utterance, and how to rely upon the verbalized semantic channel alone. The distinction between written and spoken language is that the former provides for the possibility of disambiguating the message through syntactic stylistic structures, such that a simple set of

3. For example, in everyday accounts of activities, such as a shopping trip, the precise details of car parking, getting to the store, are backgrounded, that is not mentioned, the focus will be on the actual shopping, unless something goes wrong at any stage. Too great detail or specificity in everyday life accounts seems odd. One way to recognize blind persons from sighted persons in transcribed accounts of everyday life actions is the amount of verbal scene setting and additional comments that blind persons give to accounts of everyday actions. Seeing people take for granted features of the scene and in retelling a past event are not likely to mention or even to be able to recall "backgrounded" information. Such information about the scene is not backgrounded for blind persons and has to enter into pragmatic judgments about activities in everyday settings.

written propositions, as a discourse, provide all the features necessary for the understanding of the message without reliance upon any external performance, that is, **situated** features.

SITUATED MEANING: HOW DOES MEANING GET ACCOMPLISHED IN ACTUAL SETTINGS?

By the **situated** character of a communicated event we describe how meaning gets realized interactively in everyday settings through the additional interpretive use of all the performance characteristics of spoken language, so that social meaning is accomplished during actual interaction rather than assigned on an *a priori* basis. Theoretically, it is this distinction that makes the analysis of language as spoken performance different from the analysis of written texts. At this point we should perhaps consider the theoretical implications of the term situated meaning. For these purposes three or four kinds of meaning can be distinguished.

After the long recognition by anthropologists that the norms of speaking are different from those of language as an abstract system (Gumperz 1974; Hymes 1974), it is now recognized that language-in-use represents a different set of meaning possibilities in several ways. Thus, the interpretation of language as spoken requires the recognition of more than one kind of meaning. Following speech-act philosophy, not only **referential** but also **conveyed meaning** is distinguished. **Conveyed meaning** concerns the contrastive implications generated by the use of a particular referential syntactic-lexical item in a context. The acknowledgment of conveyed meaning recognizes that language does not have a one-to-one correspondence with an established referential order of objects, but that words vary with their use in context. The same semantic string can have several meanings according to its context, including the presuppositions of the particular utterance that enters into the interpretation. Further, the semantic understanding of the string will depend both on the presupposed knowledge and the linguistic cues that provide the **performative** intent of the speaker. In this instance by performative intent we mean the intent which a sentence can be taken as expressing in its ordinary sense and in isolation from context.

To these two kinds of meaning in spoken language we will add a third—**situated meaning**. This must not be confused with situational or contextual meaning, which we have subsumed briefly within the term "conveyed meaning." Our argument is that conveyed meaning deals with the solely **semantic** sequence of implication and inference that is generated by a single utterance in its **semantic** context. Such a sequence takes into account the social presupposition of the utterance, considered as the set of possible conditions that could underly any potential "ordinary" interpretation. By **situated meaning** we are making the case for another, rather different mode of interpretation, which depends upon what actually happens within the working out of the social activity of which any utterance is a part, the interpretation that appears to be given to any utterance in a **situation** by social actors. The linguist's notion of **conveyed** meaning is considered to be a part of the actor's knowledge that enters into his situational judgments; although the linguist aims for completeness of logical analysis, an actor does not.

By **situated meaning** we refer to the essentially **performance** characteristics of speech, which add a new dimension to the interpretation of language, apart from the verbal (semantic-syntactic) channel, and which therefore indexes a very different kind of knowledge from that which can be referred to as more specifically linguistic. We can perhaps best clarify the distinction by contrasting spoken language as an organizing or concurrently recorded performance, with language, whether uttered or devised, which is written down, **as a text**, and so examined as such. Most obviously of all, **spoken** language as speech performance exists and communicates in several modalities at once, and these modalities or channels are capable of each carrying and modifying meanings (Bateson 1972; Gumperz 1974). By contrast, the interpretation of written language can be seen to rely mostly upon the meanings both referential and conveyed that are expressed by the syntactic-lexical organization. Spoken language also relies upon the meanings carried by the other performance features of language in its situated occurrence. The situated meaning of an utterance draws upon knowledge that includes accepted social conventions, as well as the negotiated features of the particular social interaction of which the utterance is a situated part. Situated meaning refers to features of context or situation that are outside of the sphere of the linguistic chain of logical inference, and therefore refers to the more specifically sociological features of the speech performances. **Situated meaning** is essential for the interpretation of speech as it conveys the speaker/listener's knowledge of how to conduct and interpret live performances. The features previously referred to as paralinguistic-intonation, stress, as well as contrastive rhythm, shifts of phonetic values—are other ways of conveying meaning that add to or alter the meaning of semantic choices. Situated meaning is also carried by the kinetic gestures and body movements that speakers use, and their conventionalized interpretative possibilities. Another component of situated meaning is the negotiation of specific semantic-lexical interpretations during the course of a particular stretch of interaction. References to meanings can range over recent time and past encounters, and can add specific interpretation to seemingly referentially "ordinary" items. Situated meaning relies upon the negotiable features of an encounter becoming apparent during the course of the interaction so that certain kinds of knowledge do not have to be linguistically realized at the outset of an encounter (Sacks et al. 1974). The process of unfolding situated meaning allows for spoken language existing in a space-time dimension where information flow is linearly sequenced in a rapidly fading modality of several channels, but where the cognitive processes shaping the encoding and decoding of the speech performance move in a different space-time dimension. Situated meaning shapes the perceptual surface of the speech and so shapes the cognitive frame by highlighting certain possible interpretations rather than others.

Both adults and children use situated meanings, but for adults situated knowledge is backgrounded, and therefore is not a normal stateable part of any verbal accounts of the interpretive process. The reasons for the appearance of the exclusively verbal-semantic dominance is the need **not** to rely on the linguistic and paralinguistic situated features to be the socially recognized carriers of meaning. Although everyday face-to-face communication can never be separated from the unrecognized dependence on situated meanings, this goes unmarked in the normal course of adult interaction. The shift from strategies which rely on situated meaning, to strategies which entail the lexical coding of intent is dependent, from our viewpoint, on growth in several areas of competence. These areas of competence include an increasing ability to manage the mapping of communicative intent into surface syntactic structure, and the ability to recognize the speech activities that contextualize the immediate proposition and that "chunk" speech into sequences of recognizable and interpretable social activity (Bruner 1975; Kay in press).

INSTRUCTION-GIVING AS A MEANS OF STUDYING THE COMMUNICATIVE STRATEGIES OF SCHOOL-AGE CHILDREN

Since entering into social areas outside of the shared communicative system of the home require the child to learn a different communication system, the school socialization experience is necessarily discontinuous with that of home in certain important respects. Although the basic universal features of realizing meaning and attributing sense of other's speech remain similar, formal schooling must necessarily be a shift away from the expectation of shared assumptions. Much of the school experience requires the child to attend to interpreting overtly lexicalized intentions rather than to rely on situated information; and the child must learn how to lexicalize the assumptions which are specific to the particular interactional setting and novel to the participants. The lexicalization of the necessary details both of the speech activity and of what is assumed as shared knowledge, provide a way of shaping the outcome and so controlling the social interaction itself.

Much of the communication the child receives in school is directive, either imperative in the sense of directing the movement and change of objects, activities, and people, or if not directly imperative, then sequences of directives to achieve certain required goals such as instructions for mathematics problems. School learning concerns the receiving and giving of explicit instructional sequences which are algorithms for action; and express the intended outcomes of activities in words rather than allowing the purpose to become apparent in the course of the unfolding of the activity, as in informal everyday learning activities. Learning how to learn (in the formal school sense) involves the planning of action sequences verbally (Scribner and Cole 1973).

Given this theoretical basis for our study, an experimental instruction-giving situation provides a paradigm case of the uses of language to communicate clearly, that is, without ambiguity of intent, in the sense of the second kind of ambiguity: the avoidable ambiguity of failing to make explicit necessary assumptions.

The Experiment and Data Base

This chapter reports on some findings from an experiment made with fifth-grade children, of both sexes in the San Francisco Bay area (Cook-Gumperz and Bowyer 1972). The data were recorded on both audio and videotape. The entire set of tasks has been examined as an example of children's understanding of the communicative requirements of instruction and direction-giving in situations that involve experimental constraints on the activity (such as occur in educational testing). These situations are similar both to the communicative requirements of certain everyday situations where the speech event involves strangers and unknown social contexts, and to the requirements of formal school learning, as we have described before. In such situations, it is necessary for the participants to lexicalize the details of the speech activity and their own personal intentions, in particular details, as a means of structuring and signaling the kind of activity they are involved in. The communicative requirements for stranger-interactional settings differ from interaction with familiars; and as we have suggested, it is the former which make up the educational standard of successful language socialization.

After the achievement of literacy, the child's communicative ability is judged not only by criteria of effectiveness—do the requisite actions get performed?—but by whether the communication meets adult criteria of contextually relevant and appropriate speech. We suggest that the acquisition and use of these appropriate and relevant speech strategies depends not only on acquiring the strategies, but also on acquiring the adults' rules (perhaps we should call these meta-rules) for the recognition of speech contexts. Contextualizing rules chunk the stream of events into speech activities, which then provide the context for the choice of appropriate strategies from the range of known or possible speech acts.

Through the analysis of one of the experimental tasks involved with instruction-giving, we hope to show that in order to recognize an instructional speech activity as different from other kinds of speech situations, the child will have to know some of the adult expectations and conventions for recognizing instructional language, and will have begun to contextualize the stream of activity. Even though the child may be able to categorize the speech activity as an instructional one, he/she may have a different range of strategies to realize this kind of activity, although those strategies may, in fact, lead to a satisfactory outcome.

The purpose of this experiment was to provide tasks suitable for face-to-face interaction and instruction, which permit the use of verbal strategies, which differ from everyday instruction-giving in context. Pairs of children were asked to make a model using a kit of color-coded straight and circular pieces of wood (Tinkertoy). One child volunteered to be the builder, the other the instructor. The builder was blindfolded so that the instructor had to rely upon verbal cues to guide the building process. The instructor was handed the instruction booklet that comes with the kit, with one of two models ringed. The builder was told, "You can say or do anything you want, to tell your friend how to make the model, only try not to touch the pieces." If the children asked for further guidance such as "Can I tell him what he's going to make?" they were again told, "You can tell him anything you want to." The only constraint was that the blindfold should remain on.

Initial Impressions of the Interactional Data

The model was correctly made in all but one case out of the sample of forty, that is, the model corresponded either completely or in most details with the picture diagram. Although the time taken by each pair differed, there was no significant difference between social class or ethnic groups (these results are reported on in Cook-Gumperz and Bowyer 1972), and time taken did not relate to successful completion of the task. Any differences can be seen to be those of different approaches to the task, differing strategies of "doing instruction-giving" rather than a differential competence to perform the task.

The first impression of the interaction can be described as one of continual movement, especially on the part of the child "model builder." This movement cannot be adequately represented apart from the actual videotapes. Once the blindfold was tied, the builder usually began to feel and explore the array of pieces on the table so that the instructor's first verbal statement, unless a beginning sequence was formulated, occurred in response to a visual cue.

The main overall difference that divided the entire sample (although not on social class lines) was the kind of interactional pattern established between the instructor and builder. This was either a cooperative pattern where instructor and builder had an ongoing dialogue, both giving and requesting information and checking out the adequacy of responses; or a pattern we have called controlling, where the instructor and builder exchange only occasional comments, and the verbal instructions take on the form of a monologue.

One of the first features to be noticed in the transcripts is that the verbal description of the visual events unavoidably gives the impression of a set of discrete actions, of "bursts" of activity, whereas in the actual viewing of the events the impression is that the activity never ceased. Something was always happening, both partners moved constantly, and the child making the model—except where this is especially commented upon in the transcript—was in constant slight movement. Perhaps we could have conveyed this better through typographical devices such as extending the spacing of the visual description to fill all the space. As it is, the visual record is given the impression of timing difference between actions and verbalization by the conventional means of syntactic devices (such as *while, when, after*) or by connecting lines which link items on the two sides of the transcript which occurred simultaneously.

The way in which a visual event is encoded verbally forces us to group the stream of events around action sequences, which appear to be goal-related, whereas in fact, the goal of the action sequence unfolds. The relationship between the two accounts, the ongoing verbal instructions and our description of the taped visual scene, indicates some of the difficulties of fully recollecting and attributing the situated character of an event. The two events, the visual and verbal, were parallel, interlocking events, and did not have a precise or "neat solution" of sequences. We were particularly concerned in these transcripts to capture something of this overlapping character and the kinds of synchronization that did exist. For, as we shall show, the semantic interpretation of the instructions depends in part on this synchronization—for this is a part of the situated character of the event (Barker and Wright 1951); (also Barker [1963] discusses problems of coding the "stream of behavior").

The Children's Strategies of Instruction-Giving

Three main questions are to be asked of the data. The first question is whether, and if so, in what ways, instruction-giving was made a recognizable and differentiated speech activity from any other activity the children were engaged in, such as joking, conversational chat, or play.

Secondly, if this activity was differentiated and this difference was acknowledged between the participants, did the activity have a sequential structure? The sequential structure of an activity would be another recognizable feature differentiating one kind of speech activity from another.

Thirdly, what kind of strategy preferences did children show and in what ways do we, *a priori,* consider these to differ from what we have referred to as the adult norm, or school standard?

Findings in Answer to the Three Hypotheses[4]

All the children could be said to have recognized the event as an instruction one; either (*a*) through the choice of imperative-instructional speech strategies which contrasted with their everyday conversational talk; or (*b*) through a special "tone of voice" or intonational, prosodic switch.

Firstly, we shall note that the entire interaction proceeds through the use of direct information expanded by comments which add useful information, or do grammatical repair to the pronominalized directives. Very little extrasituational information is used, and the verbal comments remain focused on the task.

Secondly, there is a noticeable contrast in the intonational patterns during the course of the interaction. The instructional tone of voice emerged as a negotiated feature of the interaction in that it contrasted with the noninstructional—off the record—passages of interaction, where jokes or evaluative comments are made.

By **negotiated feature**, we refer to the initial use of a particular prosodic pattern which can be deduced to carry a particular meaning from its semantic context as in the following example:

(1) C: *Yōu're wrong Trent. Nōt tha:t*

The tone and stress is a specially marked pattern of rise and fall, singsong warning tone with a repeat pattern, there is a rise on wrong and then on the elongated vowel of *that* which is made into two syllables. This pattern can be glossed as a prosodic way of marking *you're wrong* and in its repeated use it appears to have this meaning, a "warning" of being wrong:

(2) *Trent/you by the teeny one/you by the bi:g ones.*

Each of these phrases is said with the same double repeat "warning" tone, its repetition we take as evidence of its meaningfulness. Furthermore, the initial instructions have their own prosodic pattern:

(3) C: *OK, get two balls / take two balls /*
OK, now get two middlesized ones.

This is said in a flat tone, a measured tone with a normal pitch and a slight emphasis on each word. This can be said to characterize the "instructional tone,"

4. The procedures of the analysis and the findings are reported on in much greater detail in Cook Gumperz 1975.

and it occurs repeatedly throughout the interaction. It serves, at a certain point, to bring the builder back to the task from a further joking sequence, so that in the first few seconds of interchange C and T have established two distinct intonational patterns. The particular meaning of these two intonation patterns is implicitly confirmed in the course of the interaction, and they then reoccur in the interchange without further semantic marking to communicate whether "instructions" begin again, or a warning *watch out/take care.* An additional pattern of normal conversational style or joking pattern can be distinguished, and serves further to contrast the "instructional tone." These shifts between instruction and joking were semantically realized, but sometimes resulted in passages where the shift between the instructional and noninstructional talk is marked prosodically, rather than lexicalized as is the following example.

(4) T: *I think I'm making / I know, I'm making a ca:r / just like that.*
C: *Put it down / just like that.*

Here, T's comment *I know, I'm making a car* is said in a "light voice"; he turns the model pieces on their side and comments with a rising pitch in a single contour and increased emphasis on car with a slightly elongated vowel. This "light voice," characterized by rising pitch and vowel elongation, exemplifies a "joking style." It is not quite clear whether C's repeat of the phrase *just like that* is a conscious intent to be ironic, but it is said in an "instructional tone," a falling tone with measured cadences, and the two phrases have a parallel intonational structure.

These examples illustrate the negotiated use of prosody in general intonation, and particularly the work that we hypothesize would be done by further lexicalization in adult interaction.

The Sequencing of the Activity of Instruction-Giving

For this stage of the analysis we decided to take over Labov's paradigm structure for narrative (Labov 1972[b]), not in order to examine in detail the syntactic realization of this structure, as it is used by Labov (for a further elaboration of Labov's analysis of narrative, see Keenan 1974[b]; Watson 1973), but in order to regard the structure as a paradigm for the ordering of any account of sequential actions that move to a climactic or recognized conclusion. Either recounted stories of past real or imginary events, or the direction of future or present activities, require the organization of speaking in such a way that a sequence of action is made apparent in the telling.

Comparatively, we think that Labov's assertion that the structure of narrative must correspond to the real-life temporal sequence agrees well with the structure of instruction-direction giving, although less well with the telling of narrative, since here the stylistic possibilities of grammar allow the temporal sequence to be manipulated.

The structure of narrative, as outlined by Labov, would ideally include, in order, but not in the necessary presence of every category, the following sequences:

1. Abstract.
2. Orientation.
3. Complicating action.
4. Evaluation.
5. Result or resolution.

We will take this ideal structural schema as a starting point for examination of the action strategies used by children to manage a sequence of speech activity which is directed to the pragmatic resolution or climax of achieving a completed task—getting the model made according to the picture diagram. Adopting this scheme will give us an adult normative framework against which to contrast and compare the children's choices of strategies, and so to notice any differential sequences.

How the Interchanges Were Structured in Terms of the Narrative Paradigm

In this section we will consider how the children structured their performance of the instructional task in such a way that a temporally adequate account is given. In the case of the face-to-face interaction the need for the verbal message to provide this adequacy was not as great as in planned or recollected actions, the action itself unfolds and need only be guided, often in a post facto manner, by the verbal record.[5]

Abstract and Orientation

An abstract defines the action, its conditions and procedures, and so provides a précis of what action is to follow; orientation defines the marking of an actual beginning for the particular interaction. None of the 40 children interviewed began with an abstract. Summary statements such as *you're doing fine, it's nearly done,* occurred later in the action, but no overall statement which summarized the action came at the beginning of the task to set the scene for the builder. We hypothesize that adults would make use of this structural feature to give a précis of the following action:

5. For a more detailed account of the relationship between speech and ongoing action, see Cook Gumperz 1975.

Eg. *You're going to make a cat. It's not too difficult.*
O.K. the model is a cat, and I'm going to tell you, a piece at a time, which pieces to take and where to put them.

In the children's data, the main similarity between all the participants was that they regarded the task as a game where they withheld information from each other. Not one instructor told the builder what model he/she was making, nor gave any comments which would set the scene for the blindfolded person, such as a brief verbal description of what has to be made or of the array of pieces. In fact, no one described the pieces to the builder; all this information arose out of the interaction or was taken for granted at the outset.

In the case of the **orientation sequences**, these were not always directly lexicalized, often the activity began when the builder touched the pieces. The instructor followed the lead of the builder and sometimes checked the action by saying:

(5) *No wait, I'm beginning over.*

Moreover, in most exchanges the instructor did not formulate an opening sequence so that, in effect, the task "began" as soon as the builder began to put the pieces together. For example, the instructor would start his exchange by saying:

(6) *Yes keep that one you have in your hand.*
or
(7) *Put that one down.*

so that, as in Examples (6) and (7), the deictic "that" indicates *a priori*, nonverbalized beginning. The speech action could, in all cases, be said to have begun with the builder's first action. The following two examples show the negotiated character of these beginning sequences and the instructional tone of voice:

(8) Line 1. *Put that one down.*
Line 2. *This one?*
Line 3. *Put it straight down.*

David starts straight in without any introductory sequence. His pitch-stress patterns are distinctive, starting with a high pitch on the first word, staccato enunciation and a falling contour for the whole utterance, with a small elongation of the vowel of "down." This intonation pattern occurs several times again, and can be said to be characteristic of part of David's "instructional style." It seems to serve to imbed the imperative sequences and add meanings such as *O.K. let's get on with it.* Line 3 has the same pattern with an addition of a qualifying descriptor's "straight." This intonational-prosodic pattern occurs even in the course of an utterance when it marks a move into the instructional style again, in later passages.

This method of instruction-giving used by the children is different from what we hypothesized would be done by adults, who might begin by the instructor establishing his role through a formal beginning sequence. The children's strategies are much closer to everyday life because the information is subject to the negotiated meaning of the interaction, and so, more dependent on the situated character of the event.

Complicating Action

The main concern of instruction-giving is that the activity being described gets accomplished. The children had two main strategies to accomplish the interaction. One was direct guidance of the builders' actions, using pronominalized comments and imperatives:

(9) *Take that, no not that / Yes that.*

The second strategy entailed giving "clear" verbalized instructions as imperative statements with sufficient detail that after hearing the statement, the builder could put the instructions to work. Both main strategies were used repeatedly. The attempts at instructional clarity were sometimes an initial strategy, in other cases came at the end of a pronominalized sequence which was directive, in an attempt to resolve a communication block. The attempts at instructional clarity involved two basic kinds of speech strategies:

(*a*) repetition, either with changed prosodic features (such as increased pitch, shifted stress), or occasional additional words:

(10) Line 42: *It's all straight / right on the top / on the top,*
(11) Line 44: *They're the shortest thing, the shortest thing;*

(*b*) repetitious sequences, which are also elaborations or rephrases of the previous statement. Rephrasings were a very rare feature; mainly, elaborations were simple, semantic-syntactic expansions. Sometimes these expansions had a "correct" syntactic form without any change of semantic content as in the following example:

(12) *Put that down / put that one down.*

A rule for these kinds of attempts at clarity seems to be: more detail is better communication. The pronominal references are expanded into nominal phrases using "this" or "that" rather than using the same term as a single pronominal. On other occasions an entire phrase is added, to expand the pronominal:

(13) Lines 49-50: N: *Like in this one.*
D: *That, that hole which you have your fingers on.*

(14) Lines 53-54: *Connect it to the middle round, the middle round thing, the middle one.*

These repetitions seem to serve several uses. They give plenty of redundant information, a typical characteristic of everyday talk, so that the listener catches on at some point. They sometimes also add useful additional information:

(15) Line 3: *Take an orange stick, a shortish orange stick, you know.*

This repetition is particularly interesting as it shows how the term "orange," which to a blindfolded person is not of much use, has taken on a new negotiated meaning for two partners: *M* has seen *S* size a piece, so that together they both know that orange refers to the next to smallest piece (red is the smallest). Thus, the use of a color term is not an example of an inadequate communication, although, given the context of this task it could be thought to be, if the facts of the situated nature of the communication were not allowed for. The expansions are also interesting in terms of the way in which some nominalizations are expanded on the principle that **more detail is clearer instructing**. The expansions and repetitions sometimes take the form of what we have called "prowords," for example, where "thing" is a proword:

(16) Lines 26-27: *Pick that other thing up, no the thing that you're making up, put that down, put that thing down.*

The additional nominals such as "thing," or pronominal "one," do not increase the specificity of the instructions, although they do the grammatical work of producing a more complex nominal group and an expanded utterance. We would expect that adults would use a similar rule or clearer instructing but would realize it linguistically by more semantically varied rephrasing.

Evaluation

In the narrative structure this will occur at a later fixed point in the story sequence. Whereas one of the features of instruction-giving is the choice between evaluative checks occurring after each major statement, or at the end of a directive monologue by the instructor. Both kinds of interactional pattern occurred. The evaluative checks could be either limited to a *yeah,* or *OK*; or could take the form of requests for more information or a comment on inadequate instructions:

(17) T: *What you tell me color for, how do I know green?*

The verbalized nature of the evaluative checks is especially related to the **situated** character of face-to-face instruction-giving, and many of the checks emerged from a combination of visual information and negotiated special meaning, such as the use of the color term "orange" which we mentioned above.

Evaluation can proceed through the use of **visually negotiated features** where the use of *yeah* or of nonexplicated pronominal is effective in guiding the builder, because the instructor can see that the builder is performing the correct action (see the following example). These features are important because if the interaction is treated as a "test," apart from its performance these features could be coded as examples of "inadequate" communication or miscommunication, but in the situational performance of these instructions these nonexplicated pronouns instructions become shortcuts and ways of avoiding redundancy.

Furthermore, ***prosodically negotiated features*** also serve to shortcut lengthier verbal explication, and provide a shared communicative set for the interaction:

(18) *You're wrong Trent, not that.*

"That" refers to the stick Trent is feeling, and not to the stick Trent has already picked up and is holding in his hand, the action was already acknowledged by *Yeah.* The referent to this action appears ambiguous in the transcript, but not so when the action is visible, this is typical of the kind of situation where further verbal specification could be needed if the task were not a visually immediate face-to-face encounter. It is through these negotiated features that much of the evaluative checks preaccomplished. Evaluation semantically becomes a matter of saying *OK* or *yeah* to acknowledge the putting into practice the new instructions.

Resolution

A narrative differs from an instructional sequence in that it requires a verbally recognized finale or closing sequence. The resolution of a set of verbalized instructions is a correctly completed task. The lexicalization of a final closing sequence is another feature that gives to the task a special quality that separates the activity from the flow of everyday talk. The children were more likely to lexicalize a resolution to the task, or a move towards resolution, than to use an orientation statement to begin the task.

The resolution can be categorized in two ways, either comments on the progress of the task, assuming it to be nearing completion, which we have called indicative comments; or comments which marked a finale and lexicalized the end of the task:

INDICATIVE COMMENTS

(19) *OK You nearly done.*
(20) *Antony Williams/you good.*
(21) *Sorry it's taking so long.*

FINALE

(22) *We've finished tra laa.*

The marking of the end of the task is interestingly different from the pattern of everyday interaction, where it has been noticed that, for children, the initiation or beginning of a new sequence of play activity is marked, but not the end, where participants just leave the scene without comment. The fact that the children marked the end of the task linguistically and do not ordinarily do so in everyday conversation might be more related to the character of the speech event than to a developmental change.

CONCLUSIONS

In concluding this analysis we will consider the third question we asked of the data–in what ways do we consider the children's strategy preferences to differ from what we consider to be an adult norm?[6]

First, the children used prosody, especially the negotiated patterns, to convey information which we assume would be lexicalized at a later stage of development. The lack of formalized beginning sequences, but an initial shift of intonation, is such an example. The negotiated passages of intonational shifts, such as C and T's "warning tone," we would also expect to be lexicalized into verbal comments in adult interaction. That is not to say that adults would not differentiate intonationally, the instructional from noninstructional passages, but that these shifts would also be lexicalized. In this way adults give more redundancy in their interaction, which presumably compensates for the greater pace of much of the interaction.

Second, the children used mostly direct imperatives, and imperatives containing pronominals to guide the action. Only occasionally were any statements made which gave a more indirect proselike quality to the immediacy of the verbal interaction by recalling past information:

(23) C: *Remember that piece you had before / Well that one / you need another one like that one.*

The use of the direct pronominalized imperatives is an efficient way to guide action, in fact, a more efficient way than using more complex verbalized instruc-

6. In a further study (in preparation), we have explored actual adult performance, and we will contrast this with further children's data at those age ranges.

tions. The resolution of communication blocks are similarly directive, rather than making attempts to rephrase the verbal record, the verbal record is kept as a close guide to the actions. Occasionally, the symbolic constraint of providing the correct lexical referent breaks through, as in the following example, with a finally specified referent:

(24) *Don't stick it in take / well put / put it down some place where you know where it is / the little orange thing.*

Not only the fact that these interactions are between children, but between peers and friends, probably contributes to the reduced amount of lexicalized information, other than in pronominals. The interaction proceeded against a background of assumed, shared competency.[7] Such a rule for explicating the instructions where shared competency cannot be assumed is to presume an understanding such as that of adults.

Finally, the fact of the sequencing of the interaction, through introduction to finale, these usually marked, also shows a similarity to the presumed adult model, as these sequences mark the instructional interaction as a special speech activity. This separation of activity provides a contextualizing boundary for the linguistic presuppositions, which sociolinguistically makes the context an active part of the communication process.

7. Initial analysis of a similar experiment between 5- and 6-year-olds in interaction with 10-year-olds shows that in these cases the 10-year-olds as instructors attempted to rephrase instructions that did not work, rather than guide the action by pronominal imperatives.

Part II
Function and Act

Making It Last: Repetition in Children's Discourse

ELINOR OCHS KEENAN

"The counterfeit is poorly imitated after you"
(Shakespeare) *Sonnets* liii

INTRODUCTION

One of the most commonplace observations in the psycholinguistic literature is that many young children often repeat utterances addressed to them. Just as commonplace are generalizations concerning the importance of this behavior to the development of language in the child. We have, on the one extreme, those who consider all linguistic knowledge to be obtained through this vehicle, and on the other extreme, we have those who place no importance whatsoever to the repetitions of young children.

Throughout the 1960s and into the 1970s the literature is dominated by studies which purport to show that language does not develop through repetition. Typically, the class of repeated utterances of the child is compared to the class of spontaneous or free utterances. Over and over these studies show that, with the exception of the child's repetition of adult expansions (Slobin 1968, Brown and Bellugi 1964), repeated utterances are not longer nor transformationally more complex than spontaneous utterances (Ervin-Tripp 1964, Menyuk 1963, Bloom 1970).

If repetition is irrelevant to language development, we are left with the question: Why **do** young children repeat the utterances of others with such frequency? This question has not been seriously addressed. At this point in time, we still do not understand what children are doing when they repeat a given utterance. This state of affairs exists because, until quite recently, psycholinguists have been insensitive to the status of utterances as social acts. With some exception (Bloom 1970, Weir 1970, Scollon 1973, Slobin 1968), they have focused on the form of repeated utterances to the exclusion of their function in real communicative situations. An expressed intention of this chapter is to remedy this state of affairs. I present here an analysis of repetition in child language from a pragmatic perspective. By pragmatic perspective, I mean simply one that relates an utterance to its context of use. Context, of course, is an infinitely extendable notion, but can include such things as the speaker's communicative intention, the speaker-hearer relationship, the extralinguistic setting of the utterance, the linguistic setting of the utterance (e.g., prior discourse, topic at hand, etc.), and other areas of background knowledge, such as knowledge of conversational norms and conventions.

Data used to substantiate this presentation are drawn from a number of existing sources. However, I will rely primarily on observations carried out by myself on the spontaneous conversations of twin boys (2:9 at the outset). Their conversations were recorded (video and audio) on a monthly basis over a period of a year.

Children as Communicators

It is no accident that the positive function of repetition in children's speech has not been investigated. For one thing, perspectives adopted in developmental psycholinguistics are heavily influenced by current paradigms in linguistics. It is only in the past 5 years that pragmatics have been seriously considered within the field. Secondly, within developmental psycholinguistics, there has persisted a stereotype of the child as a noncommunicator. Over and over, we find attempts to set children apart from adults in their verbal activity. We are told that children are egocentric in their speech; that is, they are not interested in directing their talk to an addressee. Copresent individuals are merely used as sounding boards for the child, as the child has no interest in obtaining a response to his utterance. Furthermore, when others talk, the child experiences difficulty in attending and evaluating their communicative intentions. In short, we are told that, unlike adults, children typically do not engage in dialogue. More characteristic of their speech are collective monologues (Piaget 1955).

With this prejudice in hand, the psycholinguist quite naturally believed that the primary motive of the child in interacting with adults was mastery of the adult code. In line with this, it was quite natural for researchers to associate repetition with this goal. Why did children repeat? Behaviorists claimed that young children repeated utterances as an attempt to produce the same utterance themselves. That is, they repeated because they wished to imitate the adult form of an utterance. Repetition in the speech of young children became strongly associated with imitation. In fact, throughout the rationalist counterargument, the association of repetition with imitation was never challenged. It was tacitly accepted that children repeated as an attempt to copy a prior utterance; what was denied was that the attempt was successful, or a means by which mastery was obtained.

Notice here that contextual grounds have subtly entered into the psycholinguist's categorization of repetitions as imitation. The psycholinguist perceives these repetitions as imitations because the repeater is a young child and the initial speaker is an adult. Constrained by the current paradigm, the relationship is translated into that between master of the code and learner of the code. This is important to note as most psycholinguists try to define imitation in terms of repetition alone. That is, they try to treat imitation as a formal relation between two utterances and not as a social act.

I have argued in an earlier paper (Keenan 1974[a]) that attempts to define imitation on formal grounds alone have been unsuccessful and inconsistent. The constraints on what counts as a repetition vary enormously from investigator to investigator. Rodd and Braine (1971), Freedle et al. (1970), and Ervin-Tripp (1964), for example, consider only immediate responses to an utterance as possible imitations. Bloom et al. (1974), on the other hand, is willing to look to the next five to ten utterances for a candidate imitation. Then there is the problem of cross-utterance similarity. Just how much of the initial utterance must be repeated in order for it to count as an imitation? For many investigators, the repeated utterance could omit but not substitute items of the initial utterance. Further, the repeated utterance had to be a more or less telegraphic version of the adult string, omitting the function words but retaining some or all of the content words. For other investigators (Rodd and Braine 1971), it was sufficient that the child repeat a particular construction under investigation for the utterance to count as an imitation.

On top of these practical difficulties is the fact that repetition alone is neither necessary nor sufficient to characterize imitation. It is not a necessary criterion in that attempts to copy may not, in fact, repeat the prior utterance. Hence there may be innumerable unsuccessful imitations—e.g., inarticulate mutterings, wild stabs, false starts, and the like—which are not repetitions in any accepted sense of the word. Note here, then, that when psycholinguists address themselves to the role of imitation in language development, they are considering only successful imitations in their data base. We have no idea whatsoever of the character of these unsuccessful imitations. We don't know what type of adult utterance is responded to in such a way, and we do not know the nature of the distortion. It is evident that even on its own terms, the imitation literature stands on shaky ground.

Repetition is not a sufficient criterion for imitation in that it is possible to find repeated utterances that are not attempts to copy. Slobin illustrated this beautifully in his 1968 article on imitation. He provides the following dialogue between Adam (2:6) and his mother:

MOTHER: *It fits in the puzzle someplace.*
ADAM: *Puzzle? Puzzle someplace?*
MOTHER: *Turn it around.*
ADAM: *Turn it around?*
MOTHER: *No, the other way.*
ADAM: *Other way?*
MOTHER: *I guess you have to turn it around.*
ADAM: *Guess turn it round. Turn round.*

In this dialogue, Adam appears first to be using repetition as a vehicle for querying a prior utterance, and then as a vehicle for informing himself and/or agreeing with the mother's comment.

It is clear that all repetitions are not imitations and all imitations are not repetitions. In order to establish a given utterance as an imitation, contextual criteria must be provided as well. Further, it is not sufficient to define the context as simply that of a child interacting with an adult. We have seen that this relationship may be held constant through a variety of social uses of repetition (imitation, query, self-informing). In order to establish that an imitation has taken place, the investigator must somehow contend with the communicative intentions of the child. This is not to say that for an imitation to have taken place the child must have the conscious intention to reproduce a prior utterance. There may be degrees to which the child is aware of his own behavior. It is only to say that the presence or absence of the intention to imitate must be reckoned with. In particular, we can not accept that a repetition overtly elicited in an experimental situation can be equated in all cases with a repetition uttered in spontaneous conversation between caretaker and child. The overtly elicited repetition counts as an imitation because the child has been asked to copy the experimenter's utterance. While this sometimes may be the case in spontaneous conversation, we can not assume all repeats to be of this character. Claims made about the nature of repetition in the laboratory situation, then, should not automatically extend to ordinary verbal interactions between caretaker and child.

Once we address ourselves to the communicative intentions of the child, we can begin investigating a variety of interesting questions. For example, we know that children who repeat utterances increase this activity until about 2:6 and then it begins to decline. It would be interesting to follow a repeater through this cycle, indicating the ways in which the repetition was used in discourse. We could begin asking in what order the different communicative uses of repetition emerge. It may be the case that the child first uses repetition to imitate and later comes to use it to perform other communicative tasks. It may be the case that, as Slobin (1973[b]) has suggested for syntax, the child uses an old form for new functions. That is, some children may latch onto repetition quite early as a device for participating in discourse, and use this device to perform novel communicative tasks. Further, it may be the case that repetition is more appropriate or more efficient for some tasks than others. For example, if you want to copy the utterance of another speaker, then repetition is a good device to employ. Similarly, if the child wishes to let his caretaker know that he has understood ("communication check") the caretaker's utterance, then repetition is appropriate. On the other hand, there are only a few types of questions one can ask by repeating all or part of a prior utterance. It may be the case that as the child becomes competent in a greater number of speech acts, he finds repetition a less and less satisfying device.

A second area of inquiry opened up concerns the differences and similarities between children who rely heavily on repetition and those who rarely repeat (Bloom et al. 1974). The distinction has been posed in the literature as those children who are imitators and those children who are nonimitators. Addressing ourselves to the communicative intentions of children, we may discover that this dichotomy misses the mark. It may be the case that "imitators" are not, in fact, imitating, and that all of these children do similar communicative work; they simply differ in the formal devices used to carry out this work.

Repetition and Prior Discourse

I would like now to examine in some detail the varied uses of repetition in conversational discourse. In investigating these uses, I look for clues in prior discourse and in subsequent discourse. Here I consider the relation of repetition to prior discourse.

One of the characteristics of the literature on imitation is that it generally ignores the illocutionary force of the utterance that the child is responding to. The utterance repeated by the child is not described as a request for information, request for services, an assertion, a greeting, a rhyme, or song. All utterances are lumped together under the cover term "model sentence." The use of this term, of course, reflects the general assumption that all repetitions are imitations. Furthermore, in comparing an utterance with its repetition, the investigator judges only the extent to which the repetition succeeds as an imitation. It is typical of repetitions, in fact, not to succeed completely. Ervin-Tripp (1964), for example, mentions that only a small percentage of the spontaneous "imitations" in her data were exact repetitions. As imitations, then, the repetitions of young children are inferior reproductions.

If, on the other hand, children are repeating not to imitate but to satisfy some other communicative obligation, then inexact repetition might be the intended, not unintended, desire of the child. The fact that the child, particularly the child from 2-3 years, fails to copy in entirety a previous utterance in conversation, may reflect the child's **competence** and not his **incompetence.** Consider, for example, the model sentences used by Rodd and Braine (1971) in their study of imitation. In this study, the investigator directed to a child of 2:1 years the sentence *Is the baby sitting down?* The child's response was *Uhhuh, baby down.* Here, it is perfectly appropriate for the child not to repeat the previous utterance. In fact, it would be inappropriate for the child to produce an exact copy. Clearly, the child has grasped the communicative intentions of the investigator. The child's response shows that the child treats the investigator's utterance not as a model to be imitated, but as a question to be answered. The repetition is far more successful as an answer than as an imitation.

Repetition with omissions are appropriate in response to utterances other than information questions as well. For both adult and child alike, it is appropriate to repeat just one or two words from the utterance of a conversational partner to comment attitudinally:

EXAMPLE 1

(Toby and David at 2:9 conversing with their nanny, Jill)

JILL:	*And we're going to have hot dogs.*
TOBY:	*Hot dogs!* (excitedly)
JILL:	*And soup.*
DAVID:	*Mmm soup!*

To agree with: EXAMPLE 2

(Toby and David at 2:9 with their nanny, Jill)

JILL:	*And we're gonna build a fire.*
DAVID:	*Mmm.*
TOBY:	*Oh yeah/build fire.*

To self-inform: EXAMPLE 3

(Toby and David at 2:9 with their nanny, Jill)

JILL:	*And we're going to cook sausages.*
TOBY:	*Cook sausages.*
JILL:	*And bacon.*
TOBY and DAVID:	*Bacon.*
JILL:	*And eggs.*
TOBY and DAVID:	*Eggs.*

To query: EXAMPLE 4

(Toby and David at 2:10. Toby engaged in sound play)

TOBY:	*/diɔt/tziju/ i / u / bɔ / ɔt/*
DAVID:	ˇ*bɔt*

EXAMPLE 5

(Toby and David at 2:11)

DAVID: ˋ*My hands are cold.*
TOBY: ˊ*Cold.*

To imitate: EXAMPLE 6

(Toby and David at 2:9 with their nanny, Jill)

JILL: *Aren't I a good cook? Say "Yes, the greatest!"*
TOBY: *Yes the greatest.* (softly)
JILL: *That's right.*
DAVID: *The greatest!* (loudly)

Even in the case of explicit imitation, the child repeats selectively. For example, the child does not repeat the performative verb "say" in the previous utterance. The child has shaped the repetition to satisfy his obligations as a conversational partner. In each case the shaping reflects the child's orientation to the expectations of the prior speaker.

We have established, then, that children are sensitive to the illocutionary force of prior utterances in discourse. They repeat as an attempt to respond appropriately to particular types of utterances. I have mentioned some of these types in the previous discussion, but this mention by no means exhausts the list. In addition to its usefulness in answering questions, commenting, affirming, self-informing, querying, and imitating, repetition may be used to make counter-claims of the following sort:

EXAMPLE 7

(Toby and David at 2:9)

DAVID: *You*ˋ*silly/ you*ˋ*silly/ you*ˋ*silly/ you*ˋ*silly/ you*ˋ*silly/*
TOBY: ˋ*You/*ˋ*you silly/*ˋ*you silly/*ˋ*you silly/*ˋ*no you silly/*

Further, repetition may be used to match a claim made by a previous speaker (Keenan and Klein 1974). That is, the second speaker may claim what was predicted by the first speaker holds for the second speaker as well:

EXAMPLE 8

(Toby and David at 2:9 with their nanny, Jill)

DAVID: *Doggie bib.* (I have) *doggie bib.* (see).
I have doggie bib (2*x*). (?) *bib.*
JILL: *David's got brown flowers in his.*
DAVID: *Yeah.*
TOBY: (I) *have doggie bib.*
JILL: (You've got a) *doggie bib.*

EXAMPLE 9

DAVID: *I get them off.*
TOBY: *I get them off.*

In counterclaims and matching claims, we see that an utterance that replicates another in form does not replicate it in meaning. The utterances differ in meaning precisely because they differ in context. In each case, the meaning of the deitic item (*I, you*) depends on who the speaker is and who the addressee is. Such examples indicate the difficulty involved in earlier claims that imitations must preserve the meaning of the model utterance (Ervin-Tripp 1964). Preservation of meaning must surely be the exception rather than the norm in repeated utterances. Even if the repeated utterance contains no deitic items, the position of the utterance as a response (i.e., second pair part, cf. Schegloff and Sacks (1973) makes it pragmatically distinct from the initial utterance.

In addition to the above-mentioned uses of repetition, there are examples in the data of repeating to greet back, to reverse the direction of an order, to reverse the direction of an information question, and to request clarification of an utterance:

EXAMPLE 10
(Toby and David at 2:11)

DAVID: *(fae:b)*
TOBY: *(fae:b). You mean that/*

In short, there appears to be no end to the ways in which cross utterance repetition is employed in conversational discourse. Repetition is probably one of the most misunderstood phenomena in psycholinguistics. It is associated with the language of children, who, in turn, are underrated as communicators. It is obvious, however, that with some exceptions, the kind of repetition described here is quite characteristic of adult speakers as well. Any of the following exchanges could appear in adult discourse:

EXAMPLE 11: GREETING

A: *Hello.*
B: *Hello.*

EXAMPLE 12: SELF-INFORMING AND/OR DISPLAYING KNOWLEDGE

A: *That's Halley's comet.*
B: *Ah, that's Halley's comet.*

EXAMPLE 13: AGREEING

A: *That's dreadful.*
B: *Dreadful.*

EXAMPLE 14: MATCHING CLAIM

A: *I'm fat.*
B: *I'm fat.*

EXAMPLE 15: COUNTERCLAIM

A: *You're thinner than I am.*
B: *You're thinner than I am.*

EXAMPLE 16: QUERYING

A: *Yes.*
B: *Yes?*

EXAMPLE 17: ANSWERING

A: *Yes?*
B: *Yes.*

EXAMPLE 18: REVERSING DIRECTION OF QUESTION

A: *Well?*
B: *Well?*

EXAMPLE 19: IMITATING

A: *Say 'cheese'.*
B: *Cheese.*

EXAMPLE 20: COMMENTING

A: *But my diet.*
B: *Diet schmiet. Let's eat.*

What then is going on when a child repeats the utterance of a copresent speaker? Is the child learning anything about his language? Is there any way in which repetition is developmentally progressive with respect to language? We can say that in repeating, the child is learning to communicate. He is learning not to construct sentences at random, but to construct them to meet specific communicative needs. He is learning to query, comment, confirm, match a claim and counterclaim, answer a question, respond to a demand, and so on. In short, he is learning the human uses of language, what Dell Hymes has called "communicative competence" (1972[a]).

Repetition and Subsequent Discourse

I would like to turn now to the relation between repetition and discourse subsequent to a repetition. It has been often noted in the literature (Slobin 1968, Brown and Bellugi 1964) that when caretakers repeat and expand the utterances of children, they often do so as a kind of "communication check." The caretaker presents his or her interpretation of the child's utterance to the child for verification.

EXAMPLE 21

(Toby and David at 2:9 with their nanny, Jill)

TOBY: *Gramma Ochs/*
JILL: *Gramma Ochs?*
TOBY: *Yeah/*

EXAMPLE 22

(Toby and David at 2:9 with their nanny, Jill)

TOBY: *Airplane/*
JILL: *Oh. She went on an airplane, did she?*
TOBY: *Yeah/*

It is similarly the case that children repeat the utterances of adults to let them know they have understood their utterances at some basic level. (Examples 1-3 illustrate this point.) It is characteristic of some adults that they in fact wait for such repetitions by the child before proceeding with the discourse. These communication checks are not unique to adult-child interaction, however. They are also prevalent in child-child conversational discourse as well:

EXAMPLE 23

(Toby and David at 2:11)

DAVID: (putting head on Toby's bed) . . . *Help me/David's falling/ help me/ David's falling/ help me/ help me/ help me/ Its got me/ help me/ help me/ oooo/.*
TOBY: *Help me/. you saying help me/.* (See also Example 10)

Children often experience enormous difficulty in getting their message across (Ryan 1974), and many of them come to expect verification of their message through repetition. In the case of Toby and David, when verification was not expressed by a co-conversationalist, the child would solicit it (Keenan 1974[b]; Keenan and Klein 1974). The child would repeat his utterance over and over until it was acknowledged:

EXAMPLE 24

(Toby and David at 2:10 with their nanny, Jill, in the process of making a picture)

TOBY: *Put it Toby's room/*
JILL: *Toby's got a worm?*
TOBY: *No/ Put it Toby's room/*
JILL: *Toby's what?*
DAVID: *Room/* } (simultaneously)
TOBY: *Toby's room/* } (simultaneously)
JILL: *Toby's room?*

TOBY: *Yeah/*
DAVID: (?)
JILL: *Oh. Put it in Toby's room.*
TOBY: *Yeah/* (See Example 23 for child-child interaction)

The child might accompany his utterance with an explicit request to attend and acknowledge:

EXAMPLE 25
(Toby and David at 3:0)

TOBY: *My big tractors coming/*
DAVID: *No/* (?)
TOBY: *Its coming/* ***look*** *its coming/ its coming/*
DAVID: *Now its coming/ Its coming/ Its coming/* ***look*** *its coming/*
TOBY: *I see/*

In short, the children observed in this study established a convention, whereby given an utterance by one partner, some evidence of attentiveness or base comprehension from the other was expected to follow. It is certainly the case that adults in our society depend on communication checks (nods of the head, eye contact, mutterings of "umhum," etc.) in talking with one another. However, the dependence does not appear to be as extreme or as frequent as is the case for young children. For example, when one adult native speaker converses with another such speaker, he or she usually assumes that the message has been successfully decoded by the addressee. Adult speakers usually take it for granted that conversational partners "know" in some sense (e.g., are aware of) the messages previously exchanged in the course of a particular conversation. In the absence of a challenge from the addressee, a speaker can treat these utterances as shared knowledge (Givon 1974), and in subsequent discourse, he or she can consider these utterances to be known, or old information.

Children, on the other hand, cannot make these assumptions. Because of the production difficulties they experience on all levels (phonological, syntactic, semantic), they cannot assume that their utterances have been decoded. Simply uttering a proposition does not assure that it is "shared knowledge" between speaker and addressee. **Hence, what communication checks do is to precisely turn an utterance into shared knowledge**. That is, when an addressee repeats (expands) an antecedent utterance, he evidences his knowledge of that utterance. Henceforth, both interlocutors can treat the propositions contained in the utterance as given or old information.

It is often the case in adult discourse that known or old information emerges as the topic of a subsequent utterance. The topic is the unchallengeable or presupposed element about which some new prediction ("comment") is made. Similarly, in the discourse of young children, information made known through repetition may serve as future topics in subsequent discourse. It is often the case that an utterance is produced by one speaker, part or all of it is repeated by the addressee, and the repeated information becomes the topic of a next utterance. For example:

EXAMPLE 26
(Toby and David at 2:10, eating lunch)

TOBY: *Piece bread then/*
DAVID: *No piece bread/piece bread/ Its gone/*

EXAMPLE 27
(Toby and David at 2:11 in bedroom. An alarm clock rings.)

DAVID: *Bell/*
TOBY: *Bell/*
DAVID: *Bell/ its mommy's)*
TOBY: (?) *It/*
DAVID: *Was mommy's alarm clock/*
TOBY: *'Larm clock/yeah/goes ding dong ding dong/*
DAVID: *No/ no/ goes fip fip/ fip fip/*

These two examples bring out a number of points. Example 26 illustrates the way in which the repeated information may become the topic of a subsequent utterance in the form of a pronoun. Pronouns normally refer to an established or already known referent. In this case, it is perfectly appropriate for the speaker to use a pronoun, because repetition has given the referent this status. In Example 27, we see that the initial utterance *bell* is repeated and treated as the topic of the following utterance *Its mommy's.* Again the known information is represented in the form of a pronoun. On the other hand, the repetition of *alarm clock* later in the dialogue is incorporated directly as topic of *goes ding dong ding dong* without the mediation of a pronoun. Further, Example 27 illustrates nicely the recursive nature of topic-comment sequences in conversational discourse. We see that the new information *bell* serves as old information topic for the comment *was mommy's alarm clock.* However, part of this predicate *alarm clock* becomes old information through repetition by the other child. Having achieved this status, it then becomes the topic of the subsequent utterances *goes ding dong ding dong* and *goes fip fip/fip fip/.* Whole stretches of discourse are linked in this way: New information is transformed into old information through repetition, yielding topics for subsequent discourse. One positive role of repetition in discourse is, then, to establish topic candidates (Keenan 1974[b]). The topic candidates can be utilized in the discourse of either conversational partner. In Example 26, the child who repeats the utterance exploits it as a topic. In Example 27, we have a case in which the child who introduces the new information is the one who topicalizes it in later discourse.

(David first points out the existence of a *bell* and later makes a claim about it: *its mommy's,* etc.)

Two additional points need to be made with respect to the role of repetition in establishing topic candidates. The first is that such sequences are characteristic of many adult-child interactions as well as child-child interactions. It is often the case that an adult will present new information, the child will repeat some or all of it, and will use it as the topic of utterances:

EXAMPLE 28

(Toby and David at 2:9 with their nanny, Jill)

JILL:	*Jiji's going camping this afternoon.*
TOBY:	*Oh yeah/* } (simultaneously)
DAVID:	*Camping/ oh exciting/* }

Or the child will initiate an assertion, the adult will repeat it and use it subsequently as a topic:

EXAMPLE 29

(Toby and David at 2:9 with their nanny, Jill)

TOBY:	*Jiji's wonderful/*
JILL:	*Wonderful. I know it/*

With respect to the earlier mentioned topic of children who are imitators and those who are not, it may be worth investigating if the so-called nonimitators engage in conversations primarily like Example 29, whereas the so-called imitators engage in conversation primarily like Example 28. That is, it may be characteristic of some caretaker-child interactions that the caretaker takes an utterance of a child and makes it old information through repetition, using it as a topic in further discourse. This kind of discourse would give a "nonimitative" look to the child's utterances. In other caretaker-child interactions, however, the child himself or herself may transform the utterance of another into old information through repetition ("imitating"), providing either the caretaker or the child with a topic candidate.

Second, now that we understand some of the work that is being carried out through discourse, we can understand more clearly the meaning of any single utterance of an interlocutor (child or adult). For example, we can retrace the history of the discourse to isolate the communicative work of an utterance. In many cases (though by no means in all cases), the first mention of a referent by a child or by an adult talking to a child is simultaneously a claim and a request to be ratified as a topic candidate. The second mention of the referent (the repetition) ratifies the information as known, and subsequent mentions take for granted that it is established, old information.

Furthermore, without discourse history, it would be difficult to separate what is new information from what is old information in any single utterance. That is, it would be difficult to isolate what is being asserted from what is already taken for granted or presupposed. The linguist cannot, for example, rely on the range of syntactic cues expressing old information in adult speech. The use of pronouns to express old information is a relatively late development in child language (Bloom et al. 1975). Further, even if pronouns are available for this purpose as in the speech of Toby and David, there still is an absence of definite articles, relative clause nominalizations, and other syntactic means for codifying taken-for-granted information. For many children, taken-for-granted information is marked through discourse and not through syntax. Ratification of a word, phrase, etc., in discourse is sufficient in itself to establish these items as presupposed in subsequent utterances. This is the case in Example 27, where *alarm clock* is the old information, or topic addressed by the next two utterances *goes ding dong ding dong* and *no/no/ goes fip fip/ fip fip/*. We end this chapter with the hypothesis that cross-utterance repetition anticipates the syntactic marking of old information, and that heavy reliance on repetition gives way once syntactic devices for topicalization emerge in the child's speech corpus.

"Oh Them Sheriff": A Pragmatic Analysis of Children's Responses to Questions[1]

JOHN DORE

How do we know when an answer to a question is appropriate? Why is it that when a 2-year-old was asked, *Put the truck where?* his answer, *Put truck window,* was considered appropriate; but when the same child was asked, *Which is right, 'two shoes' or 'two shoe'?* his response, *Pop goes the weasel!* was considered a non sequitur? These examples are from a study by Brown and Bellugi (1964) who were concerned with children's acquisition of syntax and the experimental techniques necessary to get at it. Since that time a great deal has been found out about the development of syntax, but very few studies have asked, much less found out, what makes an answer appropriate. An exception was Ervin-Tripp's work (1970), which provided the necessary first step toward explaining appropriateness. She described the development of "grammatically appropriate" answers to "Wh-questions," that is, answers that "are appropriate from the standpoint of grammatical category." And, apart from this formal "category agreement," she pointed out the other relevant aspects of answering, among them that "some semantic interpretation is made of a question, unless it is merely a routine. In addition, a pragmatic interpretation may be required [p. 80]." Children's pragmatic interpretation of questions is the focus of this present chapter.

1. The laboratory facility and staff, the data collection, and some of the data analyses for the research reported in this chapter were supported by Grant No. 5-20284 from The Grant Foundation to the Rockefeller University. This research was also supported in part by a grant from the Carnegie Corporation of New York to the Rockefeller University.

The data presented here are from a study of the spontaneous responses by 3-year-old children to questions addressed to them. While many of their responses were grammatically matched, the majority were not; these responses were, however, "pragmatically appropriate" in various ways. The primary purpose of this chapter is to characterize the notion of pragmatic appropriateness, or more specifically, of "contingency relations" between questions and answers; another purpose is to propose the form of interpretive rules underlying children's responses. This will be accomplished first by briefly describing what is taken to be the domain of linguistic pragmatics and then by discussing the results of our study of children's illocutionary acts in general and their responses to questions in particular.

The Domain of Linguistic Pragmatics

Some philosophers of language have discussed the distinction between grammar and pragmatics. Stalnaker (1972), for example, claims that:

> Syntax studies sentences, semantics studies propositions. Pragmatics is the study of linguistic acts and the contexts in which they are performed. There are two major types of problems to be solved within pragmatics: First, to define interesting types of speech acts and speech products; second, to characterize the features of the speech context which help determine which proposition is expressed by a given sentence [p. 383].

To illustrate these kinds of problems, I will take an example from Grice (1975). He has been developing a theory of the **full signification** of an utterance, which involves not only **what is said**, but also **what is meant** and **what is implicated.** For example, if a speaker of English hears the utterance *He is in the grip of a vice,* Grice claims that he would know that **what was said** was "about some particular male person or animal and that at the time of the utterance (whatever that was) either (i) that x was unable to rid himself of a certain kind of bad characteristic, or (ii) that some part of x's person was caught in a certain kind of tool or instrument." Notice that one knows this much about the utterance, without knowing anything about the context, by virtue of knowing the grammar of standard English. However, Grice adds that "for a full identification of what the speaker had **said** one would need to know (*a*) the identity of x, (*b*) the time of the utterance, (*c*) the meaning, on the particular occasion of utterance, of the phrase 'in the grip of a vice' (a decision between (i) and (ii) above [p. 6]." These aspects of saying are pragmatic; (*a*) and (*b*) require knowledge about the particular context, and (*c*) depends upon whether the speaker intended his utterance metaphorically. Knowledge of the context and of another's intentions cannot be handled in the grammar (cf. Katz and Langendoen 1976).

Similarly, Grice's notion of conversational implication is also pragmatic. He would claim, I think, that if *He is in the grip of a vice* followed the question *Do you think he is the right man for the job of Archbishop?* then, on the "bad characteristic" reading, **what is meant** by the utterance might be that he is not the right man; if it followed the command *Tell him to come in here immediately!* then, on the "tool" reading, **what is meant** might be that he cannot come.[2]

To Grice's account of **what is said-grammatically** and **what is said-pragmatically** can be added the following kinds of **what is done**. In saying *He is in the grip of a vice* one performs the **act of referring** to some male and to some characteristic or tool; and one performs the **act of predicating** some characteristic or situation of this male. On another level of doing, the speaker is **describing** a situation or a location (on the "tool" reading) or he is **attributing** a certain internal state to the male (on the "characteristic" reading). Further, if the utterance follows the *Archbishop* question, we might want to say that the speaker is **denying** (albeit obliquely) the proposition in the question; if it follows the command, we would say that the speaker is **explaining** why *the man* cannot come. Notice that these responses do not overtly answer the question or acknowledge the command, at least in the sense of providing the most expected or predictable information; they are nonetheless appropriate, if oblique, responses. Finally, there are other contexts in which this utterance might be produced where we would call it a joke.

In summary, the acts of referring and predicating are **parts** of speech acts; describing, attributing, denying and explaining **are** speech acts; and jokes are probably what Stalnaker means by "speech products." The point of explicating **what is done** is to show that the acts performed by a given utterance are not determined by its grammar, though the grammar may constrain the kinds of acts that can be performed by a given utterance. I take it, then, that **what is said-grammatically** is in this sense independent of pragmatic phenomena such as **what is said-pragmatically**, **what is meant-conversationally**, and **what is done**. In this view, everything that a speaker knows about the utterance, except the phonological, syntactic, and semantic knowledge of the sentence type, can be treated as the pragmatic, as distinct from the grammatical, component of the utterance. For the purpose of discussion, we can assume that

2. I realize that Grice's example is artificial to the extent that in actual conversation hearers rarely, if ever, perceive utterances like *He is in the grip of a vice* as ambiguous. But, apart from the fact that such utterances must almost always be interpreted metaphorically, the example suits Grice's theoretical purpose. Moreover, my juxtaposition of the utterance with the preceding utterances is even more artificial. Yet in this section I am solely concerned with distinguishing the theoretical boundary between grammar and pragmatics. The following sections report results from empirical studies that provide sufficient examples of actual occurrences of utterances that are "functionally equivocal" (if not structurally ambiguous).

"semantic meaning" has to do with the reading of the proposition while "pragmatic meaning" has to do with the intentions of the speaker, the relations of utterance to contexts, and conversational skills.

Searle (1969) describes the speech act as containing two components: A proposition (defined in terms of a predicating expression taking one or more referring expressions as its arguments), and an illocutionary force (which indicates how the speaker intends his utterance to be taken). The proposition conveys the conceptual content, while the illocutionary force indicates whether the utterance should count as an assertion, promise, question, and so on. Illocutionary acts are those performed in producing certain utterances. They were distinguished by Austin (1962) from "a locutionary act, which is roughly equivalent to uttering a certain sentence with a certain sense and reference" and from "perlocutionary acts: What we bring about or achieve by saying something, such as convincing, persuading . . . [p. 108]." The following discussion of children's language is restricted to illocutionary acts.

Dore (1976) argued that the primary determinant of the illocutionary force of an illocutionary act is the speaker's **communicative intention** (CI). This is an intention to induce in a hearer two specific effects: (*a*) the **expected illocutionary effect**—that the hearer recognize the illocutionary status of the utterance; (*b*) the **expected perlocutionary effect**—that the hearer recognize what the speaker expects him to do or believe as a consequence of recognizing the utterance's illocutionary status. For example, if I ask *What's your name?* I will have achieved my expected illocutionary effect if you recognize that I have asked you a certain kind of information question; I will have achieved my expected perlocutionary effect if you recognize that I expect you to tell me your name. The clearest evidence of my success, of course, would be your actually telling me your name. Unlike other notions of intention, a CI must be linguistically marked. That is, it must be conveyed by utterances of certain grammatical forms; and the illocutionary acts determined by CIs must be conventionally governed by rules for the use of utterances in contexts so that hearers automatically recognize speaker's CIs.

However, it is important to note that form alone cannot determine pragmatic function. The hearer's recognition of the speaker's CI depends upon several factors that operate independently of the grammar. This claim is supported by the results of both of the following studies, though the two studies approach the nonisomorphism of form and function differently. In the first study, the purpose of which was to identify the array of illocutionary acts performed by children, utterances were **initially coded for intention.** Thus, one child's utterance of *Why don't you sit in the seat behind?* was coded as a **Request for Action** on the basis of the evidence yielded by the methodology employed. In the second study, which focused on the children's responses to questions, that same utterance was **initially identified on the basis**

of grammatical form as an information question; the analysis of the hearer's response—the hearer replied with *Alright* and sat in the seat behind the speaker—indicated that he interpreted the question as an **Action Request**. Therefore, although the procedures for initially categorizing utterances were different in the two studies, the results of both led to the same conclusion: It is not the grammar that conveys illocutionary intent.

Children's Illocutionary Acts

Four boys and three girls of middle-class backgrounds attended a nursery 2 hours a day, 3 days a week, over a period of 7 months, and their interactivity was videotaped about 2 hours a week. A wide variety of situations (including structured activities like snack-time and arts and crafts as well as free-play) were systematically sampled. Although the nursery school teacher was almost always present, she was as unobtrusive as possible regarding child-initiated activities. Consequently, the children appeared to engage in relatively unrestrained, spontaneous conversations and more than half of their speech was addressed to other children. The following corpus comes from videotapes of 1-hr sessions per month for the last 4 months of the study. The children ranged in age from 2:10 to 3:3 years at the first of these four sessions. The corpus consists of almost 3,000 child utterances, each of which was coded for illocutionary act.

The decision procedure for coding utterances as illocutionary acts was to determine, in the following order:

1. The literal semantic reading of the primary proposition of the utterance, on the basis of its logical subject, predicate, adverbial phrases, and other constituents (according to Katz 1972).
2. The grammatical and prosodic operators on the proposition.
3. The new, or focused, information; new in relation to both conversation and context (Halliday 1970[b]).
4. The speaker's related utterances and nonlinguistic behavior.
5. The reciprocal and contingent behavior, both verbal and nonverbal, of his interlocutors (Garvey 1975).
6. The contextual features directly relevant to the pragmatic status of the utterance (Lewis 1972).

Let me exemplify the steps in this procedure. The vast majority of the children's utterances were propositional in structure (though sometimes elliptical), consisting of at least a subject and predicate; for example, the *I* and *am painting* (respectively) in *I am painting.* Numerous kinds of grammatical operators applied to propositions: Word order converted a proposition to a Yes-No question (for example: *Are you painting?*), and a grammatically determined intonation pattern did the same (as in *You're painting?*), and an interrogative pronoun converted it to a Wh-Question (*What are you doing?*). The new information in an utterance may be new in relation to the conversation (*Nothing* might be the Wh-Answer to the above Wh-Question); or information could be new in relation to what was already given in the context (*He likes to* would be an **Attribution** about the above "painter's" internal state relative to painting).

The single most important evidence for determining the illocutionary act is the speaker's utterances that are contingently related to the target utterance being coded. For example, one boy said to a girl, *Hey, don't sit there!*, which was coded as a **Protest**; then he said *I was sitting there* which was contingently related to his first utterance by stating his right to make a **Protest**. The remarks of addressees often indicate how they interpret the speaker's intention; children often reply with *Okay* to a speaker's **Action Request** in order to verbally encode their **Compliance**. And a third source of evidence for identifying illocutionary acts is the teacher's remarks which were, though often unsolicited, contingently related to a child's utterance to another child. For example, one boy tried to make an **Action Request** appear to be a genuine **Protest** by raising his fist and saying, in an abrupt rising-falling intonation contour, *Get out of here* to a girl. The teacher immediately asked *Why does she have to?*, thereby questioning the boy's right to issue a **Protest**. The girl did not leave.

The context is often crucial in determining an illocutionary act. Contextual features, in fact, often override the literal meaning of a proposition: Instead of an **Event Description**, *I am painting* would be coded as role-playing if the child were merely waving his arms in the air as he said it. The utterance *We painted the windows* would be coded as a joke if the participants in the conversation respond with laughter because they know that it is obviously untrue, and even unreasonable. In general, the coding of individual illocutionary acts is determined by both "internal" grammatical factors, and "external" discourse-relation and contextual factors. Most often, the relations among sequences of utterances define the status of individual utterances in the sequence.

Thirty-two types of illocutionary acts were performed by the children in the study. Table 1 lists the types and gives the code, the definition, and an example of each type. We achieved a reliability of better than 82% for all sessions for classifying utterances into illocutionary act types; this was measured in terms of the initial agreements of two experienced coders who scored independently. Given the state of our knowledge about children's pragmatic processing of speech, it would be premature to argue that the illocutionary act categories we postulated have an absolute validity or even that the categories are arranged in the most descriptively adequate way. However, this initial phase of the research enabled us to group together utterances of roughly the same illocutionary value, based on definitions available in the literature and on our own intuitions. Fortunately, of all illocutionary types, questions are the easiest to identify because of their distinct grammatical form. Thus, the following question-response study was on relatively safe grounds, and we were able to focus directly on how children respond to questions.

TABLE 1

Definitions and examples of the communicative intentions we identified as underlying the children's illocutionary acts. Each definition begins with "... is an intention to induce in a listener the recognition that the speaker wants his utterance to be taken as ..."; following the ellipsis is a specification of the speaker's expectation.

	Code Definitions and Examples of Communicative Intentions
	REQUESTS ... solicit information, actions, or acknowledgment.
RQYN	*Yes-No Questions* ... solicit affirmation or negation of the propositional content of the speaker's utterance; e.g., *Is this a birthday cake?*
RQWH	*Wh-Questions* ... solicit information about the identity, location or property of an object, event or situation; e.g., *Where's John?*
RQAC	*Action Requests* ... solicit a listener to perform, not to perform, or cease to perform an action (process, etc.); e.g., *Give me some juice!*
RQPM	*Permission Requests* ... solicit a listener to grant permission for the speaker to perform an action; e.g., *Can I go?*
RQRQ	*Rhetorical Questions* ... solicit a listener's acknowledgment to allow the speaker to continue; e.g., *You know what I did yesterday?*
	RESPONSES ... directly complement preceding utterances.
RSYN	*Yes-No Answers* ... complement Yes-No Questions by affirming, negating, or otherwise answering them; e.g., *No, it isn't.*
RSWH	*Wh-Answers* ... complement Wh-Questions by providing information about the identity, etc., requested; e.g., *John's under the table.*
RSAG	*Agreements* ... complement previous utterances by agreeing with or denying the content; e.g., *That isn't a car.*
RSCO	*Compliances* ... complement requests by complying with or refusing to comply with them; e.g., *I won't wash my hands.*
RSQL	*Qualifications* ... complement utterances by qualifying, clarifying, or otherwise changing their content; e.g., *But I didn't do it.*
	DESCRIPTIONS ... represent observable (or verifiable) aspects of the environment.
DSID	*Identifications* ... label an object, person, event or situation; e.g., *That's a house.*

TABLE 1–Continued

	Code Definitions and Examples of Communicative Intentions
DSPO	*Possessions* . . . indicate who owns or temporarily possesses an object; e.g., *That's John's egg.*
DSEV	*Events* . . . represent the occurrence of an event, action, process, etc.; e.g., *I'm drawing a house.*
DSPR	*Properties* . . . represent observable traits or conditions of objects, events or situations; e.g., *That's a red crayon.*
DSLO	*Locations* . . . represent the location or direction of an object or event; e.g., *The zoo is far away.*
	STATEMENTS . . . express facts, beliefs, attitudes or emotions.
STRU	*Rules* . . . express rules, conventional procedures, analytic facts, definitions or classifications; e.g., *You have to put it there first.*
STEV	*Evaluations* . . . express impressions, attitudes or judgments about objects, events or situations; e.g., *It looks like a snowman.*
STIR	*Internal Reports* . . . express internal states (emotions, sensations, etc.), capacities or intents to perform an act; e.g., *My leg hurts.*
STAT	*Attributions* . . . express beliefs about another's internal state, capacity, intent, etc.; e.g., *He doesn't know the answer.*
STEX	*Explanations* . . . report reasons, causes, motives for acts or predict states of affairs; e.g., *He did it cause he's bad.*
	CONVERSATIONAL DEVICES . . . establish, maintain, end or otherwise regulate interpersonal contact and conversations.
CDBM	*Boundary Markers* . . . initiate or end contact or conversation; e.g., *Hi,* and *Bye.*
CDCA	*Calls* . . . make contact by soliciting attention; e.g., *Hey, John!*
CDAC	*Accompaniments* . . . signal closer contact by accompanying a speaker's action: e.g., *Here you are.*
CDRE	*Returns* . . . acknowledge the listener's preceding utterance or fill in to maintain the conversation; e.g., *Oh.*
CDPM	*Politeness Markers* . . . make explicit the speaker's politeness; e.g., *Please* and *Thanks.*
	PERFORMATIVES . . . accomplish acts by being said.
ROLE	*Role-plays* . . . establish a fantasy; e.g., *This is a train.*
PROT	*Protests* . . . object to the listener's previous behavior, *No, don't touch that!*
JOKE	*Jokes* . . . produce a humorous effect by a nonliteral, playful remark; e.g., *I throwed the soup in the ceiling.*
GAME	*Game-markers* . . . initiate, continue or end a game; e.g., *You can't catch me.*

TABLE 1–Continued

	Code Definitions and Examples of Communicative Intentions
CLAI	*Claims* . . . establish facts by being said; e.g., *I'm first.*
WARN	*Warnings* . . . notify the listener of impending harm; e.g., *Watch out.*
TEAS	*Teases* . . . annoy the listener by being provocative or taunting; e.g., *You can't come to my house.*
	Miscellaneous Codes
UNTP	*Uninterpretable* . . . for unintelligible, incomplete or incomprehensible utterances.
DOUB	*Double-coded* . . . for utterances receiving two of the above codes.

A few additional remarks about the methodology of coding illocutionary acts will indicate the kinds of problems one encounters in the pragmatic analysis of child speech. Not all utterances contained full propositions. Sometimes a child's speech was unintelligible or incomplete, or sometimes clear and complete but nevertheless incomprehensible in the given context, in which cases we coded the utterances as uninterpretable; 7.9% of the corpus was uninterpretable. In other cases, utterances were merely elliptical; a *No,* for example, suffices as the complete answer to *Are you painting?,* so it is coded as a Yes-No answer, implicitly equivalent to *No, I am not painting.* Also, the category of illocutionary acts called "Conversational Devices" are nonpropositional in structure. These include conversation-position markers like greetings and farewells, filler-returns like *Oh* or *What* to rhetorical questions, calls for attention like *Hey* or *John,* and utterances like *Here you are* (while handing over a cup), which are completely redundant with respect to the actions they accompany.

Some utterances were "double-coded," and of these there were two types. The first is definitionally double, given the coding scheme. Responses to Wh-Questions, for example, are often also descriptions: A response to *Where's John?* was *He's under the table*, which is both a Wh-Answer and a "Location Description"; 5.5% of the corpus was coded as a Wh-Answer plus another illocutionary act. The second type of double coding was problematic insofar as it involved utterances which either lacked sufficient linguistic or contextual information to determine the act, or which fell clearly into two categories. For example, in response to the teacher's request of *Paint your real name on the egg, okay?,* a child replied, *But I'm Robin Hood,* which we coded as both a Compliance (because it made explicit his refusal to comply), and a Role-Play (because it simultaneously established a fantasy). Fortunately, merely 0.3% of the corpus was of this problematic sort.

In addition to coding for illocutionary act, we also used six code tags: -R for immediate repetitions of previous utterances by the child or another, in which the form, but not the intention, changed; -F for utterances whose content was fantasy (these occur in fantasy sequences after Role-Play initiates the fantasy); -C for utterances which were contingently related to other utterances; -I for indirect forms of illocutionary acts such as *I want some juice* or *Can I have juice?* as indirect Action Requests; and -E for egocentric speech, that is, an utterance not addressed to a listener, and which the speaker apparently does not expect any contingent behavior. It is problematic to view egocentric utterances as "intentional," even if we assume that the speaker and hearer are the same person. These utterances can, however, be dealt with separately for the purpose of data analyses.

The Question-Response Study

From the protocols for the illocutionary act study we isolated all the question-response sequences in which a question was addressed to a child by the teacher or another child. We did not isolate questions addressed directly and only to the teacher because our purpose was to analyze only child responses. Thus, for example, responses to all of the eight "when-questions" in the corpus do not appear on the response tables because they were all child questions addressed to the teacher. The questions in the sequences solicit two kinds of information: Wh-questions (RQWH) solicit identifications of varying complexity (from simple object labels for most "what-questions" to complex explanations for "why-questions"); Yes-No Questions (RQYN) solicit the affirmation, negation, or confirmation of the propositional content of the question.

We identified the questions on the basis of form. RQWHs had a Wh-word as the focus of the question, almost invariably as the first word in the utterance. RQYNs were marked for interrogative by inverted word order and/or rising terminal intonation contour; they included grammatical tags and single-word queries as well as full sentences. We also listed separately RQYNs having embedded Wh-words or imperative forms. (One item had both embeddings: ***Could*** *you* ***tell*** *me again* ***what*** *it was?* Among the possible appropriate responses to such a question would be: *Yes, I could,* or *Okay, I'll tell you,* or *It was a boat,* each responsive to a different part of the question, the "could," the "tell," and the "what," respectively. The actual response was characteristically complex: *It wasn't that.*) The few disjunctive questions in the corpus of the form *Is it A or B?* were not listed because the expected response was not of the yes or no type. This procedure for identifying questions formally does not, of course, require that the child actually recognizes each utterance according to the way we listed it. In fact, one of the interesting findings of the study concerns how children interpret forms having a variety of functions, and functions having a variety of forms.

Responses to questions were determined on the basis of three criteria. First, utterances providing the information requested by the question (this is the expected or most predictable information) were considered to be direct answers. Second, utterances subsequent to questions which share their topic, or were otherwise recognizably related, were considered oblique responses. Although these do not supply the expected or most predictable information, they are nonetheless appropriate responses. Third, we counted as responses any utterances subsequent to questions and clearly addressed to the questioner, on the basis of the child's attentional orientation, regardless of whether a relation could be identified. These can be construed as "in response to," rather than direct responses to, questions. This procedure yields not only grammatically matched answers, but also pragmatically appropriate ones, as well as responses associated in vague ways with questions.

Responses were divided into three major groups. **Canonical responses** are the simplest standard forms of response—the most expected, predictable, and grammatically matched form, given only the form of the question. Responses to functionally equivocal questions (defined later) are canonical only if they supply the requested information specified by the **form** of the question, regardless of how the addressee may have intended his utterance to be taken. **Noncanonical responses** provide relevant information (except for non sequiturs), but not standard or highly predictable information.[3] Canonical and noncanonical responses correlate roughly, but not exactly, with the first two criteria for identifying responses. The third group consists of **No Answers** and these were subdivided into three kinds: **definite** no answers, where there is some behavioral evidence that the child deliberately did not answer; **indeterminate** cases, where there is no such evidence (the child is off-camera, for example); and no answers to **egocentric questions** where apparently no answer is expected. An **uninterpretable** group of responses includes inaudible, incomplete or otherwise unintelligible replies.

In addition, responses were scored along four dimensions. The first was **elliptical** responses (*yes, no,* a gesture, a single word, etc.) versus **full sentence** replies. The second was responses to **genuine** questions (where the questioner does not know the requested information) versus **examination** questions (where the questioner does know). No clear differences in response patterns were found related to either of these two dimensions, so nothing will be said about them in our analyses. The third was addresser-addressee role, **teacher-to-**

3. Predictability here is narrowly construed as what can be predicted on the basis of form alone. Thus, with an utterance such as *Aren't you going to give me the brush?* only yes-no answers are canonical responses; responses such as saying *Okay* or giving the brush to the speaker are noncanonical insofar as they do not supply the verbal information solicited by the form of the interrogative. The actual responses to such questions, of course, indicate how hearers interpret them.

child versus **child-to-child.** The fourth and most important dimension concerns the notion of equivocality. **Nonequivocal** questions are those that can take only one kind of canonical response, the one which matches the information specified by the form and function of the question. But an **equivocal** question can receive either a canonical response to its grammatical form or a noncanonical response to its alternate reading.

Occasionally children give both kinds of responses; for example, Q: *Think you need more paint in there?* R: *Yeah, okay.* The *yeah* is canonical to the form of the RQYN; *okay* is noncanonical to RQYNs, but canonical as a compliance acknowledgment (RSCO) to a request for action (RQAC). In our example, the child apparently interpreted the teacher's utterance not merely as a RQYN, but partly as a RQAC (of the form called "question directive" or "situated conventional directive" by Ervin-Tripp in this volume), as though it were equivalent to *Put more paint in there!* In our corpus, 11% of the RQWHs were equivocal in this way; all were of the forms *How about doing x. . . ?* and *Why don't you do x. . . ?* These forms, as Ervin-Tripp (1970) pointed out, are understood as directives from early on in development, at first as unanalyzed routines. Interestingly, our children gave responses which suggested that they may have semantically decoded some occurrences of these as information requests. Such "information" responses indicate the genuinely equivocal status of the questions. Moreover, of the RQYNs, 31% were equivocal. These were spread over all the RQYN-form types and they make answering such questions more difficult than one might at first expect. For example, *Can you get this off?* can be interpreted as a question about the addressee's ability or as an embedded imperative. Note that such questions are not structurally ambiguous in the sense of having different underlying propositions, rather they are functionally equivocal insofar as the addressee may not be sure of how the speaker intends his utterance to be taken. On this view equivocality is a pragmatic problem, not a grammatical one.

Finally, the "paint" example mentioned previously indicates how utterances were segmented in order to count responses. A yes, no, okay, nod, or other acknowledgment counted as one response; if anything followed it, that was counted as another response. Utterances potentially related as responses, but which occurred after many succeeding utterances on a topic different from the question, were not counted. Many questions, therefore, received more than one response, sometimes from more than one child. But no one segment was counted as more than one response.

Results and Analyses: Wh-Question Responses

Table 2 lists the children's responses to RQWHs. More than 47% were canonical, that is, grammatically matched in Ervin-Tripp's sense of category agreement.

TABLE 2

Total Number of Occurrences of Each Response Type to Each Wh-Question Type

RESPONSE TYPE	WH-QUESTION TYPE						
	What	Where	Which	Who(se)	How	Why	
Canonical							
Object	56	1	1				
Property	8						
Location	2	13					
Person				15			
Internal State	4						
Event	22						
Number					2		
Explanation	1				2	10	
							137
Noncanonical							
RSQL	1				3	2	
STIR	7	4	2		1	2	
Different Answer	7	1			3	2	
RSCO					2	5	
RQWH	6						
Clarification	4		1			1	
RSAG					1		
RQAC/PM	1	1			1	1	
							59
No Answer							
Definite	26	6	2	4	6	21	
Indeterminate	6	3			1	1	
Egocentric Question		2					
							78
Uninterpretable	6	1			2	2	11
	157	32	6	19	24	47	285

Of the canonical responses, only two were to equivocal questions:

Q: *Why don't you get up and sit in your cubby . . . ?*
R: *I'm tired.*

Q: *Why don't you sit down until you're finished?*
R: *Cause I'm all finished.*

Notice that the information in the responses matches the "why" of the questions: The responses supply reasons. For the purpose of speculating about the children's actual interpretation of the questions, there are two possibilities. Either the children semantically decoded the utterances as genuine information questions, and provided the canonical identifications; or they interpreted the utterances as action requests and, not wanting to perform the requested action (*sitting*), provided reasons as a form of noncompliance. Experimentation is necessary to decide which is the case here. At any rate, all other questions of the *Why don't you* form were either responded to as though they were RQACs or they were not answered. Of all the why-questions receiving explanation responses, half were asked by the children, none of which were equivocal. Thus, the children's why-questions to other children apparently were genuine information requests and not meant to function as RQACs. The remaining three why-questions asked by the teacher were unequivocal.

There is a curious overlap in what- and where-questions. Consider:

Q: *What's a muffet?*
R: *There's a muffet.* (while pointing to it)

Q: *Where's* **my** *chair?* (boldface word stressed)
R: *This is* **my** *chair.* (self-answered)

The first response identifies an object by indicating its location, the second does not indicate a location but identifies an object. Despite this lack of grammatical fit, we scored the responses as canonical because of the overlap in meaning between *what* and *where* in such questions.

Whereas grammatically oriented approaches to question-answer sequences give one the impression that most responses are canonical answers, the present study indicates the contrary. Several factors contribute to the fact that less than half of the responses were canonical. First of all, the seven noncanonical RSCO responses were to alternate readings of *how about* and *why don't you* questions. If these were added to the canonical group (and there are strong reasons to believe that RQAC readings do dominate interpretation of most of these question-forms), then more than 50% of the responses would be canonical. Another factor keeping the percentage of canonical responses down was uninterpretable responses which might have been canonical.

A third and major factor concerns questions which were not answered. Of these, some may not have been heard and some were equivocal. We have no way of being certain that the children processed the nonanswered questions, but we have at least some behavioral evidence that they attended to most of them (more than 83% of the questions seemed to be deliberately not answered). Almost half of the why-questions and more than a third of the how-questions were not answered, and of these, half were equivocal. Many of the equivocal cases were responded to by the performance of an action, without verbal accompaniment—after all, verbal compliance to an RQAC is optional and certainly secondary to performing the action. It seems then, that apart from the occurrence of responses to alternate readings, and apart from the difficulty of mastering the conceptual domains of reason and manner, the equivocal questions related to these domains must make answering them much more difficult. However, the largest number of nonanswered RQWHs were to what-questions, all but one of which were asked by the teacher and none of which were equivocal—in fact, none of the RQWH types but hows and whys were equivocal.

Considering all the facts about nonanswered RQWHs, and assuming that the children heard most of the corresponding questions, it is hard to believe that they felt obligated to answer. Moreover, nothing in the children's noncanonical responses would lead one to believe that they felt obligated to answer. If the first decision an addressee must make after grammatically processing a question is whether or not to answer, then no answer seems to be a viable alternative for children, and one which does not appear to violate a social obligation. The second decision an addressee must make is exactly how to answer, a rather complex matter to which we now turn.

What are the relations between RQWHs and their noncanonical responses? These responses are defined according to the illocutionary act types listed in Table 1, with two minor exceptions. The first exception is the "Different Answer" category, meaning that the child responded to a RQWH of one sort with an answer appropriate to another sort. The second is the "Clarification Question," which is a subdivision of both RQWH and RQYN forms whose function is to seek clarification of the question originally asked. Our analyses of the relations between RQWHs and their noncanonical responses focused on what they could suggest about the child's actual interpretation of the questions. We identified eight (rather heterogeneous) categories of interpretation: full, none, partial, wrong, alternate responses related by semantic presupposition, responses related by pragmatic conditions, and responses "remotely associated" with the question.

When the child replies with a canonical response we can assume that he **fully** comprehended both the propositional meaning and the pragmatic intention of the question. This is also probably the case with some instances of most response types. As an example of this type consider the rather peculiar single occurrence of an RSAG: A: *Well how can we do it when I haven't given, gotten a chance to tell you what we're gonna do?* R: *Ya, of course.* Presumably **no** interpretation takes place when the child responds with a *What?* or *Huh?* Clarification Question, as may be the case with some of the indeterminate no-answers. **Partial** interpretation occurs when a Clarification Question isolates part of the question, as in Q: *What are you two guys doing?* R: *Me?* **Misinterpretation** occurs when a child gives an answer appropriate to a different question, as in Q: *What do plants need to grow?* R: *They grow in this.* An **alternate** interpretation is one that reveals that the child interpreted a question on its functional (as opposed to formal) reading, as occurs in responses to *Why don't you?* questions.

Responses related to the **semantic presupposition** of a question reveal the complexity of children's question-response sequences. For example: Q: *What number are you making?* R: *I'm not making a number.* A canonical reply would have identified a certain number. However, the proposition underlying the question—that *you are making a number*—was false. The propositions that underlie RQWHs are presupposed, as distinct from focused, information. In our case the child responded to the presupposed information, repairing the truth value of the question's proposition. All six of the RSQLs to RQWHs were of this sort; they all contradicted some information in the question's proposition.

Presupposition can be contrasted with a **pragmatic condition** (cf. Searle's "sincerity conditions" and Garvey's "interpersonal meaning factors"). This notion is clearly exemplified by STIR responses: Q: *What kind of man is he? What does he do?* R: *I don't know.* This reply, though appropriate, is not related grammatically to the question; it does not supply the requested information nor does it take issue with the propositions of either question. Rather, it relates to a general pragmatic condition on questions and answers: The addresser believes that the addressee knows the answer and that he **can** answer. Among adults, when the questioner does not know whether the addressee knows the answer, he can ask *Do you know what kind of man he is?,* for example. Our children made this underlying condition explicit: Q: *What is that?* R: *I know, a carrot.* Bates (1976[b]) calls these "pragmatic presuppositions," defined as "conditions necessary for a sentence to be appropriate in the context in which it is used," and she points out that "there are ambiguous cases in which what seems to be a semantic presupposition will vary according to the context in which the sentence is used [p. 33]."

We had our unclear cases. Consider:

Q: *What could you use as a refrigerator?*
R: *Where is a refrigerator?*

Q: *What did we make yesterday?*
R: *Draw it!*

At first these responses might appear inappropriate. Yet they did share a topic with the questions. In the first case the child apparently did not fully comprehend the question, and her partial interpretation may explain the response. In the second it seems that the child understood the RQWH, but deliberately avoided providing the canonical response. Neither reply questions the presupposed information in the propositions, that *you could use **SOMETHING** as a refrigerator* and *we did make **SOMETHING** yesterday.* Nor do they seem to make explicit any general condition on questioning. It seems, however, that in the *refrigerator* case the child did not recognize the questioner's expectation to receive an identification, while in the *Draw it* case the child probably recognized, but ignored, the teacher's expectation. In cases like the latter the child may not be willing to provide the canonical information because of a more pressing desire.

At any rate, on the basis of our analyses of responses to RQWHs we might characterize the child's strategy for responding as follows: The child will provide canonical information if he:

1. Comprehends the proposition underlying the question.
2. Believes the proposition is true (or accurate).
3. Recognizes the addresser's expectation in asking the question.
4. Believes the addresser wants the requested information.
5. Believes the addresser does not know the requested information **or**, in the case of examination questions, the addressee wants to display his knowledge.
6. Is able to (knows the answer).
7. Is willing, that is, has no more pressing desire.

If any one of these conditions fails to apply, the child will respond noncanonically or will not answer. Our corpus provides instances of responses which make explicit most of these conditions. In contrast to Ervin-Tripp's comprehension rule (this volume) for recognizing directives, this rule is at least part of a production strategy for responding to questions once they are recognized. And, in contrast to Garvey's "interpersonal meaning factors" underlying requests for action and their responses, if the above rule is operative then 3-year-old children do not feel any social obligation to answer RQWHs.

Results and Analyses: Yes-No Question Responses

Table 3 lists the children's responses to RQYNs. Only 35% were canonical. Responses to formally equivocal questions (like the RQYN:WH *Do you know what it is?* and the RQYN:AC *Can you give me it?*) were split, with more than half being noncanonical responses to alternate readings. If we add these noncanonical responses to equivocal questions to the canonical group, the percentage of canonical responses to the total would rise to 39. But, apart from these, about 7% of the canonical responses were to equivocal questions without embeddings. Thus, there is a roughly even trade-off in canonical and noncanonical responses to equivocal RQYNs.

The number of nonanswered RQYNs is quite high, almost half. Yet, there are plausible explanations for many of these. First, every one of the RQYN:ACs that received no answer was functionally as well as formally equivocal—and 22 of the 47 were responded to by performing the act specified in the alternate reading. Now, if we add these 22 action responses to the canonical responses, the percentage of canonical rises to about 43%. Also, there may be a conversational strategy for not responding verbally to many RQYNs of the grammatical tag form. By definition tags are appended to other utterances. In our corpus, 33 tags that were not answered were equivocal to the extent that they followed utterances which could have functioned as RQACs. In about half of these cases the child physically performed the act implied in the utterance preceding the tag without verbally responding; for example, after the teacher said *He needs more room, okay?* the addressee moved over. Moreover, the teacher in our study often embedded tags within long sequences of utterances, without pausing for responses after the tag. In almost all such cases the children did not acknowledge the tag; and they may have believed that an answer was not expected. Nevertheless, even if we were to discount the no-answers to all equivocal questions and to all embedded tags, almost 30% of the questions would remain as unanswered. Assuming that the children heard most of these, we can once again safely suppose that they did not feel obligated to answer.

TABLE 3

Total Number of Occurrences of Each Response Type to Each Yes-No Question Form

RESPONSE TYPE	YES-NO QUESTION FORM						
	RQYN	RQYN: WH	RQYN: AC	Intonation	Tags	Words	
Canonical							
Yes or No	83	4	13	8	19	7	
Full sentence	13	1	3	4	1		
Gesture	12		1	4		1	
							174
Noncanonical							
RSCO	3		14	1		3	
RSWH	6	5		1		1	
RSQL	11		2	3	7		
STIR	1	1			1		
Clarification	9	2	3	1	3		
RQAC/PM	2						
Non sequitur	1				1		
							82
No Answer							
Definite	52	3	37	12	66	7	
Indeterminate	25		9	5	14	2	
Egocentric question	1		1				
							234
Uninterpretable	2		1		1		4
	221	16	84	39	113	21	494

To the noncanonical response group were added two additional categories which did not occur in response to RQWHs. The first, RSWHs, are canonical to RQWHs but noncanonical to RQYNs. Of the twelve of these, five were, predictably, responses to RQYN:Wh-forms. Of the six RSWHs to simple RQYNs (those questions with inverted word order, interrogative intonation without embeddings), five were the same answer by different children to one of the teacher's RQYNs. The remaining RSWH to a simple RQYN reveals two interesting phenomena: Q: *Does somebody else have it?* R: *Cathy has it.* Although the RQYN does not contain a Wh-word, it is nonetheless equivocal with a who-question because of the pronoun "somebody." Thus, the child must be aware that (*a*) there is an overlap in some RQYNs with pronouns and RQWHs insofar as either can be used to obtain the same information; and (*b*) rather than supply a simple yes or no, as is indicated by the form of the RQYN, one should give information beyond this when one can specify the referent of the pronoun. In terms of categories of interpretation RSWHs reflect full comprehension of the RQYN but with responses being to alternate readings of RQYN:Whs.

The second additional noncanonical response type to RQYNs is the non sequitur. It is difficult to define. In our study, it is a catch-all category for responses which have no identifiable relation (on the category level we postulated) to the eliciting question, despite behavioral evidence that it is addressed to the questioner subsequent to the question. The two in the corpus were:

Q: *Are you there?*
R: *I going to do this color.*

Q: *And after you's is going to be* **my** *turn, right?*
R: *I'm sorry a do it.*

We could not put these into the uninterpretable category because they were neither incomplete nor inaudible. At first glance they appear to be genuinely inappropriate, if not irrational. On the interpretation scale, it is easy to assume that they register almost nothing, though they could equally, as well, be partial or misinterpretations. Yet it is tempting to speculate about possible associations; in fact, where the context is rich enough, speculation becomes less necessary. In our first case, for example, the teacher had been trying for some time to get the child's attention (she was trying to get him to play with other children), but he had been ignoring her. Her final solicitation, *Are you there?*, was not meant seriously—she knew where he was. The child finally conceded, but only to the extent of telling her what he was going to do. In the second case, the two participants in the question routine had previously been competing for a toy (pushing each other), and what appears to be a response to the RQYN may well be an apology for his prior behavior. Of course, for the response code to be worthwhile, it cannot tolerate too much latitude in speculation. Nevertheless, the more one probes, the more one is left with the feeling that non sequiturs differ not in kind, but in degree of remoteness of association from other responses—never quite totally irrational. Our code is helpful in isolating non sequiturs, but clearly more data are necessary. In general, it seems clear that utterances which we have been calling non sequiturs are related to the situation and the overall discourse, if not to the local sequence.

Of the other noncanonical responses, 18 were RSCOs. Predictably, the majority of them, 14, were responses to RQYN:ACs that were both formally and functionally equivocal. The three RSCOs to simple RQYNs were of the following form: Q: *Can I leave it here and go and get the cups without anybody touching it?* R: *Sure* (two children replied). The oddity of the question is that it seems like a combined permission and action request by the teacher; but the children responded to the literal form of the utterance, perahaps intending to grant permission. RSCOs suggest full comprehension of the eliciting RQYN.

STIR responses to RQYNs are slightly odd since, unlike RQWHs, the yes-no information requested of children is relatively easy to provide in most cases. All four STIRs in the corpus had peculiarities:

1. Q: *Tape it over there. Did you ever think of that?*
   R: *No, I don't know how to.*

2. Q: *How many did we put in? Do you remember?*
   R: *I don't know.*

3. Q: *Well, when you finish you can hang yours up too, okay?*
   R: *Well I don't want to hang it up on the wall.*

4. Q: *Would you like me to help you? Yes?*
   R: *I can't do it.*

In Example 1 the first part of the answer seems to be in response to the teacher's second utterance, the RQYN; the second part of the answer may be in response to her first utterance, the RQAC, but it could have occurred in the absence of the RQAC. Because of this sequencing it was included on the RQYN table. The response in Example 2, too, seems more closely associated with the initial RQWH, but it was included because of the intervening RQYN. In Example 3 the response is clear, but notice that it implies a negative answer while the STIR functions as an explanation. Finally, in Example 4 the response, though appropriate, is again "once removed" from a straightforward manner. Such instances of oblique responses which **imply** a canonical response as well are like Grice's notion of conversational implication, and they are crucially important in understanding children's question-response sequences. There are several other kinds of oblique responses.

Consider as rather clear-cut examples, the RQAC/PM responses:

Q: *Would you like to read this one?*
R: *Start right here!*

Q: *Did you ask Martin?*
R: *Can I do that, Martin?*

In the former case the child apparently does not feel compelled to answer the question first, before getting on with the matter. So too with the latter. Perhaps this last should not be classified as a response to the RQYN at all, yet it is obviously "in response to" the question and it meets the second criterion, topic-sharing, for identifying responses. Both examples illustrate a general tendency not to answer directly, but to respond with information relevant in other ways.

All of the 26 RSQL responses exhibit this tendency. They also provide the most revealing clues to the complexity of children's responses. They can be divided into four subtypes, according to their relation to the eliciting RQYN: presupposition, pragmatic condition, "extra" information, and more "remote" association. The majority of RSQLs, 14, relate to presupposed information in the question. Examples are:

Q: *Did you do that?*
R: *Tasha did it.*

Q: *Are you finding us a book?*
R: *We're going to catch the sheriff.*

Q: *He's trying to run away, so let's catch up with him, shall we?*
R: *Oh them sheriff* . . . (inaudible) . . . *I found the sheriff.*

In each of these cases the response involves a semantic contrast with some information in the question: roughly, *you vs. Tasha, finding a book versus catching the sheriff,* and *catching the sheriff versus finding the sheriff.*

The second subtype of RSQL, of which there were four instances, involves pragmatic, as opposed to semantic, presupposition. Consider:

Q: *Shall I give you a road?*
R: *No, it's broken.*

Q: *Can you pick up the lady in the blue dress?*
R: *No, this is not home.*

In the former case the child apparently assumes that it is understood between them that there is no sense in playing with a broken road. The response does not contradict any information in the question, rather it points out a "real-world" condition on an item mentioned in the question. The second case represents a flagrant confrontation with the teacher as an authority; the response takes issue with a rule of behavior in the nursery by implying that the child is not obligated to pick up toys. As in the first case, the addressee fully comprehends the proposition and intention of the RQYN but, instead of answering directly, responds with information regarding a practical condition on asking the question.

The third subtype of RSQL, for lack of a better term, is called simply "extra" information. Examples are:

Q: *Does this look like a bean?*
R: *Those are* **green** *beans.*

Q: *Do you need* **every** *sign there?*
R: *Yea, but I got it.*

This type of response, of which there were six instances, does not involve a semantic contrast or take issue with a pragmatic condition, but merely provides information beyond that requested, and highly unpredictable information at that. The second response is interesting because the teacher intended her remark to be ironic, but the child seems to have taken it as an offer of help. Perhaps this misunderstanding explains the response.

Finally, there are two RSQLs which can only be construed as "more remotely associated with" their eliciting questions:

Q: *John, are you finished?*
R: *They're out 'cause I'm sorting them.*

Q: *Did you make a hole for the grapefruit seed?*
R: *I wan' take one of those.*

In the former, the teacher is presumably asking about the blocks that several children are playing with. The child's response, instead of a direct answer, is an explanation of why the blocks are out. He may even be explaining why he is not finished, but his response does not contrast with the "finish" constituent of the question. In the second, the teacher wants the children to make a hole in some soil before taking a seed. The child, in a sense, "ignores" the question, intent on getting a seed first.

However, of all the RSQLs, almost half were to functionally equivocal questions, and these were all asked by the teacher. For instance, the questions in the last two examples mentioned could be equivalent to *Put the blocks away!* and *Make a hole!*, respectively. It has been pointed out to me that if children interpret such questions as directives, then the responses are not as "remote" as they appear when the questions are assumed to solicit information.[4]

4. I would like to thank the editors, Drs. Mitchell-Kernan and Ervin-Tripp, for stressing the importance of this point.

The responses may, in fact, be excuses for noncompliance of the sort discussed previously regarding *Why don't you . . .* questions. This seems plausible, though not necessary: Apart from the fact that the responses would still be at least slightly odd, we have no "more direct" evidence of the children's interpretations. More fundamentally, it is possible that children rarely perceive teachers' yes-no questions as "pure" information questions. And from the point of view of intention, teachers (and adults in general) may almost always have some motive other than seeking information for asking questions. At any rate, more sophisticated analyses than have been employed in this chapter will be necessary to measure the information versus command functions of questions. Also, alternative hypotheses must be explored. Some questions may be "preparatory" to commands, so that when a question is answered in a certain (canonical) way, a command will follow.

On the basis of our analysis of responses to RQYNs, we might characterize the children's strategy for responding as follows: The child will provide canonical information if he:

1. Comprehends the proposition of the question.
2. Recognizes the addresser's expectation in asking the question.
3. Believes the addresser wants the requested information.
4. Believes the addresser does not know the requested information **or**, in the case of examination questions, wants to display his knowledge.
5. Is able to (knows the answer).
6. Is willing, that is, has no more pressing desire.
7. Believes the information in the proposition is "accurate," "appropriate" and "complete."

This last condition is rather general and perhaps vague. Unlike RQWHs, where the question presupposes the truth of the underlying proposition and solicits information about a propositional constituent, the RQYN focuses on the proposition and solicits a judgment of its truth. So a condition on answering RQYNs cannot be that the addressee believes its proposition is true, else there would be no negative replies. Rather, conditions **related** to truth seem to apply. Propositional content should be accurate to be answered canonically. For example, in the sequence where *catching the sheriff* versus *finding the sheriff,* the truth of the question's proposition is not at issue so much as its accuracy in terms of what the children would do after the question-response sequence. Similarly, the "appropriateness" condition is exemplified by responses related to questions by a pragmatic condition, as in the *broken road* case. And the "completeness" part of condition seven is made explicit by some of the responses that supply information that go beyond the information requested.

CONCLUSION

We can now suggest a characterization of the contingency relations in children's question-response sequences as consisting of at least three general levels: grammatical agreement, discourse regulation, and conversational implication. Apart from grammatical matches, many responses to questions serve the rather routine function of regulating conversations. For example, clarification responses seek information necessary for the addressee to answer the addresser's initial question. Garvey (in press) has described in detail the mechanics of these—which she calls "contingent queries"—and their structure is quite complex, even for the 3-year-olds she observed.

A second aspect of discourse regulation concerns the rational organization of conversation. Because our analyses in this chapter focused on immediate responses to questions, we did not consider superordinate relations among questions and other illocutionary acts. For example, consider what occurs *after* a straightforward question-answer sequence:

BOY I: *What are you making?*
BOY II: *A zoo.*
BOY I: *Put the animals in the zoo.*

The Wh-question here functions as what Searle calls a "preparatory condition" on issuing the command—clearly, giving the command would not be possible without first knowing the information solicited by the RQWH. More than 37% of the RQWHs asked by the children made explicit a preparatory condition operating in the "domain" of an RQAC (see Garvey, 1975, for details on the "domain"). Moreover, a fact which further demonstrates the rational organization of the children's conversations is that 49% of their RQWHs were about procedures, possession, or taking turns, all institutional facts crucial to subsequent interaction.

The third level of contingency, conversational implication, seems to be the most sophisticated, as is evidenced by the four subtypes of qualified responses (RSQLs) to RQYNs we listed. These seem to warrant the kind of detailed examination that Garvey has provided for contingent queries. My guess is that such investigations will yield an even more intriguing picture of the budding "ideal cooperative conversationalist" than Garvey describes. For instance, an addressee can either give the speaking-turn back to the addresser (as in a Clarification response), or can seize a turn by responding with an RSQL and, perhaps, elaborating on it in a direction away from the initial question. This latter choice might not be characteristic of an ideal "ideal cooperative conversationalist," but it would certainly make for an "ideal Machiavellian conversationalist." At any rate, "seizing a turn" underscores the following point: For children, questions may constrain the array of appropriate responses, but being asked a question does not obligate one to answer, much less to answer appropriately. In conclusion, just as has been shown about the grammar of child speech, the present chapter, along with others in this volume, indicates that children know much more about question-response routines (and about conducting conversations in general), than "surfaces" in their speech.

ACKNOWLEDGMENT

I am most grateful to Maryl Gearhart and Denis Newman for their expert help in collecting and organizing the data, and for their helpful comments on a draft of this chapter. I would also like to thank the editors, Drs. Mitchell-Kernan and Ervin-Tripp, for helpful comments on a previous draft of this chapter.

Wait for Me, Roller Skate![1]

SUSAN ERVIN-TRIPP

The choice of **directives** as the focus for an analysis of children's speech acts is based on several advantages. They are relatively frequent from the beginning of child languages—some counts have yielded frequencies as high as 50% of utterances. Since they make a demand on the listener for services, they display considerable sensitivity to social features. They are, perhaps, somewhat more independent of text then some other kinds of forms, in the respect that they "change the subject" rather than arising naturally out of discourse, except when discourse is activity-tied; to use Halliday's terms (1970[a]), they reflect the interpersonal more than the textual axis of contrast. And they are relatively easy to recognize.

The original starting point in the series of "choices" leading to a specific realization in speech is a state of affairs which the speaker wants changed. The speaker may not even be aware of wanting any change and may merely comment about the state of affairs. A listener who imputes a desire for change, a desire that a service be performed, may, in fact, go beyond what the speaker wants. A person can, after all, let things be, or act independently rather than induce a listener to serve as an instrument to needs. There are costs as well as benefits in these choices. The high frequency of directives from children relates to their realistic dependency. The content of directives will change with age, as the speaker's desires and scope of practical competence increase.

1. This chapter is a revision of two previous papers which were widely circulated: a colloquium with the same title at the Summer Linguistic Institute of the Linguistic Society of America in August, 1973, and "The comprehension and production of requests by children," Stanford Papers and Reports on Child Development, April, 1974. It has been prepared with the support of Fellowships from the Guggenheim Foundation and the Center for Advanced Study in the Behavioral Sciences.

ADULT DIRECTIVES

To provide a framework for the discussion of the child's abilities, we will begin with what we know about adult directives. Elsewhere (Ervin-Tripp, 1976[a,b]) we have given the detailed results of observations and analysis of transcripts of adult speech. Seven kinds of utterances appeared in the corpus with the apparent intention of eliciting goods or services, or of regulating the behavior of others. Of these, the last two—questions and hints—were frequently, systematically ambiguous with respect to function, in the sense that the directive need not even refer to the act or object desired, and that a directive was sometimes understood when none was intended.

The major finding of the adult research was that there were relatively consistent differences in the type of directive used, as a function of the social features of the speech situation. The most systematic data were obtained in white collar, task-oriented settings such as offices, laboratories and hospitals.

1. **Personal need or desire statements**: *I need a match.* Directed downward to subordinates primarily.

2. **Imperatives**: *Gimme a match; You give me a match.* Directed to subordinates or familiar equals.

3. **Imbedded imperatives**: *Could you give me a match?* The actor, verb, and object of the desired act was explicit so the directive function is obvious. Directed most often to unfamiliar people, or those differing in rank. In addition, modifications to imperatives were available such as *please,* titles, address terms, postposed tags like *OK* and *could you,* and rising terminal pitch. Imbeddings and modifications occurred when a task was special, physical distance lay between speaker and hearer, or when the addressee was in her own territory.

A wide variety of question-imbedded imperatives has been discussed in the speech act literature as the questioning of "sincerity conditions" (Garvey 1975; Searle 1969). The ability and willingness of the hearer to help, and whether the act has, or will be, performed can be questioned in imbedded imperatives. The most common of these occurred typically in our data when compliance was already likely. For example, from a grandmother to grandchildren: *Can you wash the dishes?, Do you want to wash the dishes?, Have you washed the dishes?, Are you going to wash the dishes?*

4. **Permission directives**: *May I have a match?* Were too rare in our samples to study. Possibly addressed upward more often than downward in rank.

5. **Question directives**: *Have you gotta match?* These differ from imbedded imperatives since the desired act, and often the agent of the act, are omitted, so that the resulting form is identical with an information question and misunder-

standing is possible. The form is most common when the listener might not comply, so the question turns on the likely obstacle. When there are standard situations with standard obstacles, the question directive becomes a situated conventional directive: (telephone) *Is Sybil there?*; (breakfast room) *Is there any coffee left?*; (hotel desk) *Are there any vacancies?* When the question omits reference to the desired object, it is fully indirect: *Is it six o'clock yet?, Did the W-2 forms come?, What's that on the floor?* Comprehension then rests on shared knowledge of what duties the hearer has with respect to that time, place, or object. They are cues referring to other knowledge, much like hints.

6. **Hints**: *The matches are all gone.* Hints typically require inference. They were employed when the speakers could rely on shared rules in structured situations in offices and classrooms, and on shared understanding of habits and motives in living groups and families. They were important vehicles for solidarity and humor in compatible groups: e.g., *Sal, you make a good door.*

In some hints and questions downward in rank, indirectness was achieved when the act had to be specified, by avoiding the agent: **Any declarative or interrogative is to be interpreted as a command to do if it (*a*) does not specify an agent (using passive, indefinite, question word, or *we*); (*b*) is directed to a subordinate (in the case of *we*); (*c*) refers to an action or activity within the obligations of the addressee.**

Typical examples are: *This analysis has to be done over, It's time to take our naps, Let's give him a 100 of phenobarb.*

Interpretation of Conveyed Intent

Seeking a simple interpretive rule which would account for all directives, Searle (1975) and Gordon and Lakoff (1971) have assumed that listeners could consider the literal meaning of directives first, and use inference, if necessary, to reject that interpretation and find another. But many directives are easily understood although their literal meaning is opaque, humorous, or irrelevant: *What about the salt?, What's that doing here?, How many times have I told you about the door?, Can you shut up?, Can I ask you to take your feet off my head?, Would you stop hitting your sister?* It appears that a wide variety of interpretive procedures may in fact be employed by listeners:

1. **Hearing the directive component.** Both imperatives and question-imbedded imperatives contain an imperative component which is immediately interpretable. One subclass of these contains modals, so Sinclair and Coulthard (1975) proposed the following **modal interpretive rule**:

> An interrogative clause is to be interpreted as a **command to do** if it fulfills all the following conditions: (*a*) it contains one of the modals **can, could, will, would** (and sometimes **going to**); (*b*) the subject of the clause is also an addressee; (*c*) the predicate describes an action which is physically possible at the time of utterance (1975:32).

This may be only one of a family of interpretive rules in which the second and third conditions are the same and the first is enlarged.

2. **Lexicalization of directive markers.** Some types of directive frames are so frequent as to be formulaic. A good example is *Why don't you?* or *whyntcha,* and other lexicalized imbeddings like *wanna, wouldja, canya,* and *couldja.* We hear *get in, ya wanna?, Sit down, whyntcha?* We do not know the extent to which noncompliant replies differentiate between these frames showing them to carry differential meaning to listeners.

Lexicalization can occur concurrently with other productive rules which employ more elaborate interpretive processes. We have reason to believe that this is true also of morphological and syntactic processing; high frequency forms can be interpreted by storage in the lexical unit, and by identifying as wholes. Yet, if their articulation is slow or aberrant, or they occur in a transformed state or unusual context, there may be a slower grammatically analytic route to their recognition.

3. **Logical inference.** Many directives can be understood by inference from the literal meaning. If I say *it looks like rain* as we pass the umbrella stand, the passage to a directive interpretation can be easily mapped out. Many of the hints in offices and families can be understood by virtue of the listener's knowledge of the speaker's habits, motives, obligation, and so on. If a wife says *I'm going to the winetasting tomorrow,* the husband can infer that he must prepare dinner early (because the time of dinner and tasting overlap), and pick up their daughter at school (because the winetasting normally lasts too long, plus driving is normally the wife's obligation). When such inferences are made repeatedly, they probably become routinized and shortcuts occur, but it might be hard to detect these cases.

4. **Situated conventional directives.** If a situation repeatedly occurs, the usual directive becomes conventionalized and could lose its literal force in that context. There are many instances of this principle. We can use conventional question directives even when both parties know we share the information: e.g., *Is Mr. Terrell in?* when he is in full view, or *Do you have the time?* when the addressee is looking at his watch.

The "literal meaning" is the communicative intention which maps, in any context, directly onto a surface realization: in this case, requesting information. The literal meaning of an imperative would be a directive. A good test of conventionalization is that the "literal meaning" is ignored in the appropriate situation, and one can only arouse it by deliberate marking, or making a pun, so that one is misunderstood if one intends the literal meaning. Such cases occur in *Is Sybil there?, Have you any vacancies?,* and *Is there any coffee left?*

Situated conventional directives must be defined by context. For example: *Is Sybil there?* is optimally a directive when it occurs in a telephone call directly following the greetings. If it is a shout by a mother regarding her toddler, Sybil, who disappeared upstairs, it may be heard as an information request.

The routines of nursery schools and families generate a large number of these conventions: *It's naptime!, It's clean-up time!, Twelve o'clock!, Who's ready to go?, What's that on the table?* The interpretation of conventions requires a history of shaping.

We have an instance when *Can you finish the manuscript by tonight?,* which literally is a question about possibility or capacity, was replaced by *Do you think you can finish the manuscript by tonight?* in a directive to a superior. Why? Modal imperatives are not normally used, especially by subordinates, if there is a substantial likelihood the listener cannot comply. In that case, a question directive or hint was usually used, turning on the expected obstacle. This substitution argues for the conventionalization of *Can you finish* . . . , which has lost its literal force as a capacity question, and becomes an obvious directive with a particular social marking.

5. **Rules for directives.** Sinclair and Coulthard (1975) found so many nonimperative directives from teachers that they framed some general rules. One has already been described above as the rule for modal directives. In addition, they state that:

> Any declarative or interrogative is to be interpreted as a **command to stop** if it refers to an action or activity which is proscribed at the time of utterances . . . (but) as a **command to do** if it refers to an action or activity which teachers and pupil(s) know ought to have been performed or completed and hasn't been. (1975:32-33)

This rule has certain problems since it requires that the act be explicit. We know of directives which do not specify the act. The act need only be specified in cases where variety of act is at issue. In cases where only one act is plausible, only the object need be mentioned. For instance, one can obtain the salt at table with *Where's the salt?* or *Is that salt?,* neither of which mentions the desired act. In addition, to qualify as a directive, the putative addressee must be appropriate to the act, and the discourse continuity must be broken by the directive, which is not imbedded in a relevant topic sequence. **Those utterances will be interpreted as directives which break topical continuity in discourse, and which refer to acts prohibited to or obligatory for addressees, mention referents central to such acts, or give exemplars of the core arguments of understood social rules. Examples would be *Somebody's talking, I see chewing gum,* and *Where does your dish go?***

If chewing gum and side talking are prohibited, the mention of the acts constitutes a directive to stop. If the rule is that possessions must be in their places, then the mention of thing + location (or pointing) is an adequate directive if topical continuity is broken:

There are shoes in the living room.
Why are those there?
What are those? (pointing)
Where do your shoes belong?
How did those get here?

Social Meaning

The most striking finding of the work on adult directives was that there was a consistent social distribution, as illustrated on Table 1. The social distribution permits a considerable amount of communicative work to be done.

TABLE 1

Summary of Directive Type

Directive type	Neutralized form	Discourse constraints[a]		Obvious	Social features
		Comply	Noncomply		
Need statements	yes	none	excuse	yes	subordinates
Imperatives	no	none	excuse	yes	subordinates or familiar equals
Imbedded imperatives	no	agree	excuse	yes	unfamiliar or diff. rank; task outside role or territory; expect compliance
Permission directives	yes	agree	excuse	yes	superiors(?) or unfamiliar
Question directives	yes	answer+ inference	answer	no[b]	noncompliance possible
Hint	yes	reply+ inference	reply	no[c]	noncompliance possible or familiarity or routine roles

[a]Normal expected verbal response which would always be appropriate in these social conditions to an adult, accompanied by compliance or noncompliance.
[b]Obvious directives are those which are routinely understood as directives when conditions permit.
[c]Some questions and hints have become routine directives though they retain the neutralized form.

1. Some of the interpretive rules require knowledge of the social features in order to know when to recognize a directive, if the overt form is the same as some other type of speech act. For example, a Turkish student, Ayhan Aksu, thought she was choosing a polite directive when she said to her landlady *Could we move the garbage can over there?* The landlady's reply, *Why Ayhan, I didn't know you had a roommate,* showed that she did not interpret the utterance as a directive at all, and did not hear the *we* as a second person form. Because it had violated the agent indirection rule that the addressee be a subordinate, she heard it as its homonym, a permission request. From superior to subordinate, it would be an unambiguous directive.

2. When the social features of the speaker are ambiguous, the directive forms she selects, like her address forms, may provide information about her interpretation of the social relationship. Selection of *we* directive forms implies the addressee is subordinate; a permission request implies the addressee is higher in status. An eavesdropper can guess who an addressee is by virtue of the norms for selection of directives.

3. When the listener knows the social rules for which alternative to choose, she can surmise whether speakers are being rude, funny, or sarcastic. For example, when a sister says to her little brother *Would you mind taking your feet off my face?* she is being sarcastic. In families, a hint or imperative would be appropriate. To elaborate an imbedding implies that the addressee either is lazy (the task is difficult), or is putting on high rank. The full understanding of possible verbal strategies involves knowledge of the norms from which the utterance deviates, and a calculus of the social features possibly imputed.

CHILD DIRECTIVES: REPERTOIRE

On the basis of this analysis of adult directives, we will examine the following questions concerning child directives:

1. What varieties of forms are used by children to realize directives? Do they employ the full range of realizations we find in adults?
2. Given that some adult forms specify neither the desired act nor a desired object, how well can children infer directive function?
3. What evidence is there of systematic shifts in the realization of directives depending on the social context?
4. Which social information about speech context can they infer earliest from formal information?

There are some obvious limits to the kinds of directives a child is capable of producing. One limit is structural. To the extent that complex grammatical formulation is required, we cannot expect long forms from young children. If these forms are routinized or lexicalized, they can be within the child's repertoire earlier than the grammar might imply. But even forms like *whyntcha* as alternates to imperatives may not be used unless they do some semantic work as alternatives, or have been specifically taught as politeness formulas.

A second limit may be cognitive or inferential. Certain question-directives (or obstacle-questions) and hints are elliptical, and let the listener do the work of drawing the inference about the desired act and object. Restraint in mentioning what is wanted is used by adults both to leave the choice to understand up to the hearer, as a form of deference, and to allude to shared knowledge in conditions of solidarity and humor. Yet it is easy to see that children are likely to refer to the beginning stages or preconditions of need, simply out of their own failure to specify for themselves what is wanted—as when they say *I'm thirsty* rather than *I want juice.* And then adults, being nurturant, do the rest of the work for them. To test the likelihood that children actively hint when they could do otherwise, we need to look solely at situations where we are sure they know how to identify what they want.

We shall examine briefly the evidence on directives at the earliest stages of communication, from the work of Bates (1976[a]), Carter (1974), Dore (1973), and Halliday (1975), all of which mention the onset of verbal directives.

Bates examined detailed situational descriptions for two Italian children during the first year, and searched for the child's attempts to influence the response of others, either to gain attention or to get objects. Directives, of course, are an instrumental use of language to achieve other ends. It was not until Piaget's Stage 5 in sensorimotor development that three kinds of relevant instrumental kinds of behavior were found: the use of tools, the use of adults as instruments to get objects, and the use of objects as means to get adult attention (Bates 1976[a]:55). Bates here was referring to the stages of gestural communication, antedating verbal development. Among the very first uses of language are precisely that of pointing out objects to listeners, and trying to get listeners to mediate satisfactions—through directives.

Anne Carter (1974), in an extraordinarily detailed analysis of communicative development of videotapes of one child in the second year, filled in the details of the transition from sensorimotor to linguistic devices. She found a series of gestural schemata which could be differentiated with high reliability. They provide an important reference point for identification of intentions in the early utterances she observed.

TABLE 2

Gestural Schemata Early in the Second Year (Carter in press)

Schema	Gesture	Sound	Goal	Frequency*	Total
1. Request object	reach to object	"m"-initial	Get help to get object	298	342
2. Attention to object	point, hold out	"l"-initial "d"-initial	Draw attention to object	245	334
3. Attention to self	vocalization	*David* *Mommy*	Draw attention to self	142	142
4. Request transfer	reach to person	"h"-initial	Get from or give object to other	94	135
5. Dislike	falling tone	nasalized	Get help to change situation	82	82
6. Disappearance	slapping, waving	"b"-initial	Get help in removing	4	32
7. Rejection	negative headshake	[ə̃ʔ-ʔə̃]	Get help to change situation	3	20
8. Pleasure–surprise–recognition	smile	breathy "h" with vowels	Express pleasure	–	20

*Including only instances in which gesture and sound occurred together.

Carter's analysis of a single case suggests that during the second year the earliest vocalizations accompanied gestures, that later the gestures became optional, and that the earliest vocalizations had some gross phonetic properties. Later, the vocal schemes became differentiated and more related to conventional adult words.

Dore (1973) examined videotapes of four children, and described the analysis of "request-commands" of two children early in their second year. His criteria included the mother's response, since he assumed she would correctly recognize requests. Both children had, like David in the Carter study, a typical request gesture. Both had an idiosyncratic, staccato cry, both would use the object name on occasion, and the child with the richer prosodic inventory also used other segmental forms with rising pitch as request indicators, e.g., [é'é'é'], with rising pitch on each segment. The prosodic contour for this child was analogous to the early [m + V] of David, a general, unspecified request marker.

Michael Halliday (1975) has prepared a series of analyses of one child, Nigel, from observations with pencil and notebook over a long period. The first stable semantics allowing the description of a system was at 9 to 10.5

months. There is a considerable overlap in the categories of Halliday and Carter, and differences which may derive either from method or the individual child; Dore's work showed some children were more person-oriented and developed interpersonal speech cues sooner while an object-oriented child might differentiate lexicon more. By 10.5 months Nigel (Halliday 1975:148) had a general instrumental request form, [nãnãnã (mid-pitch)], several forms to regulate repetition or immediacy in actions of others, and the first of what became the names of wanted objects. At this stage, the child depended heavily on the caregiver's ability to infer what will satisfy him better than he can know for himself. Halliday, in mapping his function categories onto the surface forms, which included their prosody, found that the first specific utterances were not polyfunctional. Indeed, one feature of development was that first words, then multiword sentences, began with a single function and then became diverse in potential function. At the stage beyond the "one-unit" production, Nigel began to combine function markers with a name or theme. The result was either a gesture-word combination, or a word-word combination, as in *oh, egg.* So, too, Dory, studied by Gruber (1973) at about 19 months of age from films, combined function markers with themes in her first complex utterances, e.g., *see hat, want shoe,* before complements for themes were mentioned, as in *baby fall down.*

Early in the second year, children have merely gestures, names of desired objects, and a limited vocabulary of function indicators like *see, want,* and prosodic cues. In the following section, we will compare studies of English, Turkish, Italian, and Hungarian children. In particular, we will look for instances of directives which create ambiguity for the listener, like the least explicit adult forms.

The English data we shall consider consist of (*a*) a transcript of six children, ages 1.39-3.6, collected in a project with Wick Miller on child syntax; (*b*) a variety of nursery school studies by my students; (*c*) role-playing sessions of children ranging over a wide age range collected by Speier (1969); and (*d*) Catherine Garvey's (1975) systematic observations of 42 to 46-month-old children in an experimental setting. Several studies in other languages were undertaken at my suggestion after the first draft of this chapter was prepared (1973), using data collected for the analysis of grammatical features.

The Turkish material was prepared by Ayhan Aksu (1973), studying texts of 15 Turkish children aged 2 to 4, recorded in their homes. MacWhinney (1974) reported the development of Hungarian requests from 1.5 to 2.0. Bates' thesis (1976[a]) was based on the detailed longitudinal study of two Italian children, 1.3-3.9.

1. **Telegraphic directives** found before two:

   1. Vocatives with situational specification of desire.
   2. Rising intonation.
   3. Desire statements: *More. I want dolly.*

4. Goal objects or locations: *More juice. More up. Here.*
5. Possessives: *That mine.*
6. Imperatives: *Gimme. Book read. Sweater off. Apple me.*
7. Problem statements: *Carol hungry.*

Bates found that there were rising intonation imperatives early in Italian speech, but believed there was an accidental coincidence with the Italian rising intonation on polite questions. She argues that directives that fail tend to be repeated with rising pitch, and that questions, permission requests, and directives all have rising pitch merely because they all request confirmation or feedback.

2. **Limited routines**: *Is there a truck?, Where is the shoe? What's that?* (Holzman 1972). Questions of this sort, which appear to have a directive function (=*get me the shoe*), occurred in the Turkish and Hungarian texts early in the third year. But since "where" questions tended to be accompanied by searching by the child, it is not clear whether the child is using them as adults do, as a pure directive with the listener, not the self, as the agent.

3. **Imbeddings and structural modifications.** In the third year there was evidence of such changes in the various studies, providing a repertoire of diverse forms available for social use in a contrasted situation. These include interrogatives, inflected forms, tense contrasts, permission forms, and modal imbeddings.

In the Hungarian study, permission requests appeared by 2. In Turkish, subjunctive and aorist interrogatives appeared by 2.4. In Italian, at 2.8 there was the past tense form *I wanted to have some raisins.* Inflectional variation in these languages is easier for children than the syntactic elaboration which serves comparable functions in English. This difference in the age of development corresponds to the contrast found in rate of development between inflectional and syntactic realization of semantic contrasts, in children of different language types:

2.9: *Would you like to play golf?*
Would you push this?
Would you stand up on my roller skate?
Will you send it to Susie?
Can I have my big boy shoes?
3.2: *Why aren't you drinking your coffee?* (Italian)
3.5: *Will you give me a car?*
Can you give me one car, please.
3.5: *Are you going to leave the toy here?* (Turkish)
3.8: *You could give one to me.*
You can make a crown.

By 42 to 67 months, Garvey found that there was a higher ratio of imbedded to direct imperatives than was found with younger children. In addition, her examples suggest that more complex and diverse forms than the prevalent English modals were in use at the later ages:

Why don't you try this on, OK?
You have to call.
Don't forget to smoke your pipe.

4. **Hints without explicit imperatives.** Garvey's children did not hint, though they clearly used as "adjuncts" statements supporting more explicit directives:

That's where the iron belongs. Put it over there.
Roll this tape up for me. I can't do it.

She did not find the children using the adjuncts alone as adequate directives to each other.

The directives studied by Garvey were to peers. At 32 months, a Turkish child said to an adult, while ironing clothes in play, *This one is finished too. This is ironed now.* Aksu interpreted this as a directive to have new clothes to iron. Further, in a study of nursery school interaction in Berkeley, O'Connell (1974) reported that 4-year-olds often hinted to adults violations of rules, or drew attention to their own incapacities:

He made sand go in my eyes.
He put the motorcycle in the "Jungle Jim."
Jean, we didn't have a snack.
Jason's trying to take my stuff.
Daddy, I can't get this out.

Mitchell-Kernan reports her 4-year-old saying *I'm sorry. My room's too messed up* in soliciting help in cleaning it.

We conclude that by 4, and possibly earlier, children do employ hints, but that texts of interaction with adults might reveal them more than child interaction tapes. In all of the cases given here, the hint consists of mentioning of an aversive condition the adult can relieve. They are a more sophisticated form of the baby's *I'm hungry.* The operative interpretation is: reverse the condition.

5. **Elaborate oblique strategems.** Even in cases where there is complete structural masking of the directive intent, the desired object is typically mentioned:

> *We haven't had any candy for a long time.* (English, 42 months)
> *Isabel likes that kind of candy. You should get her some.* (English, 56 months)
> *That house is nice inside.* (English, 5 years)
> *Mom, don't you have any pickles?* (5 years)

Of course, during this period the syntactic elaboration of the other forms continues to increase, in combination with the strategic complexity:

> *If you are good, we won't use the wolf.* (Italian, 42 months)
> *If you give me this for a while, you can have this for a while.* (English, 42 months)
> *Do you think you could put your foot right here?* (English, 65 months)

Possibly the most complex example of a child's directive strategy is reported by Garvey (1975). Children in nursery schools often manipulate each other by "pretend" directives. There is negotiation about the game, and about roles in it:

(A approaches a large toy car that B has just been sitting on.)

A: *Pretend this was my car.*
B: *No!*
A: *Pretend this was our car.*
B: *All right.*
A: *Can I drive our car?*
B: *Yes, OK.* (smiles and moves away)
A: (Turns wheel, making driving noises.)

The climax of this sequence is a permission-directive, which suggests, anticipating our later discussion of social meaning, that the child is able to use deferential alternatives appropriately. It is the shift to an inclusive pronoun that shows extraordinary deftness, however, because it suggests an imbedding set of moves, as well, and possibly a social allusion to solidarity and sharing.

In all of the well-defined early examples, the desired object is always explicit. Later, children show deviousness not only of form, as the previous examples illustrated, but of content and time. They begin to make hints and question directives which do not allude to the desired object. And they are able to displace their directives and imbed several moves:

> Six-year-old in supermarket: *Can I have a penny?*
> Mother (surprised at small request): *Why yes.*
> Ten minutes later, at another stop, child deposits penny in gum machine.

To see this as a strategic move involving foresight and restraint, one needs to know that (*a*) the child would have been denied the penny had she asked at the second stop where the goal was obvious; and (*b*) she knew the second stop was planned. And of course, the penny itself was merely a means.

The development of repertoire, as we have seen it in the sparse data we have, suggests that the first forms are gestures, names of desired objects, and a few verbal function indicators like *want* and *more.* The elaboration of vocabulary, inflections, and syntax seem to be the means to the next changes in realizations: the addition of specifications of problems, goals, imperative acts, possessives, limited routines, and structural modifications, which in English are predominantly modal imbeddings. After the middle of the third year, the children sometimes made use of elaborate statements of aversive conditions which adults were implicitly to correct; they used complex and diverse imbedding forms, and found devious ways to obtain objects through not specifying the benefactor or the desired act, and through making conditional contracts. By 4, children appear to be capable of using verbal strategies which have several steps to success, and by 5 or 6 do not require reference to the desired goal. Our notions of the timing of these steps are fragmentary and anecdotal.

COMPREHENSION OF DIRECTIVE INTENT

We have distinguished the comprehension of directive intent from the interpretation of social information and of the affect involved in the choice of particular forms in the speaker's repertoire. But these are not entirely distinct issues. In the adult directive system, some directives will not be recognized as such, unless the listener knows the rules for appropriate selection in those social conditions, since the surface forms are systematically ambiguous out of context.

A familiar example is *Is your Daddy there?* Such a question from a caller at the beginning of a telephone conversation would normally be heard by an adult or older child as a routine directive to fetch him, with a reply such as *Yes, just a minute please.* Callers wishing more information must use another form or mark the deviation from the routine. We assume that children learn this interpretation because there is a regular sequence in which the caller remedies the listener's failure to hear the directive by moving to a more explicit form, like the permission directive: *Can I talk to him?* We have evidence from recordings of family interaction of such sequences in which speakers move to increasingly explicit forms. As early as 4, some children hear the directive question not as a routine directive, but at least as a possible directive, and reply: *You want to talk to him?* Yet at 10, other children fail to make this interpretation. We do not at all understand the reasons for such a wide variation in acquisition.

There are some serious problems in deciding when a child has understood a directive. The clearest examples are excuses for noncompliance, which Garvey has noted (1975). Failure to comply or even to acknowledge a directive may be deceptive because the child may not want to comply. A systematic feature of the most indirect directives is that they provide a routine reply for noncompliance (see Table 1). For example, when a 4-year-old hears: *Why are you in the garden in your socks?* and answers *Because I took off my shoes,* it is not clear whether he understood a directive. Compliance with a more explicit directive might merely indicate that he understands differences in the speaker's choice of a directive form may be related to affect. He may think a direct imperative from his mother means she's more likely to punish him. So noncompliance alone may be insufficient evidence, unless the act is one we have reason to believe the child wants to carry out, and relative sanctions are not important.

On the other hand, there are numerous factors which influence compliance positively, in addition to the kinds of alternatives listed in Table 1. These have to be adequately controlled in a comprehension study. Among them are:

1. **The explicitness of the directive.** Does it identify the intended act, the goal, the object, the agent?
2. **The demand value of mentioned objects.** Objects may have a normal place, or have normal acts directed towards them. Thus *I lost my shoe* may elicit its return, since shoes belong together.
3. **Activity set** established by the setting: "Standing behavior pattern." Pictures are to name, puzzles are to take apart and reassemble, food is to eat, balls are to throw.
4. **Training history of the child** with respect to household or classroom rules, lexicalized or situated conventional directives, and repeated sequences of circumstances in which misunderstood directives are followed by more explicit forms or by sanctions.

We can make some general predictions. First, we expect that other things being equal, imperatives, imbedded imperatives, need statements, and permission directives are the most explicit forms. The term "indirect speech act" has been used in the philosophical literature (Searle 1975) even for forms such as imbedded directives that are extremely explicit. The belief that imbedded directives might be hard to understand rests on the assumption that young children go through a literal interpretation of syntax, rather than employ easier interpretive strategies requiring less verbal processing.

On the other hand, question directives and hints are less explicit, and in some cases do not mention the desired goal state or object at all. Their comprehension has to rest either on repeated conjunction with more explicit forms, or on active inference. Thus Aksu says a Turkish child at 2 did not interpret *Do you know any stories?* as a directive, but *Tell us one* was so heard.

We have some evidence from observational studies suggesting the early shaping of compliance (as well as of replying to questions) by children's older discourse partners. This kind of shaping has three consequences. It helps discrimination of the forms that are always directives from those that contain cues to activity, but may have other functions instead in the intent of the speaker. On the other hand, it makes for understanding of proper directives when support from the setting is minimal. And it brings about understanding of directive intent in cases that are not explicit enough or that would require inference. The forms that demand such shaping are situated conventional directives, which would otherwise always require inference (*Is Daddy there?*), and the forms that are based on general rules of the household, classroom, or peer group (*Where are your shoes?*).

My current study of early conversations (Ervin-Tripp and Miller in press) suggests that adults strategically produce questions at points when children would normally give replies anyway, for instance, they ask *What's that?* while a child is labeling pictures already. They produce "eliciting forms" which are at first redundant with the child's activity or response set in the situation. Marilyn Shatz (1974), testing the comprehension predictions in an early draft of this chapter, videotaped home interaction of mothers of 2-year-olds. She found that from 87 to 100% of the directives by the mothers of the youngest children contained redundant cues. Macnamara and Baker (1975) found that at 12 and 17 months infants were heavily influenced by gestures. However, by the later age the children already could make use of language cues to some extent when the gestures were missing. **The later skill arises from the initial redundancy**.

We noted earlier (Ervin-Tripp 1970) that the imitation task gives evidence of incidental interpretations. This is a convenient test of the "normal" primary interpretation since the task is to imitate, not to interpret, and any additional interpretations must be a kind of leakage from a stronger spontaneous process.[2] The following protocol illustrates such spontaneous interpretations:

AT HOME

Say the sky is blue.	*The sky is blue.*
Say under his foot was a snake.	*Under his foot was a snake.* (waving a cup in the air)
Say put the cup down.	*Put the cup down.* (complies)
Say what is your favorite color.	*What is your favorite color. Red!*

2. On the other hand, imitations are a poor test of perceptual salience for generalization to interpretive situations, since recognition tests show that children store more detailed information about a sentence when given a set to imitate than when given a set to interpret (Novinski 1968).

Say the water was blue.	*The water was blue.*
Say up on the shelf is a book.	*Up on the shelf is a book.*
Say where is your shoe.	*Where is your shoe.*
Say what is your name.	*What is your name.*
Say in the house is a monkey.	*In the house is a monkey.* (holds a rope)
Say throw the rope.	*Throw the rope.* (complies)
Say where is the spoon.	*Where is the spoon. There!*
Say this is a kitchen.	*This is a kitchen.*
Say why don't you stand up.	*Stand up!* (complies)

IN DOCTOR'S OFFICE

Say I have dark glasses.	*I have dark glasses.*
Say how old are you.	*How old are you. Four!*
Say my eyes have drops.	*My eyes have drops.*
Say why don't you whistle.	*Why don't you whistle.* (tried)
Say the roof is high.	*The roof is high.*
Say wherever did you kick.	*Wherever did you kick. Bang!* (kicks)
Say it's Sunday.	*It's Sunday.*
Say can you take your glasses off.	*Can you take your glasses off.* (does)
Say it's a cold day.	*It's a cold day.*
Say what color is your coat.	*Blue. My jacket's blue.*
Say why don't you have a red jacket.	*I'm not wearing it now.*
Say I can jump.	*I can jump. I can too.* (jumps)

There are examples in this sequence of loss of the imitation set as the information-supplying set takes over. There is also an example of translation of an imbedded imperative into an imperative, suggesting that another strategy for studying interpretations would be reporting or accounts in story-retelling, to find conversions of surface forms to functional equivalents.

Shatz (1975) has examined the role of such discourse contexts in creating response bias in 2-year-olds. Holding physical setting constant, she put sequences containing *can you + feasible act* into two discourse contexts. In one, the child was given a series of directives. In the other, the child engaged in information exchange, based primarily on the structure *can N. . .* as in *Can Mommy talk on the telephone?* There was a much stronger compliance or activity interpretation when the activity was a continuation of prior activity, but almost half of the responses to *Can you talk on the telephone* were activity responses even in the information exchange context, especially on the part of the linguistically less mature children in the sample.[3]

One interpretation of this result is that it is evidence of activity primacy for this structure, in a setting with appropriate objects. If one uses various other imbedded imperatives the results are not the same. In the discourse context *Why don't you*. . . with alternating feasible and nonfeasible acts, the proportion of activity replies is much higher for feasible acts than in the context *Can you*. . . with alternating feasible and nonfeasible acts. Age change suggests either that the difference is due to the strong *because* response set around three (Ervin-Tripp 1970), or to a confirmation or proof set for the "can you + feasible act" sentences. There may be a fairly sensitive relation to age in these different tasks. And, of course, we do not know with home-reared young children—unless we observe their interaction with the various others in the family—what the training history of preferred forms used to them in each home has been.

A DIALOGUE AT 3.3

M:	(in car) *I'm cold.*	C:	*I already shut the window.*
M:	*I can't see anything!*	C:	*Take your hands off your eyes.*
M:	*It's noisy in here.* (TV in next room.)	C:	*Do you want me shut the door?*
M:	*I'm too hot.*	C:	*Take off your sweater.*
M:	*I can't reach it* (on ladder reaching shelf).	C:	(No reply.)
		C:	*Ask me some other funny things.*

The last comment shows how readily the child came to see the items as a problem-solving game, perhaps drawing his maximum consideration.

By the time the child is 3, comprehension of hints and of question-directives has enlarged. The change is due not merely to the child's enlarged capacity to offer services, but to an understanding of the implications of statements regarding the needs of others, and willingness to gratify those needs. Such a change is more social than linguistic, as he develops an ability to take the perspective of others. In may require, of course, considerable knowledge in some cases of the practical, social, or technical facts to make an inference. We can expect variation in the rate of development because of these social factors. We might expect some relation between the child's capacity to view speech addressed to him as intentional, and look for the speaker's motives, and his

3. Ken Reeder (1975) believes that children by 3.5 fully distinguish request and question interpretations of neutralized utterances like *Would you like to X.* He gave contextual cues which included directives *(Leave the swing)* before the "request," to establish a set, in an experimental study.

ability to use the intentions of listeners in developing elaborate strategies such as those discussed in the preceding section, which require the child to anticipate a series of replies, and to build on each stage as a means to the ultimate goal.

SOCIAL VARIATION

By the third year, children have a number of variants in requests which overlap those with a distinctive social distribution in adult usage. They may, even earlier, have been taught formulas like *please.* We can ask, then, how early these forms show a systematic social distribution rather than random choice. The youngest child, like an animal, can discern who is most likely to provide food or change a diaper. By 2, children can differentiate age and rank in terms of request types. In Lawson's study (1967) of 50 directives at school and 50 at home, a 2-year-old child had essentially three syntactic forms used as requests, and politeness modifiers. She gave almost entirely simple imperatives to her peers, but to adults she employed either desire statements (56%), or questions (38%) including permission requests.

Even more surprising is that the child differentiated within her nursery school group between other 2-year-olds and the 3- and 4-year-olds. She gave no commands to the 4-year-old, and employed only questions, including permission requests, such as:

Can have an apple, Nida, please?
Can have the pen, Nida please?

To the 3-year-old, she was willing to give commands, but four of the five instances included postposed *please* or *OK,* of the twelve such instances to all addressees.

At home, she differentiated strongly between her father and mother. Not yet having been properly trained in the equality of the sexes, she regularly used repetition and politeness modifiers with her father more than her mother. Three-fourths of her directives to him had such forms.

The most dramatic illustration of the contrast in requests to the parents occurred in a deliberate test, in which the child's milk glass was set at her place, empty, next to a bottle of milk. Normally her milk was poured before she arrived. To her mother she said:

Mommy, I want milk.

But when only her father was present, she beat about the bush:

> *What's that? Milk.*
> *My milk, Daddy. Yes, it's your milk.*
> *Daddy, yours. Yours Daddy? Ok, yours. Ok, it's mine.*
> *It's milk, Daddy. Yes, it is.*
> *You want milk, Daddy? I have some, thank you.*
> *Milk in there, Daddy? Yes.*
> *Daddy, I want some, please? Please, Daddy, huh?*

The evidence from a series of student projects involving nursery school observations of larger numbers of children confirms the finding that there is considerable social differentiation within children's repertoire before the age of 3. There are more imperatives spoken to children than to adults, and practically no negative imperatives to adults. But it is important to control, in such observations, both the age of the child and the precise message involved.

Task, itself, strongly affects the type of directives. O'Connell (1974) found that by 4 imbedded imperatives were common in wheedling goods from other children, whereas direct imperatives were more usual in behavior control. (Though not always used; power may be a variable. Consider: *Why don't you move your feet, Mr.*) In speech to adults, need statements were used to get goods, and hints or condition statements called attention to rule violations creating aversive conditions. Requests for services to adults were usually, on first approach, condition statements or imbedded imperatives, but on a repeat, clarified by a direct approach.

The reason it is necessary to control task is that the kind of task tends to vary with addressee. Since adults have control over goods, such as juice and paints, requests for goods often are directed to them when there is no issue of competition for the goods. Adults are also the targets of requests for permission to have access to locations and privileges, and the form for access to goods and privileges may be the same. Adults are also a recourse for help in aversive conditions, and for protection when other children interfere. In all of these cases compliance tends to be assumed. On the other hand, other children more often interfere and are the targets of negative imperatives and "emergency" imperatives. They are likely to engage in squabbles over control over goods and locations. Since they are partners in games, soliciting cooperation in play, especially in pretend games, is likely to be an important part of communication.

The studies in nursery schools showed changes in age of the speaker that were important. At 3 the predominant directives were still imperatives; by 4 the other imperative types predominated, except in free play between children. The **addressee** was an important variable, not merely because of the difference in type of task. For example, if the addressee was an unfamiliar adult, a question directive was more common than the imbedded imperative or permission directive:

Do you think you could put your foot right here?

If an imbedded imperative was used to unfamiliar adults, it might be quite elaborate: *You'll see when it's done, all right?* No directives with a similar degree of elaboration were addressed to children.

In general, the greater the intimacy of the addressee, the greater the frequency of hints, which identified an obstacle, need or desire, e.g., *I can't get it out, I feel sweaty*. The less familiar the adult addressee the more likely were polite modifiers.

Sharon James (1975) has explored the intersection of situation and age of addressee in a doll-play elicitation experiment with 4.5 to 5-year-old children. The intrusion condition included cases where the addressee occupied the speaker's territory, took her possessions, got her wet; the goods and services condition was a request for help, or goods, or privileges. The doll addressees were described as strangers varying in age–younger, peer, or adult. As can be seen in Table 3, requests for goods and services were less variable than the rejections of intrusions, which were highly sensitive to the age of the addressee.

TABLE 3

Directive Forms Addressed to Different-Aged Listeners as a Function of Doll Play Situation (Adapted from James 1975)

	Rejecting intrusions			Requesting goods/services		
	Adult	Peer	Junior	Adult	Peer	Junior
Direct imperative	1%	19%	48%	0%	0%	1%
Modified imperative	50	61	38	7	8	12
Can you	8	2	2	11	11	18
Would/could/will you	27	10	7	38	36	27
Can I	14	6	5	37	41	39
May I	0	2	0	7	4	3
Please	92	59	29	76	58	45

All of these studies were of English-speaking children. We have some data from Hungarian children, studied for a dissertation on grammatical development by Brian MacWhinney (1974). He reports a contrast in addressee from the earliest age. The child used *gimme* to children. At first, politeness formulas like *thank you* were restricted to situations in which an adult demanded them. The child used at 1.8 an offering form analogous to *please* when making requests of the mother. To other adults he used the polite request form *I request* or *I request nicely* by 1.6. He continued to say *gimme* to children until 2.2 when he extended the polite request. These observations suggest that the more elaborate alternatives first appear because they are overtly required by adult addressees, who are thus the first targets for their use. Only later are they generalized to become rhetorical devices in wheedling from other children.

An experimental study of these phenomena has been conducted by Elizabeth Bates with Italian children (1976[a]). She was only interested in the politeness dimension in addressing adults. She did not study addressee distribution. She studied 60 Italian children between 2.10 and 6.2 in preschools. She asked the children to make one request for a candy to a handpuppet, and then to ask very nicely, and then in a still nicer way, thus getting two pieces of candy. The first attempt gives a rough indication of a "normal" view of requests to an adult.

Italian adults asked to rank politeness terms in this situation gave the following ordering: imperative and wish statement, imperative + please, conditional wish, interrogative, interrogative-conditional, modal-interrogative-conditional, and modal-interrogative-conditional with the formal pronoun.

Most of the younger children in Bates' study started with the simple imperative or statement: *give me a candy, I want a candy*. The next most popular was the interrogative, *give me a candy?,* and a few used *please.* When asked to be polite, 3-year-olds were rarely able to change, but some moved to question pitch. The older group began where the younger group was when probed; their favorite reply at first was the interrogative. With probing they added soft intonation or *please,* and some just reduced their voices or asked for less candy! Only a handful of the conditionals, modals, and formal pronouns were used, which are evidently structurally advanced for these children.

These children, like the American children observed in natural situations, had noted how an adult should be approached "nicely" or even normally, if one wanted to be persuasive. What we do not know from this study is the extent to which children knew that informal directives also have an appropriate context. From context-free studies we cannot find whether children know that in "emergency" tasks to younger children the elaborate, polite form would be inappropriate. But free speech and James' findings suggest they do know this.

UNDERSTANDING SOCIAL INFORMATION

We have evidence, then, that children respond to age, dominance, task, and familiarity as factors affecting request forms early, but we would like to know whether children interpret the social information in these forms in the speech of others.

Elizabeth Bates did not raise this issue. She asked children to give a candy to the frog puppet which asked the most nicely, following the production task described above. She gave paired comparisons of the various possible features of polite directives, and found an order of development of features: *Please* was discriminated earliest, then soft intonation. Conditional and formal pronouns were not successfully discriminated until the oldest age, 5.5 to 6. The treatment of interrogatives is interesting. As we have pointed out, many of the youngest Italian children use rising intonation very early, at the one word stage, for directives and other response-eliciting items. But it is not clear that the children perceive this to be a dimension of *being nice* at all, and indeed at 4, most children chose the imperative as nicer than the interrogative form. Thus the semantic contrast signaled by rising terminal pitch may change with age. Bates has concluded that children "have a concept of politeness" by 3, according to the results on the *please* item, but that different items enter this system at different ages. Politeness is probably directly taught.

Bates' technique tests recognition of a polite form, but does not test the child's sensitivity to appropriateness to audience, task, setting, and so on. By this criterion, some "impolite" forms are appropriate to certain social conditions. Appropriateness is not directly taught, but must be observed.

In exploring the knowledge of 5-year-olds, Deborah Jacobs (1973), in a term paper, extended a technique developed by Marida Hollos (in this volume) to study Hungarian pronouns. These methods have the potential for checking a variety of contextual determinants. One can vary addressee, speaker, and other variables, with two methods. One is to ask the children to judge whether the utterance is silly. That is, a kind of grammaticality or appropriateness judgment is asked of speech to different pictured addressees. Children might be more likely, in this test situation, to identify informal forms to adults as wrong than overpolite forms to small children, because of training for politeness. When 14 5-year-olds were asked to identify potential addressees of statements like *Hey, gimme a cooky,* and *May I please have a cooky,* and *Excuse me, I'm hungry, do you have any cookies?,* they almost all distinguished in age or familiarity. They expected different forms to a peer than to adults, or different forms to the familiar mother than the less familiar father and strange woman.

The children in Jacobs' study also correctly identified the *we* form as appropriate to an adult speaking downward in rank in *We don't make noise like that,* and they attributed to strange women more elaborated directives to children, with more imbedded imperatives and *please.* Thus, familiarity of adults may turn out to be a major variable in children's views of the sociolinguistic system. We assume that in sociolinguistic rules, correct production of frequent forms may appear to precede the capacity to retrieve social information or judge social appropriateness.

The evidence suggests that the social basis already exists in early years for the development of more subtle forms of deviousness than children actually use, in that they differentiate in speech between imperatives, modified imperatives, imbedded imperatives using questions, and need statements. They are sensitive to certain social variables, in particular the age of addressee, and familiarity, task, and the probability of compliance (as in evidence of wheedling tone).

However, many children of 7 still cannot comprehend account terminology, and if asked to "ask" or "tell" commands, do not differentiate. Later, they may differentiate by adding "please," at least for "ask." (Possibly this synonymity is related to the confusion of these terms in other contexts, too.)

The most notable omissions in the repertoire of young children are those forms of request that do not explicitly identify what is wanted—question directives of an indirect type, and affirmative hints. If it is the case that the strategy requiring these choices arises from offering the listener greater options not to comply, by not mentioning what is wanted, one might suppose that the low frequency of these forms arises from children's lack of restraint in explicitly mentioning what is on their minds. In addition, it is clear that they can have difficulty at first identifying these versions as requests, which is surely a necessary step to emulating these request types.

A child who correctly interprets *Is your mother there?* as a directive, may continue to produce *Can I speak with Jim?*

Adults realize directive intents through speech acts that take different syntactic forms. Just as the lexicon has polysemy, so the syntactic forms can represent diverse functions. In syntax, just as in the lexicon, ambiguity isn't normally a problem, because a given configuration of intention, rank, familiarity, and setting may normally generate a regular form for realizing the intent. Deviations then systematically carry social meaning.

Children do not, at first, understand these rules. From a very early age they have a rich system of alternations in form that is systematically related to social features. They sensitively identify social contrasts signaled by tag modals, polite forms, address terms, modal imbeddings. What they gradually learn to do is conceal their purposes. While they use diverse syntactic forms, they still refer explicitly to their desires and goals, when they are not obvious from the context. So the major differences between adults and young children is not diversity of structure, not diversity of social features—though the rules may increase in number of variables and in complexity with age—but systematic, regular, unmarked requests, which do not refer to what the speaker wants. Wide use of tactful deviousness is a late accomplishment.

ACKNOWLEDGMENTS

Data, in addition to that mentioned in the text, were supplied in term papers by Carolyn Clark and Christine Young, and by the especially rich texts and analyses of Suzanne Isola.

Pragmatics of Directive Choice Among Children[1]

CLAUDIA MITCHELL-KERNAN AND KEITH T. KERNAN

INTRODUCTION

In English, and probably in most languages, directives may take a number of forms ranging from simple commands boldly stated to hints that require inference based on shared knowledge for their proper identification as directives. In a recent study, Ervin-Tripp (1976[a] and this volume) differentiates a number of common directive types, and argues that particular constellations of social factors favor certain choices from among the total set available in English. Among the determinants of choice are factors that enter into the definition of the speech situation, such as the familiarity and relative ranks of the interlocutors, the setting, and the role relations of the speaker and addressee. In addition, aspects of the request itself, such as the difficulty of the task and whether the task is a normally expected duty, play a role in determining the form appropriate to the situation.

A competent member of a speech community has internalized the norms for the appropriate use of directive types, and has not only an intuitive knowledge of which forms to use in which speech situations, but also the ability to interpret forms as directives which, on the surface, would seem to be serving some other speech function. A speaker of English, for example, interprets *Do you have a match?* not as a speech act that seeks information, but as a request for a light (cf. Gordon and Lakoff 1971; Ervin-Tripp 1976[a]; Garvey 1975). His knowledge of the rules of speaking English permit him to assign to the utterance some other function than its surface structure would seem to indicate.[2] Knowledge of the function of the utterance is necessary for its basic semantic interpretation. A person who did not recognize the utterance as

1. We gratefully acknowledge the support of the National Institute of Mental Health who funded the research on which this chapter is based (Grant No. RO 1 MH 24340-01).

2. Gordon and Lakoff argue that such indirect requests may be accomplished through the assertion or questioning of the *sincerity conditions* underlying the speech act, request.

a request would have not, in the most fundamental sense, understood the message.[3]

Dependent upon the analytic perspective taken, however, a single speech act may serve multiple functions. As Hymes (1962, 1972[b]) has pointed out, multiple functions may be hierarchically arranged. If we view the question, *Do you have a match?* as functioning as the imperative *Give me a light,* we may ask, why the former and not the latter? The answer seems obvious. The question, in this context, is more polite than the command.[4] A second function of the utterance then, the function that at least in part dictates the form, is the communication of civility or "politeness." At one level of analysis, the question and the imperative are functionally equivalent; at another level the two utterances contrast. *Do you have a match?* serves at least two functions; that of a directive and that of a polite utterance. From a broader perspective, however, when considered within the context of ongoing social interaction, the utterance may serve still other functions. If the scene were a cocktail party, for example, and if the speaker were a young man with matches in his pocket; and if the addressee were a young woman, and if after receiving his light the young man lingered making small talk, then we might reasonably assume that the utterance functioned as a means for the young man to strike up conversation with the young woman. Perhaps we could say that the request functioned as a socially acceptable conversation opener. Which function is to be considered the more basic function depends upon the frame of reference. If the concern is with the fundamental semantics of the utterance, then the basic or most pertinent function is the directive function, since the utterance must be recognized as a directive in order that a semantic interpretation may be assigned to it. If, on the other hand, our concern is with the form the directive takes, then, for the purpose of our analysis, at least, we might consider the politeness function to be basic. Finally, if our concern is to determine the function of the speech act in ongoing social and verbal interaction, then the pertinent and basic function is that of a conversation opener. A single utterance, then, may serve multiple functions and, depending upon the analytic perspective, one of the functions may be considered more basic than the others.

Function in the sense used here has to do with the speaker's intent. To understand the functions an utterance serves, we must understand why the speaker said what he said. Intent is not always obvious nor is it always easy to

3. In speech act theory, the function of a speech act at this level of analysis is referred to as the *illocutionary force* of the speech act.

4. Ervin-Tripp has argued that although it may be possible to rank decontextualized directive forms in terms of degree of politeness, when social context is available, it can be demonstrated that politeness or civility does not adhere to particular directive forms. *Would you mind emptying the garbage* ostensibly more polite than *Empty the garbage* might be judged sarcastic if the speaker were a parent addressing a 10-year-old child and this was a duty normally expected of the child.

discover. In fact, it is not always discoverable. A knowledge of intent, or an informed guess of intent, however, is usually, and perhaps always necessary to the complete understanding of any utterance. Interlocutors continually, and often unconsciously, know or make guesses about each other's intentions. In the above example, the hearer, being a member of the same speech community as the speaker and being familiar with the linguistic conventions of that speech community, would undoubtedly recognize that the speaker's intent was not to ask an information-seeking question but to request a light for his cigarette. She would further recognize his intention to avoid seeming rude and, dependent upon what followed the request, would also recognize the speaker's intention to begin a conversation with her. She might also suspect other intentions, honorable or otherwise, on the part of the speaker, but since those intentions (or that function) could probably not be served by the single utterance under consideration, they need not concern us here.

Our purpose in this chapter is to examine some aspects of the use of directives among a group of black American children who range in age from 7 to 12 years. We will be concerned with exploring (*a*) the social distribution of directive types used by the children, and (*b*) the relationship between particular directives and broader interactional goals. The data base for our analysis consists of directives used in the role-playing speech activity of the children, augmented with examples drawn from more naturally occurring speech situations.[5]

5. With one exception, the role-playing scenes to be discussed were performed with hand puppets on an improvised stage with the children themselves hidden from view. The scenes were performed before an audience of peers ranging in age from 5 to 12 years. The only adults present were members of the research team who had been seeing the children almost daily for a period of 7 months, at the time of data collection. The activity was unstructured by the investigators in that the children used the puppets and the improvised stage only when and if they chose. The characters, situations, and the story lines were entirely of their own choice and creation. The hand puppets themselves appear to have suggested a few themes and roles that appear in the data. Some of the puppets were black, some white and some were dressed in occupationally marked clothing. The children, however, were not constrained by the appearance of the puppets in creating themes and roles. Each role-playing scene involved from two to four children, with a single individual sometimes cast in more than one role. It should be noted that choice of directive form was only one of the features used contrastively by the children in their role playing. Children engaged in considerable phonological shifting across roles and also used pitch contrastively to convey attitudinal states and sex role. With few exceptions, the role-playing scenes had a common, overall structure. They began with an introduction, which included the identification of the cast, followed by a prologue telling what the show was to be about. Typically, the dramatic complication which formed an element in the structure of the scenes centered on some conflict situation. The dramatic complications included: a daughter discovered playing hooky; family quarrels; inappropriate speech behavior from child to parent; a car accident. Both performers and audience enjoyed this activity and participated enthusiastically. The directives that derive from naturally occurring conversation were tape recorded during play activity and involve, for the most part, the same group of children who participated in the role playing. All of the recording was done at a local recreation center.

In our consideration of the social distribution of variants, we will employ the classification scheme developed by Ervin-Tripp (1976[a] and this volume).[6] We present the following tokens of each type which occurred in the role-playing data:

NEED STATEMENTS (or Statements of Personal Desire)

I want a green milk shake.
I'd like to speak to Officer Kernan.
I don't want no more fighting out of the girls.

IMPERATIVES

Be back here at three o'clock.
Let my brother alone.
Shut up, you sucker.

IMBEDDED IMPERATIVES

John, would you please tell that lady to quit?
Could you come out to 4425 Clemons Street?

PERMISSION DIRECTIVES

May I have the police?
Can I speak to her?

QUESTION DIRECTIVES

Hey, you got a quarter, Mac?
Boy, what you doin' out there?

HINTS

I'm the sergeant around here.
Last person talk to me like that is in his grave.
It's hot out here.

SOCIAL DISTRIBUTION OF DIRECTIVE VARIANTS

Of a total of 261 directives derived from the role-playing data, 15 were in the form of **Statement of Need** (Table 1). None of these actually used the lexical item "need," however. Rather, they took the forms *I want* . . . , or *I don't want* . . . , and *I would like*. . . . Directives of this type occurred in similar social situations as the "Statements of Need" discussed by Ervin-Tripp (1976[a]). That is, they

6. Our debt to Ervin-Tripp's insightful analysis should be clear.

occurred in transactional work settings (including client-supplier of goods or services situations), and in family settings. Ervin-Tripp found that those statements of need that occurred in transactional work settings were always directed from persons of higher rank to persons of lower rank, or were spoken to persons whose transactional role obliged compliance. Similarly, in our data we find:

(1) (Major to secretary) *Fraulein, I want you to type some letters for me.*
(2) (Police commissioner to prisoner) *Listen here, I want you back here tomorrow, and once you get out of prison, I want you to see probation officer once a month.*
(3) (Customer to salesperson) *We would like to order a milkshake.*

Statements of desire that occurred in a family setting, however, were not from child to parent as Ervin-Tripp (1976[a]) found, but from parent to child:

(4) (Father to daughter) *I don't want you havin' no company or friends or nothin'.*

It may be that although there is some semantic commonality between the lexical items "need" and "want," they do not overlap sufficiently to warrant the consideration of directives which employ one or the other as a single category. The choice of "need" as opposed to "want" seems to offer a more compelling reason for both making the request on the speaker's side, and for complying to the directive, from the perspective of the addressee. "Need" conveys a condition of urgency, and this is probably the reason young children may frame their directives as "needs" regardless of necessity, e.g., *I need some candy.* In contrast, *I want you to. . .* brings into focus the element of personal

7. Relative rank and situation (personal or transactional) were coded independently by three judges. There were coding disagreements in a total of 12 cases, seven involving disagreements as to situation and relative rank, and five involving disagreements regarding relative rank alone. Those disagreements involving relative rank alone were confined to adult-police and police-adult dyads. Two judges rated the policeman as having equal rank to an adult citizen and one rated the policeman a superordinate because of his officially sanctioned authority. Our decision to classify adult-police dyads as equal in rank was somewhat arbitrary, since the ideology of the community could support either classification. The seven cases, which were problematic with regard to both situation and relative rank, involved a single dyad, a general and his secretary. The actual setting was a transactional one (an office), but the general had stepped out of his transactional role and was attempting to seduce the secretary. In response to this behavior the secretary issued seven directives (all imperatives) in an effort to seek freedom from this annoyance. In this case, our final decision was to code the situation as personal, and to regard the secretary and her boss as equal, under the circumstances. Had we made different decisions, however, in these 12 cases, the generalizations we have made would not be affected substantially. Had we coded the secretary as the general's subordinate in the case above, her use of the imperative would have been consistent with the use of the imperative to superiors in tense and angry situations. Had we, however, coded the policeman as of higher rank than the citizen, this decision would have changed slightly the distribution of statements of personal desire.

desire, and may convey meaning about the relative ranks of speaker and addressee. Such semantic differences between "need" and "want" may account for the association of **Statements of Personal Desire** with superordinate-subordinate rank differences between speaker and addressee in personal situations. If there is congruence between the use of "need" and the nature of the request, it may be that this form is not easily associated with relative rank, as in the following:

(Secretary to department chairman, UCLA) *I need your signature on the Preston letter.*

(Graduate student to professor, UCLA) *I need a letter of recommendation for my NIH application.*

All situations in our study in which directives took the form of **Statements of Desire** are characterized by a clear expectancy on the part of the speaker of compliance by the addressee.

TABLE 1

Number of Each Directive Type According to Situation and Rank

		Personal desire	Imperative	Imbedded imperative	Permission	Question	Hint	*Total*
Personal[a]	+		7	2				*9*
	=	2	109	14	4	2	10	*141*
	–	4	37			1		*42*
Transactional	+		4	1			2	*7*
	=	5	10	4	3			*22*
	–	4	33	1			2	*40*
Total		*15*	*200*	*22*	*7*	*3*	*14*	*261*

[a]+: Lower to higher rank; =: equal rank; –: higher to lower rank.

By far the most common type of directive in the role-playing data was the imperative. There were 200 instances of this form.

The distribution of the use of imperatives according to social situation and relative rank is presented in Table 2. In transactional situations, 68% of all directives used were imperatives. Personal situations yielded a somewhat higher percentage (80%) of imperatives among all directive types. Situation and relative rank combined, however, appear to effect choice of directive type more than situation alone. In personal situations, 71% of all imperatives were used by speakers occupying ranks equal to that of the addressee. Equal status addressees receive only 21% of all imperatives in transactional situations. The relationship in which most imperatives were used in transactional situations was that of

TABLE 2

Use of Imperatives by Social Situation and Relative Rank

	Number	Percent
Personal or Family Situations		
lower to higher status	7	5%
equal status	109	71%
higher to lower status	37	24%
Transactional Situations		
lower to higher status	4	9%
equal status	10	21%
higher to lower status	33	70%

superordinate to subordinate (70%), almost exactly the percentage used in equal rank dyads in personal situations. In both transactional and personal situations, imperatives were more likely to be directed to persons of lower rank than to persons of higher rank than the speaker. In personal situations, over five times as many imperatives are directed to lower ranked persons as are directed to higher ranked individuals. This pattern is magnified in transactional situations where subordinates receive over eight times as many imperatives as superordinate addressees. It should be noted that three of the four imperatives addressed to superordinates by persons of lower rank in personal situations were not demands for goods or services but were frantic pleas from a child to a parent:

(SON TO MOTHER)

(5) *Oh, don't tell, don't tell him, don't tell him.*
(6) *Don't tell Daddy, oh no!*
(7) (loud cry) *Leave me alone,* (sob) *quit it, now.*

Furthermore, imperatives addressed to higher ranked individuals by subordinates have a single feature in common. All occurred in agonistic or conflict situations. There is every reason to suspect that the choice of these forms was intended by the children to be expressive of the tense character of the interaction. These imperatives were outbursts, aimed at either protesting a prior act of the addressee, or preventing an act that would have unhappy consequences for the speaker. There is a perfect correlation between the presence of voice quality features registering a state of emotional upset on the part of the speaker, and the use of an imperative to a higher ranked individual by a person lower in rank. This pattern is in keeping with Ervin-Tripp's hypothesis that departures from expected usage are expressively loaded and serve to convey attitudinal states and other aspects of social meaning.

Ervin-Tripp (1976[a]) describes six structural variants of imperatives used by adults in American English:

1. Elliptical forms specifying only the direct or indirect object of the imperative.
2. **You** + imperative.
3. Attention getters.
4. Postposed tags.
5. Rising pitch.
6. Ordinary imperatives that include a verb, an object if the verb is transitive, and sometimes a beneficiary.

Of these six types, only **ordinary imperatives** and **you + imperatives** occur in the role-playing data. There are no instances of the elliptical form, attention getters such as the use of "please" in a situation where what is desired is clear, or rising pitch. There are three instances of a postposed tag, but in all of these cases the tag is a term of address and not a modal:

(MAN TO WOMAN)

(8) *Give me a kiss on that, Baby.*

(9) *Come on, Baby.*

(FATHER TO SON)

(10) *Don't you be talkin' that talk to me, li'l big head boy.*

The absence of elliptical forms, attention getters, and rising intonation in the role-play data is a bit surprising in that the children do use these forms in their naturally occurring speech. It may be that these less direct forms are not appropriate to the dramatic conflict situations portrayed in the role-play.

There are 22 examples in the role-play data of imbedded imperatives in which agent, verb, and object are explicit but are introduced by preceding forms:

(11) (Boy to boy) *Why don't you take off your hat?*

(12) (Young man to young woman) *Would you wear my ring?*

(13) (Nurse to nurse) *Mrs. Sheryl, will you please call Dr. Bullers and tell him to send an ambulance out to 3455 Clemmons Street?*

Imbedded imperatives occurred in both transactional and personal situations and were addressed to persons of equal, higher, and lower rank than the speaker. They clustered between interlocutors of equal rank (82%). In most cases, there is insufficient background information in the role-playing to permit us to assess whether the use of imbedded imperatives to equal rank addressees is associated with any of the conditions for its use suggested by Ervin-Tripp (1976[a]). For example, Ervin-Tripp found that co-workers of long standing who were on good terms would likely favor imperatives over imbedded imperatives if the act requested was a normally expected duty. Example (13) presents a somewhat problematic case, since the relevant background information is not accessible.

Examples from our natural conversational data, however, lend support to some of Ervin-Tripp's observations regarding the conditions under which the imbedded imperative may be used to an addressee of equal rank. In keeping with Ervin-Tripp's generalizations, our data suggest that when aspects of the request are held constant, such as its difficulty, the absence of solidarity between speaker and addressee may be reflected in the favoring of imbedded imperatives over imperatives. A child temporarily estranged from the peer group tended to use more imbedded imperatives than when peer group relations were more amiable. Cooling relations between formerly close individuals also brought forth the use of more imbeddings. A few children were temporary outcasts more often than others and their marginal status is evidenced by their differential use of imbedded imperatives and "please." Since friendships waxed and waned dramatically in a short time, however, it was not always easy to determine what the particular state of affairs was between two children at a given time. This information is thus impossible to code in many cases. Without doubt, aspects of the request, such as its difficulty or cost to the addressee, are registered in the greater use of imbedded imperatives. Contrast the following:

LOW COST REQUESTS

(14) (Girl 8 years to girl 9 years) *Hey, Rita, button this last button.*
(15) (Boy 11 years to boy 11 years) *Hand me that wrench.*
(16) (Girl 8 years to girl 7 years) *Give me one of the greens.*

GREATER COST REQUESTS

(17) (Girl 11 years to girl 8 years) *Alice, will you start me off?* (This was a special request because the addressee had to stop her own work to help the speaker.)
(18) (Girl 11 years to girl 12 years) *Belinda, will you go to the store for me?* (The store was two blocks away.)
(19) (Boy 11 years to boy 11 years) *Would you ask him can we use the other room?* (Clearly, nobody wanted to do the asking.)

Permission directives take the form: modal + beneficiary (speaker) + have/verb+? They differ from the imbedded imperative in that there is a shift of focus from the addressee's activity to the beneficiary's activity. There are seven instances of permission directives in the role-play data; all are addressed to persons of rank equal to the speaker:

(20) (Woman to telephone operator) *May I have the police?*
(21) *May I have the operator, please?*
(22) (Young man to young woman) *Can I speak to her?*
(23) (Performer to audience) *Could I get a hand?*

There are only three examples in the role-playing data of question directives; two are nonexplicit and the other mentions the object of desires. This directive type occurred only in personal situations:

(24) (Wife to husband) *Honey, did I bring anything home, sugar dumpling?* (Request for husband to come to her defense because she is being accused of stealing something from a neighbor)
(25) (Father to son) *Boy, what you doin' out there?* (Telling son to come inside)
(26) (Man to man) *Hey, you got a quarter, Mac?*

Finally, there are 14 hints that serve as directives:

(27) (Girl to girl) *It's hot out here.* (Request for a rest stop)
(28) (Performer to audience) *It sure is mighty sad out there. We don't hear nothing.* (Attempt to elicit applause)
(29) (Sergeant to lower ranking police officer) *I'm the sergeant around here.* (Stop giving me orders.)
(30) (Young man to young man) *Last person to talk to me like that didn't talk to me no more.*
(31) *I don't play the dozens.* (Stop insulting me.)

Most hints occurred in personal situations between interlocutors of equal rank (71%). A few occurred in transactional situations and these are evenly divided between addressees of higher and lower rank than the speaker.

Ervin-Tripp has noted that the discourse constraints associated with hints and question directives are less coercive than those associated with other types of directives, since they do not require a noncompliant addressee to formulate an explicit excuse. Since question directives may be treated as information questions, and hints may be either ignored or responded to with replies that address a function other than the directive function, they protect both speaker and hearer from the embarrassment of an explicit refusal (1976[a]). Most of the hints and question directives which were used in the role-playing, however, do not seem to be aimed at circumventing interpersonal failure. In the case of Example (24), it would appear that the addressee is being primed to respond compliantly. That is to say, the use of an endearing form of address along with a pet name as a tag, would seem to be an effort to make it difficult rather than easy for the addressee to respond noncompliantly. In addition, the tone of voice chosen in most cases serves to press or underscore the directive implication rather dramatically.

It has been suggested that hints may be used when a speaker is reluctant to be explicit and wishes to leave the pragmatic interpretation to the solicitude of the hearer (Ervin-Tripp 1976[a]). Example (28) presents a circumstance in which the choice of a hint may be meaningful in precisely this way. A performer is attempting to elicit applause from the audience, and the indirect strategy may be related to the fact that the speaker is seeking a sign of approval for herself. Interestingly, although other attempts to elicit applause did not take the form of hints, all had in common the use of indirection at some level. *Could I get a hand?* involves the shift in focus from addressee's to beneficiary's activity; *Let's hear it* requests an effect which can only be brought about by activity on the part of the addressees, and in addition, pronominalizes applause in the absence of an antecedent.

There are probably numerous, highly idiosyncratic reasons why a speaker might be reluctant to be explicit. Some circumstances associated with hinting in our data appear to have some general significance, however, because they involve considerations which are demonstrably important in making choices among other types within the total set of conventional directives. These social factors include aspects of the request itself, and factors that enter into the definition of the speech situation, such as the role relations between speaker and hearer and their relative ranks. Aspects of the request may serve as a selector for hinting because there are certain intentions which cannot be realized politely with any of the more direct forms. We refer here to directives which are functioning to terminate interaction or encounters. A hostess cannot communicate the end of a party by saying *Would you go home now.* She is forced by social convention to communicate this indirectly (cf. Ervin-Tripp 1976[a]). Similarly, in transactional situations it would be unlikely that a doctor, for example, would terminate a consultation or therapy session by saying *Would you go now?* or *Do you mind leaving?* Rather, a termination would take such forms as *I'm afraid our time is up* or *I'd like to see you again in two weeks.* Nonexplicit question directives might occur under similar socially awkward circumstances as in the following example from the children's role-playing:

(32) (Nurse to child patient) *All right, you wanna go play baseball?* (The nurse has completed his examination of the child and is communicating that the consultation is over and the child should be on his way.)

In each of the following examples taken from the spontaneous speech of the children, the source of the child's reluctance to be explicit seems relatable to his anticipation of the possibility of a noncompliant response. In turn, the possibility of noncompliance is relatable to aspects of the request alone, or aspects of the request in combination with relative status of the interlocutors:

(33) (Male 12 years to adult researcher) *You ain't got no old tapes you wanna sell, do you?* (He wants to be given a tape.)

(34) (Male 11 years to adult researcher) *What happened to the racer?* (He wants the race car track.)

(35) (Female 11 years to female 8 years) *It's peanut shells all over that floor.* (Pick up the peanut shells.)

(36) (Male 11 years to adult researcher) *I like to talk on the mike.* (He wants to be given the microphone.)

Before elaborating further on these examples, it will be informative to mention another type of hint that occurs in the spontaneous speech of the children with some frequency. One type of statement intended to function as a directive took the form *You gave Jimmy a nickle* or *You let Beverly take the tape recorder home.* This type of hint occurred so often in the course of the research that it became a source of humor. On one occasion, one of the authors said to a boy of 11, in an accusatory tone similar to the one the children often used when hinting in this way: *Oh, you washed Karen's car.* The child responded with a puzzled look and it was a few seconds before he realized that the researcher was jokingly requesting that he wash her car. It would appear that the success of this strategem is tied to role relations. It is our feeling that the children adopt this strategy because they feel it is a persuasive one; one which compels a compliant response. A hint of this kind does a number of things. First, it alludes to a norm; second, it alludes to the fact that a norm has been broken; and third, it makes compliance a mode of repairing the breach.

Why does a child say to an adult *Oh, you took Billy and them to get pizza yesterday*; or *You gave Kay two pieces of gum*; rather than *Would you take me to get a pizza?* or *Would you give me another piece of gum?* We think the reason is that such indirect requests permit the children to circumvent other norms associated with requesting. It is considered improper for children to make such requests of adults other than very close friends or family members. Within the speech community, there is a label which is frequently given to such requests, **begging**. In Example (32) a more direct request to obtain a tape could also be viewed as "Begging." In this case, the speaker is engaging in a bit of amusing artifice as well as indirection. He does not have any money to buy a tape and his offer to purchase one is a devious attempt to get the researcher to offer one. The underlying basis for indirection in the above cases has much in common with what we feel is the motivation for the hint in Example (35). The nature of the request is incompatible with the role relations of speaker and addressee. From the perspective of the children, a direct request to *Pick up the peanut shells* could only legitimately be made by a person in authority, not a peer. It would have been a distinct possibility had the speaker chosen the more direct route that the addressee would have invoked role norms as the source of her noncompliance. In all of these cases attempts are being made to circumvent rather general normative constraints on requests.

In Examples (34) and (36), however, the motivation for hinting is different. The requests do not violate norms. Rather, the nature of the request is influencing directive choice, we believe, because of more specific contextual factors. A bit more background information may be helpful to make this point. In connection with Example (34), the research team had purchased a set of model racing cars and a track for the entertainment of the children. Several of the children also had similar sets at home. The racing cars had structural defects that caused a few parts to wear out very quickly. Some children began to appropriate parts from the office set to be used on their home sets, and replacing these parts had become a source of annoyance to the research team. In short, the racing set and its use had become a sensitive issue. Similarly, in Example (36), the speaker wants the microphone back after it has been taken away and he has been scolded for treating it roughly. Moreover, it is our view that interactional goals, only circumstantially related to the specific action being requested, are being accomplished by choice of directive type. In effect, the addressee is being "set-up" so that she has the opportunity to "offer." An offer, under the circumstances, was a more persuasive token of solicitude than a mere compliant response to a more explicit directive would have been. A sign of solicitude was being sought because it, in turn, could be interpreted as a conciliatory gesture.

Although it may not be possible to order, as systematically, the impact of interpersonal functions on choice of directive type as is possible in the case of factors such as relative rank, familiarity vs. distance, and task difficulty, our data indicate that such functions affect directive choice. In the following section, we would like to develop this point by a further consideration of the functions of directives in the role-playing scenes of the children.

INTERPERSONAL FUNCTIONS OF DIRECTIVES

In the role-playing activity of the children, directives functioned as a means of achieving other than the strictly instrumental goals of obtaining goods and services. Directives and reactions to them were constantly used to define, reaffirm, challenge, manipulate, and redefine status and rank. At times the directives involved actually served the ordinary function of directives—that of requesting goods or services—while at the same time, because of their frequency of occurrence or the particular form they took, served to test the addressee's view of the statuses involved. In other instances, however, the directives were issued with the clear expectation of noncompliance. In such cases, the intent of the speaker was only to test or manipulate the status relationship in some way.

Directives from parent to child account for a large percentage of the imperatives used by higher status individuals to subordinates. In many cases the sheer density of these directives, that is, their rapid delivery in an extended and uninterrupted series, often at the beginning of the role-play episode, indicates that their broader function in these instances was to establish a relationship of dominance–submission between the characters in the play. In the role-play parent-child interaction the children treated directives as a prerogative of the parental role and used directives to mark that role:

(37) (Father-daughter) *I'mo go somewhere and I don't want nobody in this house. Nobody around. And I better not catch you expectin' no boys. I want you to clean up this house. I don't want you havin' no company or friends or nothin'.*

(38) (Father-daughter) *Get back in this house. Who told you to get up? Sit on this couch. Get on in. Come over here.*

Another feature that serves to define and emphasize the differential status in parent-child relationships is the use of directives accompanied by threats:

(39) (Father to son) *Well, then, I'ma go in the house an I'ma pack this lunch. And if you don't be out here and you be round that corner tryin' to shoot some dice and lose all your money, I'ma tan your hide, and tighten them britches for you.*

(40) (Mother to daughter) *Well, Linda Faye, you just come up these stairs before I whup your behind.*

A third directive technique used to establish the differential statuses of parent and child, or, in one case, older man-younger woman, is the inclusion in the directive of some mention or indication of the status of the addressee:

(41) (Father-son) *Well, bring your li'l self in here.*

(42) (Father-son) *Don't you be talkin' at talk to me, li'l big head boy.* (For at least some speakers of black American English, the phrase *big head boy* addressed to a child indicates that the speaker believes the child has been behaving in a way inappropriate to his status as a child; that he has been acting as only an adult has the right to do.)

(43) (Man to younger woman) *Uh, Lady, I used to change your diapers. Don't you ever call me no boy.*

These examples, in addition to establishing or emphasizing the unequal statuses of parent and child, also function as directives in the ordinary sense in that they demand some overt behavior on the part of the child; some instrumental act that the parent wants performed, or some behavior he wants stopped or avoided.

Other directives in the role-play data, however, seem to function primarily or even solely to establish the child's subservient position. This is not to say that the directives do not demand or proscribe some overt behavior on the part of the child, but that that behavior is instrumental only in the sense that it establishes or confirms the child's subordinate position in the interaction:

(44) (Father-son) *You just turn yourself over here. You gon' get a spankin' for today.*
(45) (Father-son) *Um, look at me when I'm talkin' to you. You wanna go to the park with me?*

Some of the directives that serve this function, though appropriate to the immediate situation and delivered with the expectation of compliance, are stated in the form of general principles of appropriate child behavior and are delivered in situations in which those principles have been violated:

(46) (Father-son) *You don't hit your daddy back.*
(47) (Father-son) *You don't call your daddy big head.*
(48) (Father-daughter's suitor) *That's right. You address me as Sir.*
(49) (Father-daughter's suitor) *If you in my house you don't talk this loud. You got to respect me.*

Finally it is possible, we believe, to view the difference in frequency of directives of any type between speaker and addressee as means by which information about relative rank was conveyed, and the interpersonal goal of establishing rank was achieved. Addressees who were lower in rank than the speaker received over five times as many directives as those higher in rank (see Table 3), and this pattern holds for both personal and transactional situations. Apparently, the children view one of the prerogatives of high status as the right to direct the behavior of lower ranked individuals. The social implications of choice of directive type are salient for the children in our sample, and are frequently the source of metalinguistic comments. In their naturally occurring speech activity, as in their role-play, the children so often use directives to define and test status relationships and obligations that they react testily to directive forms which, on the surface at least, seem perfectly appropriate to the situation.

TABLE 3

Percent of all Directives by Relative Rank

Rank of Addressee	Total	Personal	Transactional
+	6%	5%	10%
=	62%	73%	32%
-	31%	22%	58%
Total number	261	192	69

In observing children in their play activities, one is struck by what appears to be an absence of strong social pressure toward civility within the peer group. It would be extremely unusual, for example, for an adult to refuse to pass a pencil or a piece of paper upon request when the object was physically closer to the addressee than to the speaker. Such events are commonplace with the children in our sample, where such a request may be responded to with retorts such as *Get it yourself* or *I ain't giving you nothin'.* Requests that have little cost are generally honored by adults and, according to Ervin-Tripp (1976[a]) familiar peers commonly use the imperative in making such requests. Although it is true that the children commonly use the imperative form to their peers and sometimes to adult addressees, it is not true that these requests are generally honored. They frequently insist upon courtesy phrases from each other and even when "please" or "pretty please" is used, compliance, although it is more likely, is not guaranteed. The frequent noncompliance to even simple requests and the equally frequent use of such responses as *Who you think you talkin to?* and *You ain't none of my mama,* indicates the children are constantly on guard against challenges to their status and to their rights; and, given the frequency of such challenges, with good reason.

A common occurrence involved the use of an imperative by a child to one of the adult researchers: *Give me a pencil* or *Drive me home.* Typically, these imperatives were not softened by tone of voice or other amending devices, but were made in the tone of a demand. The most usual response from the adult was noncompliance, frequently with some sort of comment that pointed out the inappropriateness of the directive form. When this occurred, the child would rephrase the directive by adding please, a pleading tone, or imbedding the request. The rephrasing was often accompanied by smiling and laughing as though the whole episode had been a joke performed for the amusement of the other children, and, indeed, humor and performance, as well as challenges to status, are functional elements of such speech events. We have labeled this use of directives as **imperative traps.**

(50) (7-year-old–11-year-old girl) *Bring your li'l self here.*

This directive met with a good deal of laughter from the audience and a retort from a third party: *Who you think you are?* The 7-year-old's reply was, *I think I'm somebody big.*

Indeed, to succeed in directing the behavior of a peer in this way is treated by the children as a coup of sorts. They tended to treat compliance to what was viewed as an imperious directive as a loss of face, and unless the adult researchers conformed to this system, the children intervened with metalinguistic comments.

An 8-year-old girl once interrupted a conversation between one of the researchers, who had her foot on a chair, and another adult with: *I want that chair.* Continuing to talk, the researcher removed her foot and the child began to push the chair toward a table where other children were drawing. There was a marked silence on the part of the other children present and then a flurry of comments from the children, including *O-o-o-o Claudia, you gon' let her talk to you like that?* Seeing an expression of smug satisfaction on the face of the girl, the researcher made a feint toward her as if to retrieve the chair and the child hastily added, *Please.* The other children present all laughed; satisfied and pleased with the "comeuppance," as it were.

(51) (Girl 11 years to girl 12 years) *Hey ya'll, I told Betty to come here and she came.*

The statement above was addressed to an audience of peers when Betty responded compliantly to the directive *Hey, Betty, come here* addressed to her by a peer, Sharon. Betty was the butt of an imperative trap.

The children in this study were highly sensitive to the form a directive took for a variety of reasons. Imperative traps such as the one above are a device used to gain a temporary advantage of a peer. These traps typically occur in the presence of an audience of peers, and their message to the audience and interlocutor alike seems to be *See how grand I am, I can make people do my bidding.*

Imperatives play a role in the status striving of the children in another way which may give the addressee rather than the speaker an opportunity to "score."

(52) S: (Girl 12 years–girl 12 years) *Gimme that ruler.*
A: *Huh?*
S: *Gimme that ruler, girl.*
A: *Huh?*
S: *Will you please gimme the ruler before I knock you down.*

In the above case, the addressee is attempting to force a courtesy phrase from the speaker because courtesy phrases have a value as submissive gestures. That is to say, the use of a courtesy phrase is viewed as self-subordination, which, in turn, gives status to the individual who is the target of the deference. In this case, however, the outcome is a standoff. The submissive value of please is offset by the threat, and compliance was achieved.

The majority of efforts to subordinate a peer are not serious. They are, nevertheless, efforts to gain an advantage at the expense of a peer, and the garget of this kind of ploy is generally irritated and embarrassed unless, as in the previous case, he is quick enough to reply in a way that leaves both egos intact. Similar events occurred, however, in a more serious tone. They are especially aggravating to the children, because there is the expectation that these ploys, and many other forms of verbal abuse, are supposed to be taken in stride. Like insults, imperative traps may function as jokes. There are, however, occasions when a hearer feels that the more central function of the trap is a more serious put-down, and that the speaker is embedding his aggressive verbal gesture in a joke. As with an insulting joke, real indignation seems out of place as a response, as does anger. What is necessary is a similar insulting joke (see Mitchell-Kernan and Kernan, 1975).

In the example which follows, this appears to be what is happening. An 11-year-old girl was narrating a fight she recently had with a peer, emphasizing how she had gotten the best of the other child. A member of the audience let it be known in a series of oblique remarks that who won the fight was not as clear as the speaker was attempting to convey. A short time later, the "kibitzer" attempted to gain possession of the microphone from the girl whose boastful claims had been challenged.

S: *Lemme see the mike for a minute.*
A: *Huh?*
S: *Aw come on girl.*
A: *Huh.*
S: *I ain't gon beg you.*

The addressee's effort to elicit a courtesy phrase was viewed by the speaker as a serious attempt to force a submissive gesture. The speaker, however, refused to supply an amended request, because she viewed the motivation for this ploy on the part of the addressee, as a desire for retaliation for her own previous challenges to the addressee's veracity.

SUMMARY

On the basis of the directives exhibited in the role-play data, and in their spontaneous speech, we can say that the children in our sample have acquired all of the conventional forms that directives may take in American English. The children use all of the six major types of directives described by Ervin-Tripp (1976[a] and this volume) for adult American English. Although the children ranged in age from 7 to 12 years, there was no apparent difference by age in their ability or willingness to use the various types. Not only have the children acquired all of the forms appropriate for directives, they show an awareness of at least some of the social factors that help to determine which directive form is to be used on a particular occasion. Imperatives, for example, were directed much more frequently to persons of equal and lower rank than they were to persons of rank higher than the speaker. While it may be the case that more of the role-playing situations involved persons of equal status than persons of unequal status, it is nevertheless the case, that in every interaction in which one person is of higher rank, there must be one other person of lower rank. Yet imperatives were directed to persons of lower rank more than five times as often as they were directed to persons of higher rank. The preponderance of imperatives used in the role-playing data was, in part, a function of the situations portrayed in the role-play, and the type of interpersonal functions they were intended to serve. That is to say, the directives were used to accomplish interpersonal functions in addition to serving more strictly instrumental purposes.

The communicative competence of the children in regard to the use of directives, then, includes at least two of the functional aspects of directive use: the identification and comprehension as directives of utterances that have some other surface form; and the selection of particular directive forms on the basis of situational appropriateness.

The interpersonal goals that influence the choice of directive type among the children are in some cases peculiar to children's culture in the way they are elaborated. It is not that adults do not engage in status striving, but, rather that the means by which this is accomplished by the children represents a particular tradition of children's culture. In our consideration of interpersonal functions, we have engaged in some speculation about the underlying motives of the interlocutors. We acknowledge that the attribution of motives is inherently problematical, but view such attribution as integral to the interpretive process that takes place in much social interaction. That this is the case seems dramatically exemplified in the status games played by the children. These status games put in bold relief the interpersonal functions that choice of directive type may serve. Such games would, of course, be impossible in the absence of a set of normative constraints on directive choice. The use of an imperative as a status elevating device would be impossible in the absence of the conventional association of the use of this form to an addressee of rank lower than the speaker.

From the perspective of the addressee, there are interpretive problems involved in the use of the imperative by a peer. These problems arise from the status meaning which adheres to the imperative, and are accentuated by the importance of imperatives in status manipulation ploys. Unlike the ambiguity which may result from the use of a sentence modality type that permits a directive to be interpreted as an information question or a statement, the ambiguity inherent in the use of an imperative to an equal does not lie at the level of speech act

Part III

Social Meaning

Comprehension and Use of Social Rules in Pronoun Selection by Hungarian Children[1]

MARIDA HOLLOS

INTRODUCTION

Although there is increasing evidence in psychology, psycholinguistics, and sociolinguistics that social, cognitive, and linguistic development in children should be perceived as the development of separable but interdependent systems, the nature of this interdependence is just now beginning to be explored. Ervin-Tripp and Cook-Gumperz (1974), for example, view the relationship in the following manner:

> We can argue that the social development of the child and linguistic development have a mutual dependence; his communicative needs motivate his development of the formal means. On the other hand, his strategies are constrained by his **capacities** to handle the formal devices available in his grammar, phonology, and sociolinguistic norms around him [p. 3].

This position is basically in agreement with that of Piaget and his collaborators (Piaget 1970, Sinclair deZwart 1969), who claim that language development is preceded by the development of logical operations which provide an underlying structure for the former. Similarly, Slobin (1973[a]) believes that

> Every normal human child constructs for himself a grammar of his native language. It is the task of developmental psycholinguistics to describe and attempt to explain the intricate phenomena which lie beneath this simple statement. These underlying phenomena are essentially cognitive. In order for the child to construct a grammar: (*a*) he must be able to cognize the physical and social events which are encoded in language; and (*b*) he must be able to process, organize and store linguistic information [p. 175].

1. This research was supported by NIMN Research Fellowship MH 32855-01.

Others, for example, Bruner and his associates (1966), claim that it is language that provides the major stimulant and the major mode of developmental reorganization in conceptual growth. There is increasing evidence (Shatz and Gelman 1973) that even very young children have a considerable range of alternate linguistic repertoires and forms which demonstrate their sophistication in understanding social situations and rules. The interesting problem, then, is the relationship of these social and linguistic skills to logical or extralinguistic cognitive operations. What kinds of cognitive operations does the child have to be capable of before he can communicate certain ways? Obviously, his knowledge of social features will influence his strategies and rules in communicating, but is it this **knowledge** that enables him to communicate successfully? Is the comprehension of social and linguistic rules a sufficient precondition of communicative competence, or is there another kind of cognitive operation that is required? Or conversely, can we argue that it is a knowledge of social and linguistic rules that may serve as a stimulant for the development of cognitive structures? Since operational structures develop, and the knowledge of social and linguistic rules are acquired in some sort of a social context, examining the effects of different environments on these areas should illuminate their relationship and order of development.

This chapter explores the differences between the understanding or knowledge of, and the use of, certain social rules in pronoun selection by children who grow up in two different social settings within the same culture area. Three age groups of children living in two locations were tested on two tasks. The tasks, a multiple choice test and a role-playing test, were designed to measure the differences between the children's knowledge of the adult personal pronoun system, and their ability to play the role of various adults by utilizing that knowledge. The tasks also allowed the examination of the differences in strategies that are utilized by the different age groups in both comprehension and production. Since it was assumed that different social environments would have an effect on both the acquisition of sociolinguistic knowledge and the development of perspectivism or role-taking ability (the operational component), two locations were chosen that differed systematically on those dimensions, which presumably would have most impact on these areas, namely, the relative complexity of the adult role system and the amount of verbal and social interaction that children were exposed to. The measures and their relation to the social settings are used to examine the interrelationships between the acquisition of social and linguistic rules and the development of logical structures.

The tasks that were developed for this research are based on the complexity of the Hungarian personal pronoun system. Social roles and relationships in Hungary are linguistically marked and categorized by a system of address terms and pronouns that are used each time individuals interact, and which involve a series of morphological and syntactical changes on the sentence level. The use of a particular term depends on the relationship of both the speaker and the listener and the context of the social situation. The terms communicate such metalinguistic features as deference, intimacy, solidarity or distance. The adult system contains four terms: familiar (T), formal (V), polite (P) and formal-polite (VP); the children's only two: familiar and polite. Space does not permit the more detailed description of either system here. (For details, see the appendix.)

The child in Hungary hears the differences in the adults' speech from the time he begins to understand it and from the time he begins to communicate. From an early age on, he must not only learn to differentiate between the category of persons with whom he uses the familiar or the polite, but he also becomes aware of a more complex differentiation used by the adults around him. In one sense, this can be considered social and linguistic rule learning, in another it might be thought of as a training in role differentiation and cognitive complexity. Children who grow up in an environment that is relatively nonverbal, and where interaction between individuals is infrequent, might receive less training in both of these areas than children who are exposed to constant interaction between large numbers of people. On the other hand, children in both these environments learn the same language and the same linguistic rules, the major difference being that the isolated children have less opportunities for actually observing the rules in operation and for practicing their skills at interaction and communication. The following, then, is a comparison of children growing up in relative isolation with children living in a town on two tasks designed: (*a*) to measure the comprehension of the adult personal pronoun system, as measured by their ability to recognize the appropriate form used between different adults, and (*b*) to measure the ability to play the role of others by acting out the role of these adults. The comparison of the two groups' performance on these tasks should enable us to understand some of the problems related to cognitive and linguistic development. For example, it will be possible to see whether the isolated children learn to comprehend the rules of the adult pronoun system as well as the town children, and whether they are also able to take the role of others as well. If they perform equally well on the task designed to measure the understanding of the adult system, but are less capable of assuming the role of others, we will be able to answer some of the questions posed at the outset, and advance suggestions regarding the relationship between the development of linguistic and logical structures.

METHOD

Settings

The two groups of children came from two communities in rural Hungary (Hollos 1975[b]): from a dispersed farm area where families live in relative isolation and the opportunities for interaction with peers and adults is limited, and from a town in the same general culture area. There were no systematic religious, linguistic, or ideological differences among the communities. All of the children who were tested lived in intact nuclear families. All families were "working class" or peasant, with relatively low incomes, and the type and amount of schooling received by parents and children in the two groups were virtually identical.

The dispersed area is situated in the middle of the Hungarian plains, surrounding the town of Nagykőrös. Families of the children studied reside on isolated farms within an area owned and cultivated by one of the local cooperatives. There are no paved roads in the area, and the majority of the nonpaved roads are only semipermanent and become almost completely nonnegotiable in the winter and rainy season. Most of the residents are members of the cooperative and work in groups on assigned tasks that most often take them some distance away from the homestead. Since cooperative members are entitled to a privately owned parcel on the communally owned land which they independently cultivate, the majority of the women also work. The combination of cooperative labor and private cultivation results in adults leaving the home at an early hour, and returning late in the evening when they occupy themselves with the feeding and care of the animals.

Most of the early learning experiences of the children take place in and around the farm, either in the company of the mother, the grandparents, or an older sibling. Prior to school age, the children rarely leave the farm, with the possible exception of being taken to the grandparents' homestead by a mother on her way to work, or to the family's parcel where they spend the day while the mother occupies herself with her tasks. Since the average number of children per family is two and the average age difference between siblings is about 3 years, interaction takes place only with older or younger individuals, almost never with contemporaries. Children spend most of their time within the farmyard, or in colder months in the kitchen, in solitary play or observing others. Most adults are either absent during most of the day or are engaged in performing a variety of chores in the immediate proximity of the child. Older siblings are also recruited for work from an early age on. Schoolchildren walk to attend the local district school for half a day during the first 4 years. Their walk most often leads through unoccupied farmland where they only infrequently encounter other residents. Opportunities for after-school social interaction, or for the development of play groups are limited, since children are required to help contribute to the family's economy by taking care of the animals, and must return home immediately after school.

Interaction and communication between adult members of the family is limited to the evenings. Adults return late from their day's work on the cooperative's fields and during most of the evening are occupied with chores. By the time they are finished, the younger children have gone to bed. Older children are allowed to remain up longer, but since most of the farms have no electricity, especially in the dark winter months, adults also go to bed relatively early. Interaction with nonfamily members occurs infrequently. Godparents visit on the child's birthday or name's day, and occasionally a farmer may briefly stop by on his way home from work to exchange information or to drink a glass of wine. Children are almost never taken to visiting. The only opportunities for leaving the farm community come when they accompany adults to the town's market, to the yearly fair, or possibly to the doctor.

The town, Nagykőrös, with a population of 15,000 inhabitants, is the major marketing and administrative center for this area, as well as a traditional cultural and educational center of some importance for this part of the country.

Most of the houses are one-family dwellings surrounded by yards, vegetable gardens, or orchards. The structure of the families here is similar to that of the farm area. Most of the mothers also work, and the care of young children (over age three) is entrusted to grandparents, neighbors, or older siblings. From an early age on, children are allowed to leave the house alone and play with neighbor children. They have large peer groups with whom they spend a large amount of their time, and are free to roam around inside or outside of the town without adult control. They are only infrequently required to help around the house or perform chores, since most of these families do not have animals that need pasturing or feeding. Taking care of younger siblings is the most usual task entrusted to the older children, which they frequently perform by taking or carrying the younger children around all day, paying only minimal attention to them. Most of the activities of the town children occur in groups. Interaction, however, is not limited to peers; children also encounter a number of known and unknown adults in a variety of social settings (their friends' houses, shops, markets, etc.). The time spent at home or alone is relatively short.

Interaction and communication between family members is more frequent than on the farms. Since the adults have no or less evening chores around the house, evenings are often spent at home with the others in the family, or with neighbors or relatives who often come by. In general, these families seem to be more verbal than their isolated counterparts.

In summary, while the communities and the samples of children tested were similar in many aspects, the major differences between the two environments were due to their relative size and complexity which, from the child's point of view, resulted in different opportunities for social-verbal interaction. The farm children spent a great deal of time with one adult, and without peers, and met a limited number of other adults outside of the family, and participated in a less verbal family setting in the evening.

Subjects

In each setting 15 children were tested, 5 at each of three age levels: first group (7-year-olds), second group (8-year-olds), third group (9-year-olds). Approximately equal numbers of males and females were selected. At both locations, the subjects were chosen on the basis of random sampling.

Measures

In constructing a measure testing the children's **role-taking** ability (see Hollos 1975[b]), the basic assumption made was that there are three specifiable levels of development (based on Piaget's and Flavell's work), which should be reflected in the children's ability to use the adult personal pronoun system: (*a*) The child is egocentric and is only able to project his own knowledge; (*b*) the child can imitate the external behavior of others; and (*c*) he can play the role of a hitherto unknown other by extrapolating from the role system.

Field observation in the two communities has shown that the individuals a child comes in contact with may be divided into three groups ranging from the most to the least familiar. For the purposes of the test, a set of pictures were drawn, depicting a variety of individuals in different kinds of interactions. The pictures were of three principal types, corresponding to the three levels of development mentioned above. The pictures designed to elicit the first level required the child either to play a child's role, or the role of an adult talking to a child. In the second level, the child had to play the role of an adult in a familiar role, thus making imitation easy (examples are such as: the mother in the grocery store, the father talking to the mailman, and father talking to grandfather). In the third level, the children had to be able to extrapolate from the pronoun system and could not imitate since the roles were more or less unknown (examples: father talking to his boss at the cooperative office, a farmer talking to a tractor driver). Since the role and the personal pronoun system is considerably complex in Hungary, the measure was constructed so that even the least familiar roles depicted in the pictures were local and not totally unknown to the child.

The child was shown the pictures and the various figures were identified by the examiner. Questioning then took forms such as: "How does your mother greet the shopkeeper when she goes shopping? Ask for some eggs, as your mother would." If the child could not supply the entire sentence, it was given by the examiner in indirect discourse. The child then had to change it to direct discourse appropriate to the adult in the picture.

A point system for scoring was devised, based on a scoring system devised by Flavell for a role-taking task (1968). As expected, the children found the use of the reciprocal V, which is not used in their own system, and which is not used between family members and between adults most familiar to them, the hardest.

No child of any age group in either social setting was able to consistently use this form throughout the pictures. The highest score (4 points) in this age group was therefore given for an inconsistent use of the reciprocal V, which required a recognition of the existence of the form, and an attempt at playing virtually unknown roles. On the other extreme, the majority of the children, even in the youngest groups, were able to play all child roles and the roles of the adults interacting with children. Successful playing of these roles was therefore set as minimum requirement and received the score of one. Two points were given for imitation of less familiar but frequently encountered adult roles which required the use of the P (for example, mother/storekeeper), and which were easy to imitate. Three points were given if the child played those roles which were unfamiliar but did not require the use of the V (for example, friends/parents). In all instances, the judgment of correctness of the children's response was based on information elicited from the adults in that community.

The multiple choice test was based on the choice of the three levels of personal pronouns–familiar, polite, and formal–and their use by the adults in the two communities. A set of 12 pictures and 16 cut-out figures were drawn by a local artist depicting familiar figures of different ages, sexes, kinship positions, and occupations. The person in the picture was supplied with a statement (request or question) that he presumably addressed to one of three cut-out figures, which were identified and arranged in a group next to him. The three figures, if possible, were selected so that there was a different personal pronoun appropriate from the sender to each of them, and therefore the sentence in the form given would be correctly addressed to one of them. The child had to select the correct addressee and explain the reason behind his choice. In some situations, when more than one person could be addressed by the same term, or when the use of the same term could reasonably be justified with more than one of the characters, and the child could explain his choice, it was also considered correct. In any case, if the child gave an incorrect answer he was quizzed about his choice, and frequently, even if his first choice was appropriate, he was asked how the major figure would address all three individuals. Some examples are the following: Mother, using P asks: *Did you leave the door open?* The choice is between: (*a*) grandfather (appropriate form P); (*b*) child (appropriate form T); and (*c*) veterinarian (appropriate form V). Doctor, using V, states: *You have to take this medicine three times a day.* The choice is between: (*a*) a stranger from the city (appropriate form V); (*b*) grandmother (appropriate form P), and (*c*) teacher (appropriate form V).

In evaluating the results, the interest was not only in correctness vs. incorrectness, but also in determining the different strategies used by the different age groups of children, and the semantic features that their systems contained. At this point the town and the farm children will be discussed together since there was no difference in the strategies the two groups employed.

As in the role-taking task, errors made on the multiple-choice test clearly differentiated between adult roles, which were more or less familiar to the child. Similarly, children at this age level found the recognition of the distinction between the choice of P or V in the adults' speech problematic. On the basis of the most common errors, the development of the children's comprehension of the adult system may be arranged in the following order:

1. The items in which one of the addressees was a child, and the speaker (adult or child) was speaking in T, or where children were speaking in P (to adults), were found to be the easiest. Most of the children encountered no difficulties with this set, probably due to the fact that this was essentially a reproduction of the child's own system.
2. Nor did they have difficulties, in general, in assigning the mutual T to adults speaking or being addressed by adults. In most cases, the children clearly differentiated between adults who are on familiar terms from those who are not, probably since this is used most frequently between family members and other well-known adults.
3. A large number of children correctly assigned the V where familiar adults were using it. However, in the youngest age group the following type of error was often found: **Godmother**, using V, addresses the mother, the doctor, and the storekeeper. The appropriate choice is the storekeeper, but younger children frequently answer as the child would do.
4. Familiar adult (mother), using P, was a frequently missed item. For example, **Mother**, using P, addresses the veterinarian, the grandfather and the child. Instead of correctly choosing the grandfather on the basis of his age, children chose the veterinarian, basing their choice on his higher status or on his strangeness, perhaps assuming that strangers are addressed in P. Unfortunately, no other item existed where a familiar adult spoke in P, however, this example may be contrasted to the following one: **Father**, speaking in V, addresses the doctor, grandmother, and godmother. The appropriate choice here is the doctor and most children select this, so that it seems the problem lies in the use of the P by familiar adults to strangers.
5. By far the most common error was on items where unfamiliar adults were speaking in P or V. It seems that in the case of adults children were not familiar with, the simplest strategy to assume was an egocentric one. The child extended his own system and assumed that P is used by unfamiliar adults to adults of any category since this is what he would do.

In summary, the younger children used the following rules in differentiating the system used by adults and children:

1. Children use T to children and receive the same from other children.
2. Children use P to adults and receive T in return.

3. Adults who are friends or family use the reciprocal T with other adults unless one of them is considerably older. Adults who are not friends do not do this.
4. Familiar adults use V to unfamiliar adults of the same status and P to people with higher status (or to strangers).
5. Unfamiliar adults use P to all other unfamiliar adults.
6. When confronted with unfamiliar adults using V, the children in this age groups are confused.

The results seem to suggest that even at the earliest of the age levels the children distinguish between the P/V use of familiar adults, but have difficulties in assigning the same distinction to unfamiliar adults. By the time they reach the highest age level (9 years), the number of errors becomes very small in both of the groups, most of which occur with unfamiliar adults using V.

On the basis of these features, a point system for scoring was devised which was basically very similar to the scoring used on the role-taking test. Four points were given to the children who almost always correctly distinguished between the unfamiliar adults' use of P and V. Three points were given to those who made errors on these items but dealt successfully with familiar adults, two to those who could not distinguish the features any adult (familiar or unfamiliar) would apply to differentiate between the use of P or V, but who differentiated between these and the adults' use of T. Children who had a good knowledge of the children's system only received a score of one.

The children were also ranked on the basis of the absolute number of errors they made. However, it was found that the "number of errors" score closely corresponded to the point score and since the point score was more directly comparable to the scoring used on the role-taking task, the "number of errors" score was not used in the final data analysis.

Results

In the following, the differences between the performance of the town and farm children on the two tasks will be discussed. Mean values for the role-taking and the comprehension tasks for the three ages at the two locations are given in Table 1.

An analysis of variance indicated significant **location** effects for both the role-taking task (*F* for 2 and 23 *df* is 7.81, p .01) and the comprehension task ($F = 4.13, p < .05$). Also, the mean values in Table 1 indicate that the town children achieve higher scores on both measures for all comparisons at all ages, with the exception of one, the comprehension scores for 8-year-olds where the means are identical. The farm children never do better at any age level on either measure.

TABLE 1

Mean Values on Role-Taking and Comprehension for 7-, 8-, and 9-Year-Old Town and Farm Children

Age	Role-Taking	Comprehension
Farm		
7	1.80	2.00
8	2.80	3.20
9	3.00	3.40
Town		
7	3.00	3.20
8	3.00	3.20
9	3.80	3.80

The analysis for **age** effects revealed a significant effect for both measures (F for role-taking with 4 and 46 df is 4.84, and F for comprehension is 4.90). The difference between the measures is much less pronounced for the age groups than it is for location effects, although inspection of the mean values of Table 1 suggest that the town 7- and 8-year-olds are not differentiated by either measure as much as are the farm 7- and 8-year-olds. Interaction of age and location effects was not significant.

As can be seen by inspecting Table 1, the mean values for the comprehension task are always higher for all groups at all ages, than those for the role-taking tasks, with the exception of the 9-year-old town children, where the means are identical. This, however, is not surprising since the mean score of 3.80 indicates a near perfect performance by this group on both tasks. The differences in the value of the F statistic for the two measures (7.81 for role-taking and 4.81 for comprehension), clearly indicates the more difficult nature of the role-taking task. The groups are differentiated much more by the effects of this task than by those of the comprehension task.

DISCUSSION

The results indicate that although there is a significant difference in the overall performance of the town and the farm children, both groups scored higher on the comprehension test than on the role-taking measures. In other words, their different exposure to social situations and adult roles in the two environments, as previously described, made a less significant difference in their **comprehension** or **knowledge** of the appropriate linguistic form to be used. On the other hand, the difference in their ability to **process** and **use** this knowledge by playing the

FIGURE 1

Graph of Mean Values on Role-Taking and Comprehension for 7-, 8-, and 9-Year-Old Town (T) and Farm (F) Children. (——): Role-Taking. (– – –): Comprehension.

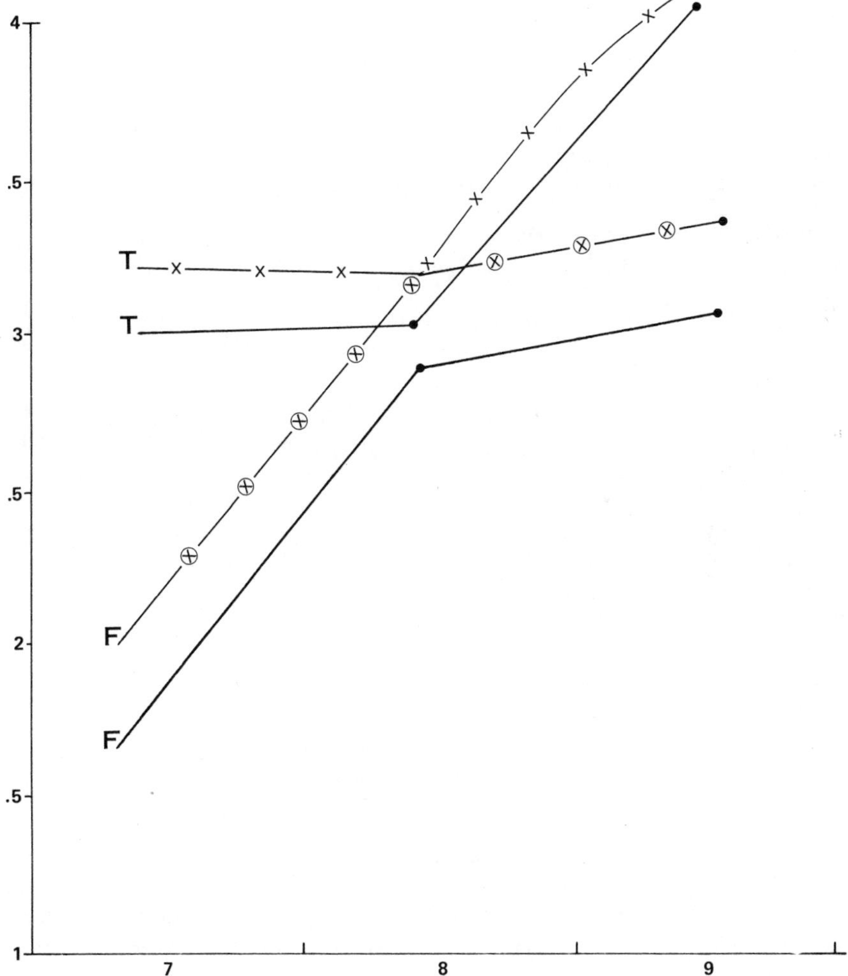

role of others was strongly affected by their environment. (Thus, general communicative ability should be considered to consist of two distinct operations,[2] linguistic and extralinguistic.) Since children who could not yet perform the role-playing task performed well on the comprehension task, the data suggest that the acquisition of the linguistic forms and comprehension of the social features that govern their use may precede the development of this general communicative ability, but in itself is not a sufficient precondition for it. A knowledge of linguistic forms and social rules alone does not enable the child to play different roles, for which he has to acquire a cognitive operation, which enables him to switch perspectives with others.

APPENDIX

Hungarian Personal Pronouns and Rules for Pronoun Selection

When addressing others, Hungarian adults choose between four alternative levels as reflected in the following constructions:

1. Familiar, **te** plus 2nd pers. sing verb. (T)
2. Formal, **maga** plus 3rd pers. sing verb. (IV)
3. Polite, a construction of title plus last name, honorific plus last name, honorific plus first name plus 3rd pers. sing. of the verb tetszeni (to wish, to like, to please) plus infinitive of the main verb. (P)
4. Formal-polite **on** plus 3rd pers. sing verb. (VP)

The children's system contains only the familiar (T) and the polite (P).

With some modifications, the semantic dimensions of the adult system might be depicted on Brown and Gilman's (1960) two-dimensional figure:

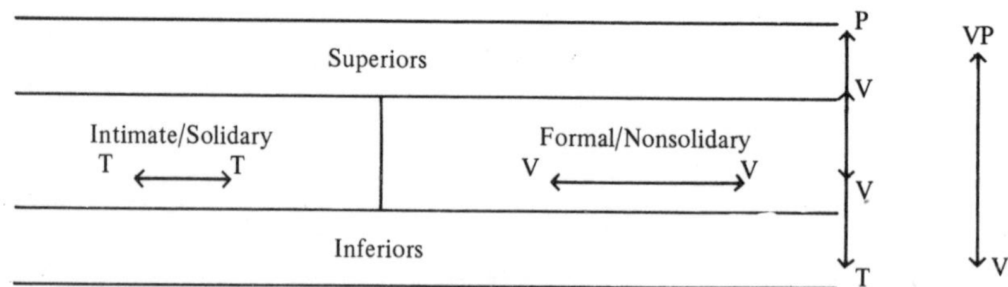

2. The particular type of logical operation referred to here as a possible precondition to performance may be called **reversibility of perspectives,** a component in perspectivism or the ability to take the other's perspective (role-taking). This kind of logical operation is extralinguistic. The difference in scores in comprehension vs. performance seems to indicate that comprehension is possible before this operational component is present, but for performance it is a precondition.

In the adult system, the **reciprocal T** is used between kin of the same ages, between all kin up to two generations removed in the town, and in both communities between same sex friends, same sex co-workers, or organization co-members, and between opposite sex intimates. A range of subtle differences along the power, or status, difference axis, and in formal distance may be communicated by the choice of various nonreciprocal forms or the reciprocal V. The **reciprocal V** is used between persons of the same status who are neither solidary nor intimate (for example, between most males/females, customer/clerk), in situations where the status difference is minimized by working together (for example, boss/worker), and in cases where the status or age difference is not considered sufficient for using the nonreciprocal forms (for example, waiter/customer, officer/soldier). The **nonreciprocal P/T** is used between adults who have a considerable age difference, the younger adult addressing the older with a P and receiving T. (Formerly, this form was also used between persons of considerable status difference, as for example, master/servant.) Persons with considerable status difference (especially in the rural area) use the **nonreciprocal P/V** (as for example, veterinarian/farmer). The **nonreciprocal VP/V** is used mostly in formal applications, or in situations where, not venerance (as with using P/T and P/V), but formal distance, is communicated (for example, in addressing a high functionary or maitre d'/customer). This form is only rarely used in rural areas and was, therefore, not included in the task given to the children.

Children use the **reciprocal T** with other children or younger persons of both sexes (until they reach adolescence) and in the town with all kin, except with the grandparents. In the rural areas the reciprocal T is not used with any older kin: parents, grandparents and godparents receive P and return T to the children. In the town, this nonreciprocal system is used with all nonkin adults.

Acquisition of an Aspect of Communicative Competence: Learning What It Means to Talk Like a Lady

CAROLE EDELSKY

LANGUAGE AND SEX: AN INTERPRETIVE SOCIOLINGUISTIC VARIABLE

Communicative competence, according to Hymes (1970:72), is the knowledge speakers have of the structure and meaning of sentences, the structure and meaning of the social world, and the relationship between the two. In subcategorizing that relationship, Hymes (1964[a]) has proposed several factors of speech events. Knowledge of characteristics of these factors (speaker, receiver, audience, channel, code, setting, message form, topic, and type of communicative event) and their interrelationships are proposed as fundamental to a speech community's system of communication. In systematically describing the communicative competence within a speech community, one may then start with any one of the factors and relate the others to it (Hymes 1964[b]:110).

There is ample documentation for some of the ways in which two of these factors, sex as a speaker characteristic and message form, are related in the productive communicative competence of widely varying speech communities (see Edelsky 1974, chapter 2). Communicative competence, however, involves both production and interpretation, including interpretations of social intent and judgments about appropriateness. People not only talk; they interpret language (including its absence) in the light of their expectation that the social structure will be enacted linguistically. In view of the power positions of the sexes, and the role attributes assigned and inculcated on the basis of sex, it is reasonable to expect that not only do people produce language differently depending on their sex, but, also, that they have the competence to interpret language as sex-linked. In other words, people in our society should have knowledge of the roles of women and men, should have a stereotype involved in "acting like a woman/lady," and as a subset of that, should have a stereotype encompassing "talking like a lady." They should have competence, then, with judging the appropriateness of hypothetically produced alternations (Ervin-Tripp 1971) involving speaker sex and language. The judgments would constitute part of a stereotype, part of the general knowledge of adults, regardless of whether that knowledge conforms to actual language production (Labov 1972[d]). As such, this knowledge would allow people, if they were inclined to make use of the stereotype, to evaluate the language (and by extension, the speakers), they might hear. Such general knowledge would enter into identifying, via actors' lines, the degree to which characters portrayed in the media play out traditional sex roles; understanding jokes whose point is homosexuality and which depend on both linguistic and paralinguistic cues to depict this; and making social evaluations of others. In short, they would enter into understanding the social meaning that can be conveyed by the choice of linguistic items.

THE STUDY

The purpose of this study was twofold: First, to document the agreement on sex stereotypes for linguistic features in the beliefs of adults (of "regular folks," not simply sophomores in psychology courses or linguists); and second, to find out changes with age in agreement on sex attributes of linguistic features. It is important to emphasize that the focus of, and data derived from this study, did not directly concern any differences in language production according to the sex of the speaker. Rather, this was a study on judgments, eliciting adults' and children's beliefs about how men and women talk.

The major findings were as follows: Adults exhibit knowledge that proves that a language/sex of speaker stereotype exists, and they show agreement on many of the particulars of the details concerning that stereotype; children show a gradual progression in their acquisition of the adult norms for linking language and sex roles, with first graders' interpretive competence bearing a minimal resemblance to adults; and with sixth graders' competence appearing quite like adults'; children can make judgments about the sex-appropriateness of language, but at different ages they use different strategies for making these judgments; and older children have more stereotyping of judgments about sex linkage of some linguistic forms than do adults.

Method

The subjects were 122 adults and 122 first, third, and sixth graders. There were 70 women, 52 men, 58 girls, and 64 boys, approximately evenly divided according to grade and sex of the experimenter. The adults were those present at a PTA meeting at a school in a white, middle-class, native English-speaking neighborhood in Albuquerque, New Mexico, and also some older graduate students enrolled in late-day courses at a university. Several of these people lived in the neighborhood of the school previously mentioned. The children were those first, third, and sixth graders (from two classes at each grade level) who had received parental permission to participate in the study. The children were enrolled at the school from which the PTA-attending adults comprised the adult sample.

All subjects were presented with a list of 24 printed sentences and were asked to choose who would most likely say each sentence, men, women, or both men and women with equal likelihood. Adult subjects were instructed to include in their concept of women or men all English-speaking American females or males of all ages, all social classes, all life-styles; in short, to think of women or men **in general**. Children were "trained" to answer the test (they had to put an *X* on one of three pictures; a man, a woman, or a woman and man pictured together) with four preliminary sentences. The "adult answers" (male, female, neutral, neutral, respectively) to these four sentences *(What in blazes is going on here? What for good gracious sakes is going on here? What exactly is going on here? What's going on here?)* were given to the children. This served a double function: First, it allowed for ensuring that children knew how to mark the intended answer (an *X* on the man's head pictured with the woman would be considered a neutral response. If a child intended to indicate that "men say that" rather than "both men and women say that," the child had to mark the picture which showed only a man); it also suggested to children that they were to try to imagine how adults would answer the test sentences, that they were to use adult-like interpretations.[1] The sentences presented to children were read aloud (in a flat voice while pointing to each word–to convey the impression that the reader was not encoding the language, but was merely reading aloud already encoded language) by either a male or a female experimenter. This was to ensure that the test results would not be influenced by reading ability.

There were 12 language variables presented in the 24 sentences. Each variable or form appeared twice, combined with two topics which were deliberately chosen for their sex-neutrality in order to encourage people to focus on the form

1. At this point, it is necessary to point out that children and adults had different tasks to perform. The language and the speakers about which judgments were to be made were adult. That means that adults were "native speakers," making judgments about their own culture. Children, on the other hand, were "immigrants," making judgments about their destined reference group, but not about their own child-culture. If each group had been asked to interpret language as appropriate to their peers of each sex, a more comparable task would have been presented to all groups. However, since acquisition of a particular set of language beliefs was the major issue, providing a comparable judging task for each group would have precluded an examination of acquisition of the adult norms. I found no satisfactory solution to this dilemma.

rather than the topic. The 24 sentences are presented below in pairs with the forms in bold type. On the test, the pairs were separated, no bold type appeared, and the presumably male, female and neutral items did not appear in clusters:

1. *That's an* ***adorable*** *story.*
2. *That's an* ***adorable*** *movie.*
3. ***Oh dear,*** *the TV set broke!*
4. ***Oh dear,*** *I lost my keys!*
5. ***My goodness,*** *there's a friend of mine!*
6. ***My goodness,*** *there's the president!*
7. ***Won't you please*** *get me that pencil?*
8. ***Won't you please*** *close the door?*
9. *I was* ***just*** *exhausted.*
10. *I was* ***just*** *furious.*
11. *I was* ***so*** *mad.*
12. *I was* ***so*** *tired.*
13. *I was* ***very*** *mad.*
14. *I was* ***very*** *tired.*
15. *That was a great show,* ***wasn't it?***
16. *They did the right thing,* ***didn't they?***
17. ***Close*** *the door.*
18. ***Get*** *me that pencil.*
19. ***Damn it,*** *the TV set broke!*
20. ***Damn it,*** *I lost my keys!*
21. ***I'll be damned,*** *there's a friend of mine!*
22. ***I'll be damned,*** *there's the President!*
23. *I was* ***damn*** *mad.*
24. *You're* ***damn*** *right.*

The variables (in bold type) are message forms which Lakoff (1973) has proposed are linked to a particular sex because they are linguistic signals of traits such as powerlessness, strength of expression, confidence, etc., which are also assigned on the basis of sex. The variables, as has been noted, each appeared twice on the written instrument. This provided a measure of consistency. From that measure, it was possible to infer whether people were responding to the form in question or whether they were being influenced by a shift in topic.

Another source of inference about the part of the sentences on which all the people at a given age focused when making their written responses came from interviews which were conducted with 10 subjects at each age chosen at random from the group that had already taken the written test. During these interviews, people were asked again to judge the sentences[2] for sex-appropriateness, to identify the sex-linked cue in the sentences, and to explain the sex-appropriateness of the cues they identified.

The two kinds of responses, written forced-choice and oral open-ended, provided several kinds of information about one aspect of the communicative competence of four age groups as groups, and of individuals within those groups. It is possible that communicative competence is the property both of the community and of an individual. If it belonged, in some sense, only to individuals, then the notion of shared knowledge of sociolinguistic rules would exempt from membership in a speech community those people whose rules did not completely overlap, those who were "dialect deaf" (Labov 1966), and those whose production of registers differed (Weeks 1970). Since even judgments of grammaticality vary from speaker to speaker (Labov 1971:161), it is hardly reasonable to expect unanimity in the interpretation of sociolinguistic variables. It seems appropriate, then, to talk about interpretive communicative competence in terms of percentages of people within a group who make a given judgment. Using the written responses, which provided such percentages, a variable was designated as having a group definition, so that *Oh dear,* for instance, was defined as female by adults but not by first graders. Although the definitions were derived from nonunanimous written responses, the fact that a specific definition accurately reflected adult knowledge of the stereotypes was revealed during the interviews. Although it happened that a variable just barely met the criteria (which appear on Table 1), on the basis of written responses, during the interviews, **all** adults could focus on and sex-link that variable. The reverse (a large percentage of sex-linked written responses leading to an unquestionable group definition, and an inability of adults to agree on and to identify the variable in question) never happened.

Both written responses and interview data also revealed the possibility of a substantive, rather than merely a numerical, division between high and low consensus interpretations. The high consensus variables may be ones which are perceived as categorically sex-linked. Labov (1971) notes that there may be a receptive factor which causes people to be consciously oblivious to a certain variable (a dropped final "g" in "-ing," for instance) when it is produced up to a certain frequency and which, when production exceeds that frequency, causes a categorical perception expressed in a judgment that Speaker *X* "always drops his 'g's'." Such categorical perceptions, according to Labov, often occur in relation to behaviors for which there exist strong social values about standards of role performance. If people tend to perceive Speaker *X* or speakers from

2. Children who were interviewed were presented with some additional sentences which had not been included in the written instrument. These were nonsense sentences (such as *Oh dear, the flig jibbed*), and also sentences where a conflicting topic and form were deliberately juxtaposed (for example, *Won't you pretty please get me that hammer?*).

Category *X* as always using language Item *Y*, it is possible that they might also perceive language Item *Y* as always (or only) used by speakers from Category *X*. Language items which would be perceived in this way, as always being associated with one or the other sex, would get near unanimous agreement as to sex-linkage from judges, would not be influenced by topic in their interpretation, and would receive the same interpretation regardless of variations in the judging task.

Adult Judgments

Adults' written responses revealed that they share Lakoff's (1973) beliefs concerning linguistic differentiation by sex, as can be seen on Table 1.

TABLE 1

Definitions of Variables According to Age of Subjects[h]

Variable	Age[a]	Response types: M	M/W	W	Definition[b]	Difference between adjacent groups
Adorable	A	.005	0	.995	W*	**[c]
	6	.01	0	.99	W*	
	3	.01	.19	.80	W*	
	1	.12	.26	.62	W	
Damn it	A	.65	.32	.03	M	****[d]
	6	.89	.11	0	M*	
	3	.86	.09	.05	M*	
	1	.77	.16	.12	M*	
Won't you please	A	.03	.39	.57	W	++++[e]
	6	.02	.27	.71	W*	
	3	.04	.36	.60	W	
	1	.27	.29	.44	El.	
Damn + adjective	A	.69	.27	.04	M	****
	6	.87	.11	.02	M*	
	3	.73	.22	.05	M*	
	1	.64	.15	.21	El.	
My goodness	A	.01	.11	.88	W*	+++[f]
	6	0	.18	.82	W*	
	3	.04	.34	.62	W	
	1	.22	.40	.38	El.	
I'll be damned	A	.85	.12	.03	M*	++++
	6	.96	.04	0	M*	
	3	.81	.14	.05	M*	
	1	.51	.21	.28	El.	

Table 2–Continued

Variable	Age[a]	Response types M	M/W	W	Definition	Difference between adjacent groups
So	A	.03	.52	.45	W	+++
	6	.05	.59	.36	W	
	3	.30	.51	.19	El.	
	1	.22	.40	.38	El.	
Tag question	A	.11	.59	.30	W	+++
	6	.11	.56	.33	W	
	3	.14	.60	.26	M/W	
	1	.25	.45	.30	El.	
Very	A	.04	.54	.42	W	**
	6	.12	.38	.50	W	
	3	.26	.47	.27	El.	
	1	.40	.26	.34	El.	
Oh Dear	A	.01	.03	.96	W*	**
	6	0	.04	.96	W*	
	3	.06	.22	.72	W*	
	1	.30	.12	.58	El.	
Just	A	.03	.31	.66	W	***[g]
	6	.13	.43	.44	W	
	3	.18	.50	.32	El.	
	1	.41	.27	.32	El.	
Command	A	.33	.63	.04	M/W	***
	6	.45	.45	.10	M	
	3	.42	.39	.19	El.	
	1	.51	.21	.28	El.	

[a] A = Adults; 6 = sixth graders; 3 = third graders; 1 = first graders.

[b] W* = Female, high consensus; W = female, low consensus; M* = male, high consensus; M = male, low consensus; M/W = neutral; El. = eliminated (did not meet criteria for definition).

[c] Form for which the number of consistent, predicted responses were different beyond .05 on chi-square analysis for third and sixth graders, but not for sixth graders and adults, with older subjects' responses of this type exceeding those of younger subjects.

[d] Form for which number of consistent, predicted responses were different beyond .05 on chi-square analysis for sixth graders and adults, with sixth graders' responses of this type exceeding those of adults.

[e] Same direction of difference as ****, but not significant beyond .05.

[f] Same direction of difference as ***, but not significant beyond .05.

[g] Form for which number of consistent, predicted responses were different beyond .05 on chi-square analysis for adults and sixth graders, with adults' responses of this type exceeding those of sixth graders.

[h] Criteria for Definitions: *Sex-linked on Basis of High Consensus* (M* or W*) = 70% or more responses at one sex-linked pole and less than 15% opposite sex responses. *Sex-linked on Basis of Low Consensus* (W or M) = Less than 60% M/W responses and less than 15% opposite sex responses. *Neutral* (M/W) = 60% or more M/W responses.

We have distinguished as high consensus those judgments about which there was maximum agreement, and as low consensus those judgments about which there was partial agreement. Supporting evidence for the distinction comes from the fact that there was more reliability or intrasubject consistency in judging those forms for which there was considerable intersubjective agreement. The form **adorable**, for instance, elicited a female judgment, regardless of the topic with which it was paired **(intrasubject consistency)**, and regardless of the subject making the judgment **(intersubject agreement)**. This was not the case with *very* or *so* or the other low consensus sex-linked items.

Although the extent of intersubject agreement was built in to the definition that divided the two kinds of forms, the extent of intrasubject consistency was not. It would have been possible, according to the criteria for definition, for people to respond consistently to two sentences containing one form and to still disagree with each other. It was less likely, however, that a form would be defined as high consensus sex-linked in the first place (all responses to both instances of that form were tabulated in order to arrive at each definition), if each subject did not also respond consistently to that form. Therefore, three chi-square analyses were performed on intrasubject consistent responses to items defined as low as opposed to high consensus variables. One analysis compared inconsistent responses made to categories based on the definitions derived from counting responses to both sentences. The other two analyses took the definition of one sentence for each form, categorized the sentences (W*, W, M*, M, or M/W), and compared the categories reflecting amount of consensus on one sentence with consistency in regard to both sentences. All the analyses revealed a difference significant beyond .001 between inconsistent responses to low as opposed to high consensus forms. For adults then, high consensus female language, for example, was judged female always, regardless of the judge and regardless of the topic. Interpretations of low consensus female language varied, depending on the judge, the topic with which it was paired, and the judgment task.

The effect of task became clear when adults were interviewed. At that time, all adults were able to isolate all the language variables being tested from their sentence frames, to identify them as the ones carrying the social meaning, and to justify their sex-appropriateness by matching features of the forms with assigned sex-role traits. Even though many of the adult interviewees frequently disclaimed any personal belief in, or approval of, the interpretations they gave, they all clearly shared knowledge of the language/sex-role stereotype.

Since acquisition of adult norms of interpretation was the orientation of this study, and since, as we have seen, the adult group definitions derived from percentages of written responses were verified during the interviews with adults, at each age level each subject's response to a sentence could be considered right or wrong against the standard of the adult definition for the variable contained in that sentence. A *t*-test performed on responses congruent with the group's definitions, and a chi-square analysis of sex of subject differences in types of responses revealed that women more often made sex-linked rather than neutral responses, more often agreed with the total group's definitions, made fewer responses which were polar opposite to the definition, and were less influenced by a shift in topic.

Children's Knowledge of Adult Norms

Children's performance clearly differed from that of adults. Table 1 shows both the distribution of response types to each variable at each age and the definition each group gave to the variables. Table 2, the summary of Table 1, presents a clearer picture of the gradual nature of the acquisition of this particular aspect of communicative competence.

TABLE 2

Variables Meeting Criteria for Definition, and Definition, According to Age of Subjects[a]

	Age groups			
Variable	First graders	Third graders	Sixth graders	Adults
Adorable	W	W*	W*	W*
Damn it	M*	M*	M*	M
Damn + Adjective	–	M*	M*	M
I'll be damned	–	M*	M*	M*
Oh dear	–	W*	W*	W*
My goodness	–	W	W*	W*
Won't you please	–	W	W*	W
Tag question	–	M/W	W	W
So	–	–	W	W
Very	–	–	W	W
Just	–	–	W	W
Command	–	–	M	M/W

[a]W* = Female, high consensus; W = female, low consensus; M* = male, high consensus; M = male, low consensus; M/W = neutral; – = not meeting criteria.

At first grade, children could agree among themselves enough to provide a group definition for only two variables, *damn it* and *adorable.* Children's responses were submitted to the same three kinds of chi-square analyses for consistency of response that were performed on the adult data. Whether sentences were categorized, for the purposes of the analyses, according to the adult definitions concerning high or low consensus or according to children's definitions for each sentence in a pair, the high/low consensus distinction was irrelevant intrasubjectively for first graders. They responded as inconsistently to both instances of *adorable* as they did to both instances of *damn it* or commands (they defined one sentence containing a command as high consensus male; the other did not elicit enough agreement to reach a definition).

The strategy first graders used in making written responses could be inferred from the interviews. Very few of these youngest subjects were able to identify the forms at all as carriers of sex of speaker meaning. Instead, even though the topics had been chosen for their neutrality, first graders focused on topic as the factor in speech events which signaled sex-linked meaning to them. In fact, they did this to a desperate extent. Not only did some believe *Oh dear, the TV set broke* was male "because my dad watches TV" or female "because my mom watches TV when she's ironing," but they sought topical justifications everywhere. They linked words like *broke, movie, tired* and *I* to one or the other sex and gave topical justifications. Even nonsense sentences *(The wik slupped my damn flip)* evoked these interpretations. Some children assigned this sentence to women "because women say 'wik' more" possibly associating *wik* with candles, candles with home, and home with women. When a sentence was presented with a conflicting form and topic, even a form for which first graders had a stereotype *(Damn it, get me that perfume!),* topic outweighed form in saliency.

The two forms whose adult-like sex-linkage had been learned by first grade required two areas of knowledge: first, that a particular domain (home, clothing, babies, small things) was sex-linked and that an adjective used in describing this domain (*adorable*) carried the same sex-linkage; and second, that a particular sex-linked stereotype concerning anger/meanness/badness could be signaled linguistically via *damn it* and was therefore more likely for the angry/mean/bad sex. To first graders, *damn* in any other context, however, was not heard as either profane or male. In strong contrast with adult norms, *damn* used in connection with nonanger, as in *I'll be damned,* had its male association especially reduced. Although (+rough) was one of the male features of profanity for adults too, other features adults used were (+strength) and (+conviction). Comments like "if you say, 'My gracious, the TV set broke', it doesn't mean anything" and "Men would use 'damn' any old place, not just when something awful happens, to let you know they mean business" were heard from adults. First graders, on the other hand, kept referring to *damn* as a "mean word" in connection with catastrophe or explicitly stated anger. Without that specific emotional content, a sentence containing *damn* was often interpreted using topical strategies again. (*I'll be damned, there's a friend of mine!* was female because "ladies like to go places with their friends.") For young children, then, there was no all-inclusive concept of profanity with the same content as the adult concept. Instead, they had a notion of "bad word" with the features (+anger), (+mean), and (+bad).

By third grade, there was enough agreement among subjects to provide a group definition for all adult-defined male items, all female items adults defined with high agreement, and one other, *won't you please.* The low consensus female forms, the adverbs and tag question, were still responded to on the basis of topic by some children. A new competing strategy, besides the topical one, had emerged, however, at this age. When some children did not immediately recognize some form as sex-appropriate, rather than hunting for a topic/sex-role activity link, they simply claimed neutrality for that sentence, whether in written responses or during the interviews.

The high/low consensus distinction and its implication for consistency was made by third graders. Chi-square analyses revealed that when third graders agreed with each other (or when they agreed with adults), they also were more likely to agree with themselves, and respond consistently to both sentences containing a single form rather than shift their responses with a shift in topic.

During the interviews, third graders were able to identify more of the forms being tested as carriers of social meaning, although none could identify them all. That they were in a transition period between strategies focusing on form and strategies focusing on topic, can be seen from the following exchange which took place during an interview:

EX: *Who says "Won't you pretty please hand me the hammer?"*
CH: *The lady.*
EX: *Why?*
CH: *Cause of "pretty please."*
EX: *How about "Won't you pretty please hand me the baseball uniform?"*
CH: *Maybe a boy.*
EX: *Why?*
CH: *Cause of "baseball uniform."*

Where sixth graders, because of their commitment to associating language forms and speaker sex, defended their case for claiming that females might talk about a cross-sex topic (a baseball uniform), the third graders, new to that association, switched their allegiance from form back to topic when the conflict became too great for them. When third graders did link topic and speaker sex, they agreed with each other about the sex of the topic (men get mad, watch TV, and take women to shows). This was not the case for first graders.

By third grade, interview responses to the forms whose sex-linkage had been learned revealed a knowledge of clichés (*"men swear but ladies don't," "ladies are polite"*) and their linguistic expression. Also, they showed an awareness of the linguistic means to signal niceness and absence of swearing in addition to meanness.

Sixth graders defined all the variables, except for command, the way adults did, although to some forms, profanity and *won't you please,* their intersubject agreement exceeded adults'. While adults differentiated between the profane forms, granting more influence to topic in connection with *damn it,* but assigning *damn* in connection with surprise or conviction more consistently to men, sixth graders (and third graders also) assigned all profanity overwhelmingly to men.

While most of the definitions were verified by interview responses, sixth graders' definition of tag question appeared to have been accidentally adult-like. In the sentence *That was a great show, wasn't it?,* many identified *great* as the sex-linked cue. It should be noted here that *great* is a form, not a topic. As was mentioned earlier, the major difference between third and sixth graders was the latter's ability to maintain a focus on form. When they were not able to make judgments using the same form adults used, they used another form, but their strategy remained message-form oriented as adults' was.

Chi-square analyses showed that, like adults and third graders, sixth graders made more consistent responses to those forms on which they showed maximum intersubject agreement, and also to those forms which received categorically sex-linked responses from adults.

In the interviews, many sixth graders were able to identify almost all the variables being tested, including the adverbs, as the sex-linked language items. No third graders had this ability. Only two sixth graders, and no younger children, were able to isolate tag questions.

By the sixth grade, the justifications given for the sex-appropriateness of linguistic forms concerned role attributes more varied than meanness and niceness. Sixth graders said that *"they can get away with more," "men need to feel relief,"* while women would be stigmatized for using relief-giving forms. They said that other language forms were more appropriate for women on the basis of appeals to Nature (*"Eve talked that way so now all women do too"*), and because women are more religious, have less power, are more concerned with setting a good example for their children and making an impression, and are more patient. Furthermore, several children at this age felt that certain forms (*just, adorable, so*) were examples of unusual, slightly inferior, and "mooshey" language, and that men would not use such language because they, but not women, talk like (are?) regular people.

Responses to the items learned between third and sixth grade showed that sixth graders had the knowledge that weakness and elaboration of expression are presumably sex-linked traits, and that some adverbs, since they weaken the relation between the speaker's convictions and the topic following the adverb, are a linguistic means for displaying such traits. The item that only adults were aware of, tag questions used to elicit agreement rather than information or the instigation of a conversation, requires a knowledge that a reduction of conviction can be accomplished by violating a rule of speaking—the rule that the speaker believes that the addressee will believe what is said. The relation of syntax, of tag questions, to underlying rules of speaking is evidently the most difficult relationship to understand and to identify as being linked to the sex of the speaker.

The Judging Process

It is interesting at this point to speculate on the nature of the judging process as it changes with age. During the interviews, it appeared that even though adults were told that they were not being asked about what they believed particular people they knew would say, or whether they believed that language **should** be viewed as sex-appropriate, but that they were merely being asked if they were aware of some folk-linguistic notions, they were not immediately able to reveal their awareness in relation to all the items. Categorically female items, *I'll be damned,* and *damn right,* immediately called forth knowledge of the stereotype. In one sense, it was almost as though adults used a formula to make judgments about these items; a formula that would include casual profanity as male, absence of profanity in exclamations as female, and adoring and trivializing adjectives (*darling* and *divine* were two additional adjectives presented to adults), as female. However, it was not simply that adults appeared to make judgments in these cases using formulas, but also, that only in these cases, they believed those formulas to be representations of reality. Subjects said men would never use *divine* unless they were mimicking women or homosexuals. Others believed that although some subgroups or women might swear even more than men, on the whole, women would not use casual profanity as often as men. Even in the face of discrepancies between performance and beliefs about performance, this insistence on the truth of these formulas was maintained. One subject, male, said men would not use *Oh dear* "because it's a protected word, more passive, that men don't use." This statement was separated by an interval of about 10 minutes from the following one, made by the same subject. "I can't come up with anything. Oh dear, I'm just going to run the tape down."

The remaining variables, however, did not elicit this immediate outpouring of the stereotype. Instead, adults may have done several things simultaneously: reflected on their experience with the heard frequency of the variables; tried to invent a range of contexts in which each sex might conceivably say that sentence; and matched those inventions with the reflections on their experience. Evidence for these invented contextualizations comes from volunteered comments such as "Well, men would talk politely to their secretaries more than to their wives," "I'll bet when women are with other women (male subject), they swear just as much as men," "If it's a male character on certain TV shows and he's saying 'I was so mad,' I know he's playing a homosexual or effeminate character." These volunteered contextualizations were usually initial responses. Initial sex assignments for the sentences were also often neutral. It was only after further questioning ("Some people say that sentence is female. Do you know why they would think so?") that the subjects were willing to tap their knowledge of the stereotype.

The nature of the judging process in children appeared to be similar, but different in the extent to which the strategies could be used. Children, too, appeared to invoke and believe in a formula when it was available to them. At first grade, the formula par excellence was *angry, bad word* = ***damn it*** = *man.* At third grade, there were two: *profanity* = *male; niceness* = *female.* At sixth grade, niceness had become subdivided into politeness, substitutes for profanity, and "love word" adjectives. When a formula was not available, however, children, like adults, tried to match their experience with the sentence and choices presented. The youngest used their parents as reference points, including comments about *my mom* or *my dad* in most nonformula explanations. The ability to reflect on men or women (with the exception of *damn it* and men) in the abstract, in relation to these sentences, was not apparent until at least third grade.

The sentences where a topic and a form or two forms may have conflicted (*please* + *hammer, damn it* + *lipstick, I'll be damned* + *adorable,* etc.), which were presented unsystematically and to which responses were not subjected to any formal analysis, may have artificially helped children contextualize somewhat. When such sentences were presented, as mentioned earlier, the older children found it necessary to justify their maintenance of a formula in the face of a change of context. The younger ones shifted their focus entirely and reverted to topical strategies.

Information on possible reflections on experience and invented contexts was not volunteered by younger children. When they said a sentence was neutral, further questioning produced fidgeting, apparent discomfort, and utter silence. Sixth graders were better able to endure and respond to further questions, and also volunteered information about the contexts they were imagining. Commands, for instance, were heard as being directed to children. Directives, both the naked command and the elaborate *won't you please,* were contextualized with home as the setting and the child as the addressee, according to both a formula and a political reality: *She* ***has*** *to be polite because we won't do it if she doesn't say 'please', but if a man doesn't say it, we sure will anyway,* and *The man is thought of as the king of his house or something and he can tell you what to do, and the lady just* ***wants*** *you to close the door while the man tells you to and* ***expects*** *you to do it.*

Two Patterns of Acquisition

The picture displayed so far has been one of a gradual movement toward adult norms in the acquisition of knowledge of the language form/sex-role stereotype. In terms of an ability to provide a group definition for all the forms, to isolate those forms, to explain them using role attributes, to use form rather than topic strategies, and to give more consistent written responses to the entire test, increasing age and increasing abilities were related. This picture, however, is slightly misleading. As can be seen on Tables 1 and 2, some of the language variables which were identified as sex-linked on the basis of low consensus among adults were defined as sex-linked on the basis of high consensus among children. If we only look at the written responses, it appears that more children than adults were aware of the language stereotype in regard to those items. The interviews showed that this was not true. Nevertheless, some account must be made for the fact that significantly more predicted, consistent responses to profanity and *won't you please* were made by sixth graders than by adults, while for other items, consistency increased significantly with age.

Since it was apparent that first graders were responding overwhelmingly to topic, if first graders' responses are eliminated, and each language variable being tested is analyzed separately in order to compare only responses that were at the same time consistent intrasubjectively, consistent intersubjectively, and adult-like in response type, it is possible to begin a stepwise comparison of oldest to next oldest subjects to see if the differences in numbers of predicted, consistent responses are significant. The farthest right column on Table 1 shows that for all female items (except *won't you please*) and command, either the adult and sixth grade consistent, predicted responses were alike and exceeded third grade responses, or that more adults responded with predicted, consistent response types. In other words, there was no significant drop-off in stereotypy for these items. The other four items, profanity, and one rather superficial example of politeness, on the other hand, do not show this steady increase. Instead, predicted, consistent responses to these items peaked at the sixth grade level and then decreased at adulthood. Figure 1 is a graphic representation of the division of variables into two patterns, depending on the peak age of predicted, consistent responses.[3] The two patterns may be related to two kinds of learning of sociolinguistic knowledge.

3. Elsewhere, these two patterns have been divided differently because only raw numbers, rather than statistical analyses, were used. When using only raw numbers (converted to percentages) of consistent, predicted responses, the division is as follows: Pattern A–*adorable, oh dear, my goodness, just, so,* tag question, command (as a neutral variable); Pattern B–*damn it, I'll be damned, damn* + adjective, *won't you please, very,* and command (as a male variable). The inclusion of command (as male) and *very* in Pattern B is still consistent with the argument of availability of clichés that aid in judgments and lead to overgeneralization in childhood. *The man is the king of the house* and *Men are the boss* appeared in the interview data. *Very* may be a more obvious mechanism to children than *so* or *just* for "adding extra words" and therefore for fitting the cliché that "ladies gab."

FIGURE 1

Percentage of Consistent, Predicted Answers to Pattern A Variables

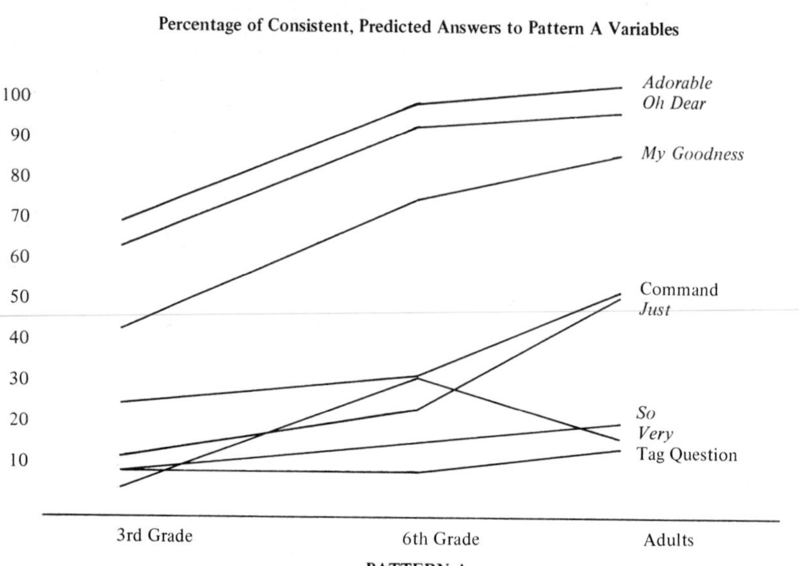

PATTERN A

Percentage of Consistent, Predicted Answers to Pattern B Variables

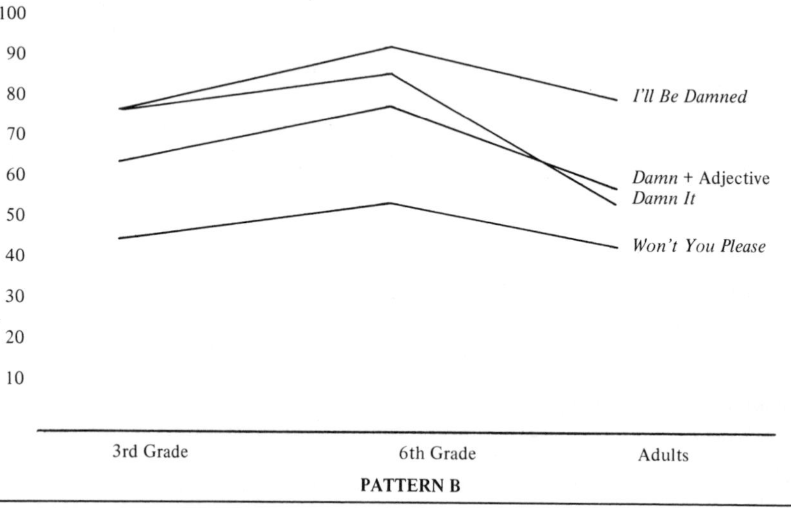

PATTERN B

Pattern B, one of an increase in intersubjective agreement until older childhood, and then a decrease at adulthood, may partially arise through explicit statements or available clichés, and may therefore be learned deductively. Clichés such as *men swear but ladies don't* and *ladies are polite* not only exist generally, but were also repeated by children during the interviews. They were mentioned by adults, too, it must be noted, but usually after adults had said the statements were neutral and had then been subjected to the *Some people say. . .* variety of further questioning. It appears, in relation to profanity, at least, that with first graders, an isolated routine (*damn it = bad word = man*) is learned first. Then an abstract rule is learned deductively with the help of explicit cultural teaching (the inductive learning enters when children have to learn what constitutes swearing linguistically), and is overgeneralized to the point where anything profane is male. The overgeneralization shows up as greater stereotypy in childhood. Later, at adulthood, the rule is differentiated to account for other contextual features which adults consider at first (topic, setting, audience, event, etc.), factors which are not implied in the overstatement contained in the cliché.

When looking at written responses only, then, it appears that adults and younger children, in their low consensus and their inconsistency, are using similar judgment strategies in relation to these items. However, we are claiming here that adults' susceptibility to the influence of topic was a different and more educated strategy than was young children's. For all the sentences presented during the interviews, adults eventually isolated all the forms being tested as the sex-linked variables, even though they also volunteered knowledge to the effect other factors might have, often giving *it depends* answers–*it depends on who you're talking to, what's happening, who's there, etc.* Further, adults never justified their associations topically; i.e., they never said that watching TV or using pencils or seeing friends was sex-linked, that, therefore, one sex or the other would talk about these topics more, and that, thus, the presence of that topic in the sentence was the reason for their choice of sex-assignment. The youngest children were not able to isolate the forms in question, maintained their focus on topic, and almost exclusively gave the kind of topical justifications just mentioned.

Pattern A, on the other hand, was one of a steady increase in consistent, correct responses with no decrease at adulthood. The recognition of the sex-appropriateness of these variables would have to be learned inductively. (Probably no one tells children, "Women say 'adorable', but men don't.") This implies that there might be a "kernel of truth" in peoples' beliefs about the sex-linkage of certain linguistic forms in order for the inductive learning to occur. Studies of actual usage rather than beliefs about usage would, of course, be necessary here. Because the variables in this pattern either have no corresponding cliché (*adorable*), are negative instances of folk-sayings (*my goodness* and *oh dear* can be considered examples of not-swearing), are more subtle examples of role stereotypes (the adverbs and tag questions are less obviously related to notions that women cannot make up their minds, lack conviction, do not mean what they say, etc.), or are non-sex-role associated (command as an adult-defined neutral variable), children would be less likely to have an abstract statement ready and accessible to help them mediate their judgments. Their responses would then be less likely to take on characteristics of overgeneralization. Adult responses to these variables, however, may occasionally take on those characteristics.

The use of the term **overgeneralization** in this study has several meanings, and needs to be explained further. The meanings concern undifferentiated categories, consensus, and maintenance of belief in the face of conflicting evidence.

First, by overgeneralization we mean the use of a single rule encompassing only factors of form and sex of speaker to interpret several variables (a rule that would make all the variables equivalent instances of one category), while the more mature members might use several more complex rules (including factors of topic, audience, settings, etc.) for interpreting these same variables (rules that allow the judge to rank the variables on the dimension named by the category). The numerical data reported on Figure 1 and on Table 1 and the responses during the interviews provided evidence for the claim of overgeneralization in this regard. Interpretations of profanity were overgeneralized in this sense by older children, while judgments about female-linked adjectives and expletives were overgeneralized in this sense by adults.

Second, by overgeneralization we mean more consensus among the immature than the mature members of a speech community. Numerical data from Table 1 alone provide the evidence for this. It is questionable that children were more aware of the sex-of-speaker meaning signaled by profanity and *won't you please* than adults were. Instead, it is probably the case that children, again, were not accounting for other contextual factors when they made their responses. The interviews revealed that adults did recognize the sex-linkage of these variables, but their explanations also included a recognition of the influence of participant relationships, settings, and topics on the use of such forms. It is presumed, therefore, that their written responses, displayed on Figure 1, also took such factors into account, and resulted in a greater number of neutral responses from adults than from children.

A third meaning of overgeneralization is rigidity of belief even when reality violates the content of the belief. Nonnumerical evidence for this meaning was provided in the interviews. Before starting the taping of several of the children, the experimenter fumbled around with the cord and said, *Damn it, I can't get this thing plugged in.* Later, in response to follow-up questions such as *Do women ever say 'Damn it!'*, many of the older children responded negatively despite their recent exposure to a female speaker uttering that same form. The cliché children articulated (men swear, but ladies don't) evidently had more impact on their beliefs than empirical evidence. It should be remembered that adults did this too in relation to overwhelmingly female-judged expletives. (Although adults' greater sophistication may have precluded their use of the straightforward rule contained in the cliché in regard to profanity, they may still have been applying the latter part of the cliché when judging items they categorized as absence-of-profanity.)

Sex of Subject Differences

The finding that women were more sensitive to the sex-linkage of forms was not apparent in young children. First grade boys were somewhat superior to girls in their ability to consider that there might be linguistic correlates of sex roles. By the third and sixth grade level, girls had caught up to boys so that both sexes were equally aware of the sex-appropriateness of forms.

CONCLUSION

This study of the knowledge and strategies displayed at four age levels in interpreting language in line with a language/sex-role stereotype shows that people at all ages were willing to make such judgments, although the judgments, focus, and strategies used at various ages differed. It also showed that the area of communicative competence involving knowledge of certain language stereotypes is subject to considerable change during the elementary school years.

Bibliography

Abrahams, Roger D.
1970 *Deep down in the jungle* (2nd ed.). Chicago: Aldine.

Aksu, Ayhan
1973 "The development of request forms in Turkish children." Unpublished manuscript, Berkeley, California.

Ames, Louise Bates
1966 Children's stories. *Genetic Psychological Monographs.* 73:2 337-396.

Austin, John L.
1962 *How to do things with words.* Cambridge, Massachusetts: Harvard Univ. Press.

Bailey, Charles-James N. and Roger W. Shuy (Editors)
1973 *New ways of analyzing variation in English.* Washington, D.C.: Georgetown Univ. Press.

Barker, Roger G. (Editor)
1963 *The stream of behavior: Explorations of its structure and content.* New York: Appleton.

Barker, Roger G. and Herbert F. Wright
1951 *One boy's day: A specimen record of behavior.* New York: Harper and Row.

Bates, Elizabeth
1976[a] *Language and context: The acquisition of pragmatics.* New York: Academic Press.

Bates, Elizabeth
1976[b] Pragmatics and sociolinguistics in child language. In *Language deficiency in children,* edited by D. Morehead and A. Morehead. Philadelphia: University Park Press.

Bateson, Gregory
1956 The message "this is play." In *Group processes: Transactions of the second conference,* edited by B. Schaffner. New York: Josiah Macy Foundation.

Bateson, Gregory
1972 *Steps to an ecology of the mind.* New York: Ballantine.

Bernstein, Basil
1971 A sociolinguistic approach to socialization: With some reference to educability. In *Class, codes and control: Theoretical studies towards a sociology of language,* edited by Basil Bernstein. London: Routledge and Kegan Paul. Pp. 143-169.

Bernstein, Basil and Dorothy Henderson
1969 Social class differences in the relevance of language to socialization. *Sociology* **3**: 1-20.

Bernstein, Louise
1969 Humor as an indicator of social relationships among Hawaiian children. Unpublished senior honors thesis. Department of Anthropology. University of Hawaii.

Bloom, Lois
1970 *Language development.* Cambridge, Massachusetts: M.I.T.

Bloom, Lois, Lois Hood, and Patsy Lightbrown
1974 Imitation in language development: If, when and why. *Cognitive Psychology* **6**: 380-420.

Bloom, Lois, Patsy Lightbown, and Lois Hood
1975 *Structure and variation in child language.* Monograph of the Society for Research in Child Development.

Blurton-Jones, Nicholas C.
1972 *Ethological studies of child behaviour.* London: Cambridge Univ. Press.

Boggs, Stephen T.
1972 The meaning of questons and narratives to Hawaiian children. In *Functions of language in the classroom,* edited by Courtney B. Cazden, Vera P. John, and Dell Hymes, New York: Teachers College Press. Pp. 299-327.

Boggs, Stephen T.
1974 "Summary of speech events involving part-Hawaiian children five years old and younger." Unpublished manuscript. Honolulu, University of Hawaii.

Boggs, Stephen T.
n.d. From the mouths of babes: Reflections of social structure in the verbal interaction of part-Hawaiian children. In *Adaptation and symbolism: Essays on social organization presented to Sir Raymond Firth by his students in North America, 1968-1974,* edited by Karen Ann Watson-Gegeo and S. Lee Seaton. Honolulu: Culture Learning Institute Monograph Series, East-West Center, University Press of Hawaii (in press).

Brady, Margaret K.
1975 "This little lady's gonna boogaloo": Elements of socialization in the play of black girls. In *Black girls at play: Folkloric perspectives on child development.* Austin, Texas: Southwest Educational Development Corporation.

Britton, James
1970 *Language and learning.* London: Allen Lane.

Brown, Roger
1973 *A first language: The early stages.* Cambridge, Massachusetts: Harvard Univ. Press.

Brown, Roger and Ursula Bellugi
1964 Three processes in the child's acquisition of syntax. *Harvard Educational Review,* **34**: 133-151.

Brown, Roger and Albert Gilman
1960 The pronouns of power and solidarity. In *Style in Language,* edited by Thomas Sebeok. Cambridge, Massachusetts: M.I.T. Press.

Bruner, Jerome S.
1975 The ontogenesis of speech acts. *Journal of Child Language.* **2**: 1-19.

Bruner, J.S., R. Olver, and P. Greenfield
1966 *Studies in cognitive growth.* New York: Wiley.

Carter, Anne
1974 Communication in the sensori-motor period. Unpublished dissertation. Berkeley, California: University of California.

Carter, Anne
n.d. The development of systematic vocalizations prior to words: A case study. In *Development of communication: Social and pragmatic factors in language acquisition,* edited by Natalie Waterson and Catherine Snow. New York: Wiley.

Cazden, Courtney B.
1974 Play and metalinguistic awareness: One dimension of language experience. *The Urban Review,* 7: 28-39.

Cedergren, H. and D. Sankoff
1974 Variable rules: Performance as a statistical reflection of competence. *Language,* **50**: 333-355.

Chomsky, Noam
1965 *Aspects of the theory of syntax.* Cambridge, Massachusetts: M.I.T. Press.

Chong, Edison, M.C.
1969 Untitled. Unpublished paper. University of Hawaii, December

Chukovsky, Kornei
1963 *From two to five.* Berkeley, California: Univ. of California Press.

Cicourel, A. V., K. H. Jennings, S. H. M. Jennings, K. C. W. Leiter, R. McKay, H. Mehan, and D. R. Roth
1974 *Language use and school performance.* New York: Academic Press.

Clark, Eve V.
1973 "What's in a word?" On the child's acquisition of semantics in his first language. In *Cognitive development and the acquisition of language,* edited by Timothy E. Moore. New York: Academic Press.

Clark, Herbert H. and Peter Lucy
1975 Understanding what is meant from what is said: A study in conversationally conveyed requests. *Journal of Verbal Learning and Verbal Behavior,* **14**: *56-72.*

Cook-Gumperz, J.
1975 The child as a practical reasoner. In *Sociocultural Dimensions of Language Use,* edited by Mary Sanches and Ben G. Blount. New York: Academic Press, pp. 137-162.

Cook-Gumperz, J. and J. Bowyer
1972 "The development of communicative skills in school sciences: An experiment using the SCIS program." Unpublished paper. University of California, Berkeley, Lawrence Hall of Science.

Corsaro, William
1975 Sociolinguistic patterns in adult-child interaction. Paper presented at American Sociological Association, San Francisco, August, 1975.

Davison, Anni
1974 Linguistic play and language acquisition. In *Papers and reports on child language development, special issue: Sixth child language research forum,* edited by Eve V. Clark. Stanford: Committee on Linguistics. Pp. 179-187.

Dore, John
1973 The development of speech acts. Unpublished doctoral dissertation. New York: City University of New York.

Dore, John
1976 Children's illocutionary acts. In *Discourse: Comprehension and production,* edited by R. Freedle. Hillsdale, New Jersey: Lawrence Erlbaum Associates.

Duncan, Starkey
1972 Some signals and rules for taking speaking turns in conversations. *Journal of Personality and Social Psychology,* **23:** 283-292.

Duncan, Starkey
1973 Toward a grammar for dyadic conversation. *Semiotica,* **9:** 29-46.

Eckhardt, Rosalind
1975 From handclap to line play. In *Black girls at play: Folkloric perspectives on child development.* Austin, Texas: Southwest Educational Development Corporation.

Edelsky, Carole
1974 Evidence for the existence and acquisition of an aspect of communicative competence: Recognition of sex of speaker from linguistic cues–or–knowing how to talk like a lady. Unpublished doctoral dissertation, University of New Mexico.

Ervin, Susan M.
1964 Imitation and structural change in children's language. In *New directions in the study of language,* edited by Eric H. Lenneberg. Cambridge, Massachusetts: M.I.T. Press, pp. 163-189.

Ervin-Tripp, Susan
1970 Discourse agreement: How children answer questions. In *Cognition and the development of language,* edited by John R. Hayes. New York: John Wiley. Pp. 79-107.

Ervin-Tripp, Susan
1971 Sociolinguistics. In *Advances in the sociology of language, Vol. 1,* edited by Joshua Fishman. The Hague: Mouton, pp. 15-91.

Ervin-Tripp, Susan M.
1973 The structure of communicative choice. In *Language acquisition and communicative choice: Essays by Susan M. Ervin-Tripp,* edited by Anwar S. Dil. Stanford: Stanford Univ. Press, 302-373.

Ervin-Tripp, Susan
1976[a] Is Sybil there? The structure of some American English directives. *Language in Society,* **5**: 25-66.

Ervin-Tripp, Susan
1976[b] Speech acts and social learning. In *Meaning in anthropology,* edited by Keith H. Basso and Henry A. Selby. Albuquerque: Univ. of New Mexico Press.

Ervin-Tripp, Susan and J. Cook-Gumperz
1974 "The development of communicative strategies in children." NIMH Grant Application MH26063, University of California, Berkeley.

Ervin-Tripp, Susan and Wick Miller
n.d. Early discourse: Some questions about questions. In *Interaction, conversation and the development of language,* edited by Michael Lewis and Leonard Rosenblum. New York: Wiley.

Fillmore, Lily
1976 The second time around: Cognitive and social strategies in second language acquisition. Unpublished doctoral dissertation, Stanford University.

Flavell, John H.
1968 *The development of role-taking and communication skills in children.* New York: Wiley.

Freedle, Roy O., Terrence J. Keeney, and Nancy D. Smith
1970 Effects of mean depth and grammaticality on children's imitation of sentences. *Journal of Verbal Learning and Verbal Behavior,* **9**: 149-154.

French, Robert
1975 An ethnography of speaking of the Belize Creole speech community. Unpublished doctoral dissertation, Harvard University.

French, R. and Keith Kernan
1974 "Art and artifice in Belizean Creole." Unpublished manuscript. University of California, Los Angeles.

Gallimore, Ronald, Joan Whitehorn Boggs, and Cathie Jordan
1974 *Culture, behaviour, and education: A study of Hawaiian-Americans.* New York: Russell Sage Publications.

Garvey, Catherine
1974 Some properties of social play. *Merrill-Palmer Quarterly,* **20**: 163-180.

Garvey, Catherine
1975 Requests and responses in children's speech. *Journal of Child Language,* **2**: 41-63.

Garvey, Catherine
n.d. Contingent queries. In *Interaction, conversation, and the development of language,* edited by Michael Lewis and Leonard Rosenblum. New York: Wiley, in press.

Garvey, Catherine and Robert Hogan
1973 Social speech and social interaction: Egocentrism revisited. *Child Development,* **44**: 562-568.

Givón, Talmy
1974 "Towards a discourse definition of syntax." Unpublished manuscript.

Gleason, J.
1973 Code-switching in children's language. In *Cognitive development and the acquisition of language,* edited by Timothy E. Moore. New York: Academic Press.

Goffman, Erving
1963 *Behavior in public places.* Glencoe, Illinois: Free Press.

Gordon, David and George Lakoff
1971 Conversational postulates. In *Papers from the VIIth regional meetings.* Chicago, Illinois: Chicago Linguistic Society.

Grice, H.P.
1968 Utterer's meaning, sentence meaning, and word meaning. *Foundations of Language,* **4**: 225-242.

Grice, H.
1975 Logic and conversation. In *The logic of grammar,* edited by I.D. Davidson and G. Harman. Encino, California: Dickenson Press.

Gruber, Jeffrey
1973 Correlations between the syntactic constructions of the child and the adult. In *Studies on child language development,* edited by D.I. Slobin and C. Ferguson. New York: Holt.

Gumperz, John J.
1972 Verbal strategies in multilingual communication. In *Language and cultural diversity in American education,* edited by Roger D. Abrahams and Rudolph C. Troike. Englewood Cliffs, New Jersey: Prentice Hall, pp. 184-197.

Gumperz, John J.
1974 Sociolinguistics of interpersonal communication. Working Paper No. 33. Centro-Internazionale di Semiotica e di Linguistica. Universitra di Urbino, Urbino, Italy.

Gumperz, John J.
1976 On the sociolinguistic significance of conversational code-switching. Working Paper No. 46. Language-Behavior Laboratory, University of California, Berkeley.

Gumperz, John J. and Eleanor Herasimchuk
1972 The conversational analysis of social meaning: A study of classroom interaction. In *Sociolinguistics: Current trends and prospects,* edited by Roger Shuy. Washington, D.C.: Georgetown Univ. Press, pp. 99-134.

Gumperz, John J. and Dell Hymes (Editors)
1964 *The ethnography of communication. American Anthropologist,* **66:** 6, Pt. II.

Gumperz, John J. and Dell Hymes (Editors)
1972 *Directions in sociolinguistics: The ethnography of communication.* New York: Holt, Rinehart, and Winston.

Halliday, Michael A.K.
1970[a] Functional diversity in language as seen from a consideration of modality and mood in English. *Foundations of Language,* **6:** 322-361.

Halliday, Michael A.K.
1970[b] Language structure and language function. In *New horizons in linguistics,* edited by John Lyons. Harmondsworth, England: Penguin, pp. 140-165.

Halliday, Michael A.K.
1973 *Explorations in the functions of language.* London: Edward Arnold.

Halliday, Michael A.K.
1975 *Learning how to mean: Explorations in the development of language.* London: Edward Arnold.

Holden, Majorie H. and Walter H. MacGinitie
1972 Children's conceptions of word boundaries in speech and print. *Journal of Educational Psychology.* **63:** 551-557.

Hollos, Marida
1975[a] Logical operations and role-taking in two cultures. *Child Development,* **46:** 638-649.

Hollos, Marida
1975[b] "If you please: The development of directives among Norwegian and Hungarian children." Paper presented at American Anthropological Association, San Francisco, November.

Holzman, Mathilda
1972 The use of interrogative forms in the verbal interaction of three mothers and their children. *Journal of Psycholinguistic Research,* 1: 311-336.

Hymes, Dell
1962 The ethnography of speaking. In *Anthropology and human behavior,* edited by Thomas Gladwin and William C. Sturtevant. Washington, D.C.: American Anthropological Association, pp. 13-53.

Hymes, Dell
1964[a] Formal discussion. In *The acquisition of language,* edited by U. Bellugi and R. Brown. Monographs of the Society for Research in Child Development, **29**(1): 107-112.

Hymes, Dell
1964[b] Introduction: Toward ethnographies of communication. In *The ethnography of communication,* edited by J. Gumperz and D. Hymes. *American Anthropologist,* **66:** 6, Pt. II, pp. 1-34.

Hymes, Dell
1970 Bilingual education: Linguistic vs. sociolinguistic bases. Washington, D.C.: Georgetown Univ. Press.

Hymes, Dell
1972[a] On communicative competence. In *Sociolinguistics,* edited by J.B. Pride and Janet Holmes. Harmondsworth: Penguin.

Hymes, Dell
1972[b] Models of the interaction of language and social life. In *Directions in sociolinguistics: The ethnography of communication,* edited by John J. Gumperz and Dell Hymes. New York: Holt, Rinehart and Winston, pp. 35-71.

Hymes, Dell
1974 *Foundations of sociolinguistics: An ethnographic approach.* Philadelphia: University of Pennsylvania Press.

Jacobs, Deborah
1973 "Request form alternations of five-year-old children." Unpublished term paper. University of California, Berkeley.

James, Sharon L.
1975 The effect of listener and situation on the politeness of pre-school children's directive speech. Unpublished doctoral dissertation, University of Wisconsin.

Jefferson, Gail
1972 Sides sequences. In *Studies in social interaction,* edited by David Sudnow. New York: Free Press.

Johnson, Harriet M.
1928 *Children in the nursery school.* New York: John Day.

Katz, Jerrold J.
1972 *Semantic theory.* New York: Harper and Row.

Katz, Jerrold J. and D.T. Langendoen
1976 Pragmatics and presupposition. *Language,* **52**: 1-19.

Kay, Paul
n.d. Language, evolution, and speech style. In *Sociocultural dimensions of language change,* edited by Mary Sanchez and Ben Blount. New York: Academic Press (in press).

Keenan, Elinor O.
1974[a] Again and again: The pragmatics of imitation in child language. Paper presented at the Annual Meeting of the American Anthropological Association.

Keenan, Elinor O.
1974[b] Conversational competence in children. *Journal of Child Language.* **I**: 163-183.

Keenan, Elinor O. and Ewan Klein
1974 Coherency in children's discourse. Paper presented at the Linguistics Society of America Meetings (summer).

Keenan, Elinor O. and B. Schieffelin
1976 Topic as a discourse notion: A study of topic in the conversations of children and adults. In *Subject and Topic,* edited by Charles Li. New York: Academic Press.

Kirtley, Basil F.
1971 *A motif-index of traditional Polynesian narratives.* Honolulu: University of Hawaii Press.

Labov, William
1964 Stages in the acquisition of standard English. In *Social dialects and language learning,* edited by Roger W. Shuy. Champaign, Illinois: National Council of Teachers of English. Pp. 77-104.

Labov, William
1966 *The social stratification of English in New York City.* Washington, D.C.: Center for Applied Linguistics.

Labov, William
1971 The study of language in its social context. In *Advances in the sociology of language,* Vol. 1, edited by Joshua Fishman. The Hague: Mouton. Pp. 152-216.

Labov, William
1972[a] *Language in the inner city: Studies in the black English vernacular.* Philadelphia: Univ. of Pennsylvania Press.

Labov, William
1972[b] Narrative analysis. In *Language in the Inner City: Studies in the black English vernacular.* Philadelphia: Univ. of Pennsylvania Press.

Labov, William
1972[c] Rules for ritual insults. In *Studies in social interaction,* edited by David Sudnow. New York: The Free Press, pp. 120-169.

Labov, William
1972[d] *Sociolinguistic patterns.* Philadelphia: Univ. of Pennsylvania Press.

Labov, William, Paul Cohen, Clarence Robins, and John Lewis
1968 *A study of the non-standard English of Negro and Puerto Rican speakers in New York City,* Cooperative Research Project No. 3288. New York: Columbia University.

Labov, William and J. Waletzky
1967 Narrative analysis. In *Essays on the verbal and visual arts,* edited by June Helm. Seattle: Univ. of Washington Press.

Lakoff, Robin
1973 Language and woman's place. *Language in Society,* **2:** 45-80.

Lambert, Wallace E., R.C. Hodgson, R.C. Gardner, and S. Fillebaun
1960 Evaluational reactions to spoken languages. *Journal of Abnormal and Social Psychology,* **60:** 44-51.

Lawson, Craig
1967 "Request patterns in a two-year-old." Unpublished manuscript. Berkeley, California.

Leventhal, Constance
1976 Sounding and verbal dueling among non-black students in integrated schools. Unpublished Master's thesis, University of California, Los Angeles.

Lewis, D.
1972 General semantics. In *Semantics of natural language,* edited by I.D. Davidson and G. Harman. Dordrecht, Holland: Reidel.

Macnamara, John and Erica Baker
1975 "From sign to language." Unpublished manuscript. Montreal, Quebec.

MacWhinney, Brian
1974 "Some observations on requests by Hungarian children." Unpublished manuscript. Denver, Colorado.

Menyuk, Paula
1963 A preliminary evaluation of grammatical capacity in children. *Journal of Verbal Learning and Verbal Behavior.* **2:** 429-439.

Mitchell-Kernan, Claudia
1971 *Language behavior in a black urban community.* Monograph No. 2, Language-Behavior Research Laboratory. Berkeley: University of California.

Mitchell-Kernan, Claudia and Keith Kernan
1975 Children's insults: America and Samoa. In *Sociocultural dimensions of language use,* edited by Mary Sanches and Ben G. Blount. New York: Academic Press, pp. 307-315.

Nelson, Katherine
1974 *Structure and strategy in learning to talk.* Monograph of Society for Research in Child Development. Vol. 37, No. 4.

Novinski, Lorraine
1968 Recognition memory in children for semantic versus syntactic information. Unpublished doctoral dissertation, University of California, Berkeley.

O'Connell, Beth Ann
1974 "Request Forms as a Measure of Social Context." Unpublished manuscript. Berkeley, California.

Opie, Iona and Peter Opie
1960 *The lore and language of school children.* Oxford: Clarendon Press.

Piaget, Jean
1955 *The language and thought of the child.* Cleveland: Meridian Books.

Piaget, Jean
1970 *Structuralism.* New York: Basic Books.

Reeder, Ken
1975 Pre-school children's comprehension of illocutionary force: An experimental psycholinguistic study. Unpublished doctoral dissertation, University of Birmingham, England.

Reisman, Karl
1970 *Contrapuntal conversations in an Antiguan village.* Penn-Texas Working Papers in Sociolinguistics No. 3. Austin: Univ. of Texas Press.

Reynolds, P.
1972 Play, language, and human evolution. Paper presented at the Annual Meeting of the American Association for the Advancement of Science, Washington, D.C.

Rodd, Linda J. and Martin D.S. Braine
1971 Children's imitations of syntactic constructions as a measure of linguistic competence. *Journal of Verbal Learning and Verbal Behavior.* **10:** 430-443.

Ross, John Robert
1970 On declarative sentences. In *Readings in English transformational grammar,* edited by Roderick A. Jacobs and Peter S. Rosenbaum. Waltham, Massachusetts: Ginn. Pp. 222-272.

Ryan, Joanna
1974 Early language development: Toward a communicational analysis. In *The integration of the child into a social world,* edited by Martin P.M. Richards. London: Cambridge Univ. Press, pp. 185-213.

Sacks, Harvey
1972 An initial investigation of the usability of conversational data for doing sociology. In *Studies in social interaction,* edited by David Sudnow. New York: Free Press, pp. 31-74.

Sacks, Harvey, Emanuel A. Schegloff, and Gail Jefferson
1974 A simplest systematics for the organization of turn-taking for conversation. *Language,* **50:** 696-735.

Sadock, Jerrold M.
1974 *Toward a linguistic theory of speech acts.* New York: Academic Press.

Sankoff, G. and P. Brown
1976 On the origins of syntax in discourse: A case study of Tok Pisin relatives. *Language,* **52:** 631-666.

Sankoff, G. and S. Laberge
1973 On the acquisition of native speakers by a language. *Kivung: Journal of Linguistic Society of Papuan New Guinea.* **6**: 32-47.

Schegloff, Emanuel A.
1968 Sequencing in conversational openings. *American Anthropologist.* **70**: 1075-1095.

Schegloff, Emanuel and Harvey Sacks
1973 Opening up closings. *Semiotica.* **8**: 289-327.

Scollon, Ronald
1973 A real early stage: An unzippered condensation of a dissertation on child language. Department of Linguistics, University of Hawaii, Working Papers in Linguistics. **5**:6, 67-81.

Scribner, Sylvia and Michael Cole
1973 Cognitive consequences of formal and informal education. *Science* **182**: 553-559.

Searle, John
1969 *Speech acts: An essay in the philosophy of language.* London: Cambridge Univ. Press.

Searle, John
1975 Indirect speech acts. In *Syntax and Semantics,* Vol. III, edited by Peter Cole and Jerry L. Morgan. New York: Academic Press.

Shatz, M. and R. Gelman
1973 The development of communication skills: Modifications in the speech of young children as a function of listener. Monographs of the Society for Research in Child Development. **38**: Serial No. 152.

Shatz, Marilyn
1974 The comprehension of indirect directives: Can two-year-olds shut the door? Paper presented at Linguistic Society of America, Summer Meeting.

Shatz, Marilyn
1975 How young children respond to language: Procedures fo answering. *Papers and reports on child language development,* No. 10. Stanford: Committee on Linguistics.

Sinclair-de-Zwart, Hermina
1969 Developmental psycholinguistics. In *Studies in cognitive development,* edited by David Elkind and John Flavell. London and New York: Oxford Univ. Press, pp. 315-336.

Sinclair, John and R.M. Coulthard
1975 *Towards an analysis of discourse: The English used by teachers and pupils.* London and New York: Oxford Univ. Press.

Slobin, Dan I.
1968 Imitation and grammatical development in children. In *Contemporary issues in developmental psychology,* edited by N.S. Endler *et al.* New York: Holt, Rinehart and Winston, pp. 437-443.

Slobin, Dan I.
1973[a] Cognitive prerequisites for the development of grammar. In *Studies in Child Language Development,* edited by C. Ferguson and D.I. Slobin. New York: Holt, pp. 175-208.

Slobin, D.
1973[b] *The Ontogenesis of Grammar.* Working Paper No. 33, Language Behavior Research Laboratory. Berkeley: University of California.

Snow, Catherine E. and Charles A. Ferguson
n.d. *Talking to children: Language input and acquisition.* London: Cambridge Univ. Press. (in press)

Speier, Matthew
1969 The organization of talk and socialization practices in family household interaction. Unpublished doctoral dissertation, University of California, Berkeley.

Stalnaker, Robert
1970 Pragmatics. *Synthese,* 22: 272-289.

Stalnaker, Robert
1972 Pragmatics. In *Semantics of natural language,* edited by D. Davidson and G. Harman. Dordrecht, Holland: Reidel.

Stern, C. and W. Stern
1907 *Die kindersprache.* Leipzig.

Stern, D.N.
1974 Mother and infant at play: The dyadic interaction involving facial, vocal, and gaze behaviors. In *The effect of the infant on its caregiver,* edited by M. Lewis and L. Rosenblum. New York: Wiley.

Stewart, William
1964 Urban Negro speech: Sociolinguistic factors affecting English teaching. In *Social dialects and language learning,* edited by Roger W. Shuy. Champaign, Illinois: National Council of Teachers of English. Pp. 10-19.

Sudnow, David (Editor)
1972 *Studies in social interaction.* New York: Free Press.

Sugarman, Susan
1973 A description of communicative development in the pre-language child. Hampshire College.

Turner, Roy (Editor)
1974 *Ethnomethodology.* Harmondsworth, England: Penguin.

Vygotsky, Lev S.
1962 *Thought and language.* Cambridge, Massachusetts: M.I.T. Press.

Watson, Karen Ann
1972 The rhetoric of narrative structure: A sociolinguistic analysis of stories told by part-Hawaiian children. Unpublished doctoral dissertation. University of Hawaii.

Watson, Karen Ann
1973 A rhetorical and sociolinguistic model for the analysis of narrative. *American Anthropologist,* 75: 243-264.

Watson, Karen Ann
1975 Transferable communicative routines: Strategies and group identity in two speech events. *Language in Society.* 4: 53-72.

Weeks, Thelma
1970 Speech registers in young children. In *Papers and reports on child language development,* No. 1. Stanford University, Committee on Linguistics. Pp. 22-42.

Weir, Ruth H.
1962 *Language in the crib.* The Hague: Mouton.

Index

A

Abrahams, Roger D., 64
Abstracts, 93–94, 102, 115
Accommodation, 9, 10, 16
Account
  indirect speech, 188
  terminology, 188
Acknowledgment, 134
Acquisition
  of communicative competence, 6, 105
  language, 3, 103–104
Activity
  social, 1, 2, 4, 109
  speech, 111, 112, 203
Address
  forms of, 198
  terms, 3, 11, 46, 188, 212
Addressee, 184
  age of, 11, 23, 185, 188
  familiarity of, 11
  power of, 11
  rank of, 3
  sex of, 3
  status of, 11, 23, 192, 202
Adjunct, to directive, 5
Africans, West, 15
Age
  of addressee, 11, 23, 185, 188
  relative, of subjects, 10, 16, 233
  of speaker, 2, 16
  variants in speech, 46
Age change, in narrative structure, 101, 102
Agreeing, 128
Aksu, Ayhan, 171, 174, 176, 179
Allegations, 89
  sexual, 15, 70–75
Alternation (rules), *see* Rules
American
  adult English, 206
  blacks, 15, 191–208
  children, 21, 49–65
  girls, 16, 91–103
Ames, Louise Bates, 68, 88
Analysis
  level of, 2
  linguistic, 2
  see also Pragmatic analysis
Appropriateness
  norms of, 104
  pragmatic, 140
  situational, 207
  see also Judgments
Arguments, 49–65
Assertions, 52–53, 59–60, 137
Assumptions, shared, 105
Attention, getting, 4
Attributing, 141
Audience, 4, 241
  stimulation by, 85
Austin, John L., 142

B

Babbling, 30
Baby talk, 4, 45–46
  in role playing, 45
Background features, *see* Features
Bailey, Charles-James N., 4
Baker, Erica, 180
Barker, Roger G., 112
Bates, Elizabeth, 104, 105, 154, 172, 174, 186, 187
Bateson, Gregory, 28, 108
Begging, 200
Belize (West Indian), 15

Bellugi, Ursula, 125, 133, 139
Berkeley, 176
Bernstein, Basil, 17, 64
Bernstein, Louise, 74, 84, 90
Black American, 13
  children, 191–208
  English, 91
  girls, 16, 91–102
Bloom, Lois, 125, 127, 129, 138
Blurton-Jones, Nicholas C., 105
Boggs, Stephen T., 14–17, 21, 27, 67–90
Bowyer, J., 110, 111
Brady, Margaret, 27
Braine, Martin, 127, 130
Brenneis, Donald, 14, 15, 19, 49–65, 76
Bribes, 15, 51
Britton, James, 34
Brown, Penelope, 3
Brown, Roger
  and Bellugi, 125, 133, 139
  and Gilman, 222
Brunner, Jerome S., 41, 105, 109, 212
Burke, Kenneth, 53

C

Categories
  function, 174
  lexical, 13
  social, 10, 22
Carter, Anne, 12, 172–174
Cedergren, Henrietta, 2
Chong, Edison, 87
Chukovsky, Kornei, 27
Cicourel, Aaron, 106
Clark, Carolyn, 188,
Clark, Eve, 103
Chant, 31
Checks, 134, 135
Codas, function of, 96
Code
  elaborated, 18
  restricted, 18
  switching, 2
Cognitive development, 22, 211
Cognitive operations, 212, 222
Cole, Michael, 110
Commands, 52, 168, 169, 189, 190,
    238–239
Communication
  ethnography of, 1, 5, 15
  system, 103
Communicative ability, 222
Communicative competence
  acquisition of, 6, 105, 225–243
  defined, 225
  functions, 226
  interpretive, 225
  within age groups, 229, *see also*
    Competence
Communicative intent, *see* Intent
Communicative skill, 105
Communicative strategies, 199, 211, 212
Competence
  communicative, 90, 130, 133, 207, 212
  difference in by milieu and age, 219–223
  grammatical, 19
  linguistic, 6
Compliance, 144
Comprehension, 22, 211, 223
  task, 219–222
Constraints, relevant, 4
Context, 126, 140
  linguistic, 2
  semantic, 107
  situational, 1
  social, 1, 2, 171
  speech, 110, 171
Contextual factors, 201
Contingency relations, 140
Contradicting routines, 15, 75–82, 89
Contrapuntal structure of narratives, 69, 75,
    80, 89
Conversation, natural, 1, 3
  entering, leaving, 4
  see also Rules
Conversational analysis, 1
Conversational implication, 162
Conversational postulates, 40
Conversational strategies, 156
Co-occurrence rules, 4
Cook-Gumperz, Jenny, 9, 10, 17, 18,
    103–121, 211
Corsaro, William, 19
Coulthard, R. Malcolm, 4, 5, 10, 167, 169
Creole, 3

D

Davison, Anni, 41
Day, Richard, 70
Deference, 205, 213
Demands, 53, 179, 204
Denials, 52
Denying, 141
Describing, 141

Development
cognitive, 22, 211
grammatical, 19
linguistic, 22, 103–104, 125, 211
Dialectic, 8, 15
Dialogue, *see* Narratives
Digressions, handling of, 4
Directive, 5, 11, 20–21, 109–110, 142, 160, 165–208, 238
domain of, 162
marker of, 168
types of, 166–167
permission, 166, 179, 185, 192, 194, 197
question, 166, 170, 183, 185, 192, 194, 198
Discourse
children's, 125–138
regulation, 162
rules, 49
structure, 11, 60
types, 10
units, 2, 55
Distance, 213
Dominance, 202
Dore, John, 20, 139–163, 172–174
Duncan, Starkey, 4

E

Eckhardt, Rosalind, 27
Edelsky, Carole, 22–23, 225–243
Egocentrism, 10, 149
Elaboration
linguistic, 22
narrative, 91–102
Emphasis, 101
English
American, 91, 195, 206
British, 174
Standard, 91
Environment, social, 212
Ervin-Tripp, Susan, 1–23, 64, 125, 127, 129, 132, 139, 150, 155, 160, 163, 165–199, 204, 206, 211, 226
Escalation, 56, 62
Eshleman, S., 30
Ethnography of communication, *see* Communication
Evaluation
clauses, 95, 98–100
in teaching, 118–119
Exchange, 162
Expansions, 19
Explaining, 141
Explicitness, 179

F

Face-to-face interaction, 111, 115
Family situations, 195
Features
background, 104
interpretive, 104
negotiated, 113, 119
speech, 21
stylistic, 53
Fiji, 14, 56
Fillmore, Lily, 10
Flavell, John H., 216
Focus, of speaker, 208
Focused interaction, 4
Foregrounding, 105
Freedle, Roy O., 127
French, Robert, 15
Function
of abstracts, 93–94, 102, 115
categories, 174
of codas, 96
of communicative competence, 226
of directives, 199, 202, 203, 206, 207
of evaluation clauses, 95, 100
expressive, 101, 102
interpersonal, 201
of introducers, 93–94, 102
of language, 2–3
of orientation clauses, 94, 102, 115–116
see also Speech functions

G

Gallimore, Ronald, 86
Game, 9, 11, *see also* Play
Garvey, Catherine, 4, 5, 12, 13, 14, 20, 21, 27–47, 143, 154, 155, 162, 166, 174, 176, 177, 179, 189
Gearhart, Maryl, 163
Gelman, Rochel, 10, 45, 212
Genres, 12
Gilman, Albert, 222
Givón, Talmy, 135
Gleason, J., 11, 45, 46
Goffman, Erving, 4, 5
Gordon, David, 21, 167, 189
Grammar, 2, 211
Grammatical
agreement, 162

analysis, 3
competence, 19
development, 19
operators, 143
Grammaticality, 1, 229
Greeting, 43
Grice, H. P., 40, 104, 140–141
Gruber, Jeffrey, 174
Gumperz, John, 1, 4, 5, 14, 106, 107, 108

H

Halliday, Michael A.K., 3, 28, 104, 105, 143, 165, 172–174
Hawaiian, 15–17, 21, 67–90
Herasimchuk, Eleanor, 5, 14
Hints, 167, 170, 172, 176, 185, 188, 189, 192, 194, 198
Hogan, Robert, 29
Holden, Marjorie H., 35
Hollos, Marida, 16, 19, 21–23, 187, 211–223
Holzman, Mathilda, 175
Hymes, Dell, 1, 6, 12, 53, 64, 96, 107, 133, 190, 225

I

Illocutionary acts, 140, 144, 147
Illocutionary force, 129, 131, 142, 190
Imbedding, 11
Imitation, 83, 85, 126, 130, 131, 137
Imitations, 21
Imperative
communication, 109–110, 113
force, 104
traps, 204–206
Imperatives, 3, 17, 120, 166, 170, 179, 181, 183–184, 186, 188, 190, 192, 194, 197, 201, 204, 207
imbedded, 166, 181, 184–185, 188, 192, 194, 196–197
modified, 188
negative, 184, *see also* Directives
Indians, West, 17
Indicative force, 104
Indirectness vs. explicitness, 179
Inference
active, 179
logical, 168
Information, identifying, 10
Instruction, 114–115, 118
Instructional style, 17, 116
Instructions, 103–121
Insults, 51, 58, 73, 77, 78, 80–87, 206
Intent, 4, 191, 201
communicative, 104, 126, 128, 142, 145–147, 168
conveyed, 167
deflection of, 9
directive, 176, 178, 188
lexicalized, 105
multiple levels, 191
performative, 107
Intentional focus, 208
Interaction
adult, 114
focused, 4
Interpretation, 5, 20
Interpretive ability, 104
Interpretive features, *see* Features
Interpretive rules, *see* Rules
Interview, 1
Intimacy, 213
Intonation, 17, 43, 55, 83, 108, 114, 116, 117, 187, 196
Introducers, 93–94, 102
Introspections, 1
Inventions, 7
Inversion, 51, 56
Isola, Suzanne, 188
Italian, 19, 21, 172, 174, 175, 177, 186

J

Jacobs, Deborah, 187
James, Sharon, 185, 186
Jefferson, Gail, 4
Johnson, Harriet M., 31
Jokes, 10, 206
Joking, 114, *see also* Pun
Judgments
appropriateness, 22, 187
categorical, 229–230, 232–238
language and sex association
adults, 230–233, 237–243
children, 233–243
methods, 22
over-generalized, 241–243
of politeness, 186–187
of profanity, 233–237, 239–243
sex of judge, 233–240
social, 22
strategies, 234–238

K

Katz, Jerrold J., 141, 143

Kay, Paul, 109
Keenan, Elinor, 4, 9, 14, 18–20, 33, 35, 104, 105, 114, 125–138
Kernan, Keith T., 3, 5, 7, 11, 15, 16, 17, 21, 22, 53, 91–102, 189–208
Key, 12, 13, 28
  humor, 41
Kinesics, 83, 85, 89, 104, 106, 108, 143
Kirtley, Basil F., 73
Klein, Ewan, 131, 134
Knowledge, 17, 220

L

Laberge, Suzanne, 3
Labov, William, 1, 2, 7, 16, 22, 64, 65, 91–93, 95–96, 100–101, 114–115, 226, 229
Lakoff, Robin, 21, 167, 228, 230
  and Gordon, 189
Lambert, Wallace E., 22
Langendoen, D. Terrance, 140
Language
  acquisition, 3, 104
  change, 2, 3
  development, 22, 103–104, 125, 211
  functions, 2–3
  planning, 3
  and sex role stereotypes, 225–243
  shifting, 3
  socialization, 9, 103–121
Lawson, Craig, 183
Lein, Laura, 14, 15, 19, 49–65, 76
Leventhal, Constance, 9
Lewis, D., 143
Lexical categories, 3
Lexicalization, 168
Lexicon, 188
Lieberman, Alicia, 29
Linguistic
  analysis, *see* Analysis
  competence, *see* Competence
  context, *see* Context
  elaboration, 22
  pragmatics, *see* Pragmatics
  repertoires, 188–212
  rules, *see* Rules
Location effect, 219–222

M

MacGinitie, Walter H., 35
Macnamara, John, 180
Mac Whinney, Brian, 174, 185
Mays, Violet, 70
Meaning, 11, 104, 105
  conveyed, 17, 107–108
  literal, 143, 168
  negotiated, 18
  referential, 17, 107
  situated, 17, 107–109
  social, 3, 22, 170–171
Menyuk, Paula, 125
Message, 105–106
Miller, Wick, 174
Mimicry, 82–85
  in narrative dialogues, 16
Miscommunication, 105
Misnaming, 40–41
Mitchell-Kernan, Claudia, 1–23, 49, 53, 91, 160, 163, 176, 189–208
Mocking, 15, 83

N

Narrative, 16, 67–102, 114–115
  dialogue in, 16
  extended, 93
  orientation in, 16, 17, 68, 88
  skill, 16
  structure, 16, 92–93, 114–115
  see also Mimicry
Negotiation, 9, 10, 108
Nelson, Katherine, 103
Newman, Denis, 163
Nonsense, 12, 13
Nonsense verse, 38–40
Nonverbal behavior, *see* Kinesics
Norwegian, 21
Norms, of peers, 7
Novinski, Lorraine, 180

O

O'Connell, Beth Ann, 176, 184
Ojibwa, 21
Opie, Iona and Peter, 7, 27
Orientation
  in narratives, *see* Narratives
  in teaching, *see* Teaching
Orientation clauses, 94, 99–100, 102, 115–116

P

Paralinguistics, 2, 85, 108, 109
Paraphrase, 98–99

Participants, 2, 4, 189, *see also* Speaker, Addressee, Audience
Performance, 20, 22, 106, 108
Performatives, 3
Perlocutionary effect, 142
Personal situations, 193, 196, 198, 203
Persuasion, 9
Phonology, 108
Piaget, 13, 16, 19, 126, 172, 211, 216
Pidgin, 3
Pitch, 196
Play
  definition of, 28
  pattern practice, 34
  pragmatic, 40, 155
  procedure, 162
  ritual, 30
  role, 3, 11, 13, 15, 16, 21, 22, 23, 32, 45–47, 50–51, 83, 89, 191–192, 194, 196–199, 201–202, 206, 207
  sound, 12, 13
  speech, 27–47
  verbal, 27, 30, 67–90
Poetry, poems, 7, 8
Politeness, 9, 184, 185, 188, *see also* Judgments of politeness
Polynesian, 73
Pragmatic analysis, 139–163
Pragmatics, 40–45, 154
  linguistic, 140
Praise, 52
Pretending, 9, 12
Principle of contrastivity, 28
Production, 22
  joint, 15, 80, 87
Profanity
  judgment of, 233–237, 239–243
Pronouns, selection, 2, 11, 22, 211–223
Prosody, 104, 106, 113, 117, 119–120 143, 173–176
Protest, 144
Psycholinguistics, 127–131
Pun, 168

Q

Querying, 4, 79, 128, 162
Question, 20
  directives, 166, 170, 183, 192, 194
  egocentric, 149
  as imperatives, 188
  information, 207
  responses to, 139–163
  tag, 46, 233, 236, 239

R

Rank of participants, 3, 193–196, 199, 201, 203, 207
Reduplication, 31
Reeder, Ken, 182
Referential function, 100
Reisman, Karl, 75
Relationship status, 201
Repertoires, 3, 19, 22, 178, 188, 212
Repetition, 8, 9, 18–19, 35, 43, 56, 61, 77, 96–97, 117–118, 125–138
  in insults, 58
Requests, 3, 21, 30, 43, 185–186, 190, 199, 245
  action, 143
  begging, 200
  indirect, 200
  permission, 183–184
Replies, 149–151
  answering questions, imitation in, 130
Resolution, 119–120
Reversibility of perspectives, 222
Reynolds, P., 28
Rhyming, 13, 35, 38
Rodd, Linda J., 127, 130
Role
  norms, 5
  playing test, 212
  relations, 189, 199, 200
  role play, *see* Play
  sex, 3, 191, 225, 243
  social, 10, 212
  stereotypes, 225–241
Ross, John R., 3
Round, 14
Routines, 67–90
  contradicting, 75–82, 89
  definition of, 43
  dramatization, 82–85
  primitive, 10
Rules
  alternation, 3
  contextualizing, 110
  conversation, 79
  co-occurrence, 4
  for directives, 169
  discourse, 49
  interpretation, 2
  interpretive, 15, 140, 167, 168, 171
  linguistic, 3, 212, 213, 218–219

normative choice, 5
realization, 3
selection, 11
sequential, 4, 5
social, 212, 222
sociolinguistic, 3, 187
speech event, 4
systems, 29
violations of, 4, 41
Ryan, Joanna, 104, 134

S

Sacks, Harvey, 4, 10, 109, 132
Sarcasm, 51, 171
Sadock, Jerrold, 3
Sankoff, Gillian, 2, 3
Schieffelin, Bambi, 4
Schlegloff, Emanuel A., 1, 4, 43, 132
Scollon, Ronald, 19, 125
Scribner, Sylvia, 110
Searle, John, 41, 142, 154, 166, 167, 179
Semantic
choices, 116
context, 107
presupposition, 154
strategies, 14, 15
Sequences, 55–56, 61–62, 115
in arguments, 55
beginning, 120
closing, 119–120
joking, 114
of turns, 43
Setting, 1, 2, 4, 102, 104, 105, 106, 107, 126, 179, 225, 241
family, 193
linguistic, 126
social, 212–215
work, 193
Sex, 2
and language association, *see* Judgments of speaker, 235
Shatz, Marilyn, 10, 45, 180, 181, 212
Shuy, Roger, 4
Sinclair, John, 4, 5, 10, 167, 169
Sinclair de Zwart, Hermina, 211
Sincerity conditions, 189
Situation
family, 195, 197
personal, 193, 196, 198, 203
social, 195, 212, 213
speech, 189, 199
transactional, 193–195, 203
Slobin, Dan, 104, 125, 127, 128, 133, 211
Social, system, 10, *see also* Specific categories
Socialization, language, 9, 103–121
Sociolinguistic rules, *see* Rules
Sociolinguistic skills, 9
Sociolinguistics, 1–2
child, 5–12
Speech acts, 18–22, 36, 41–44, 51–52, 96, 110, 129, 132–133, 141–142, 165, 188, 189, 207–208
coding of, 143–148
indirect, 179
taxonomy of, 20
see also Individual speech acts
Speech
non-social, 29
private, 35
Speech community, 92, 189, 191, 200, 225, 242
Speech events, 3, 12–18, 23, 49, 65, 67–90, 225
Speech features, *see* Features
Speech functions, 19, 78, 189–190
Speech play, *see* Play
Speech situation, 189, 199
Speech strategies, *see* Strategies
Speed, 53, 54
Speier, Matthew, 7, 11, 13–14, 174
Stalnaker, Robert, 40, 140
Statements, 77, 146, 207
desire, 183
need, 188, 192
Status, 10, 46, 205, 207
of addressee, 23, 194, 202
relationship, 201
Stern, Clara and William, 36
Stern, D.N., 30
Stewart, William, 7
Story, 67–90, *see also* Narrative
Strategies, 5, 49, 176–178, 217
children's, 117
communicative, 109, 211, 213
conversational, 156
indirect, 199
judgment, 236–238
semantic, 14, 15
speed, 110–111, 113
stylistic, 61
topic, 239
Stress, 31–32, 53, 54, 108, 116, 117
Structure
discourse, 11, 60

narrative, 16, 92-93, 114-115
sequential, 15
surface, 15, 189
syntactic, 106
Style, 55, 65
joking, 114
switching, 4
Stylistic
elements, 61
features, *see* Features
strategies, *see* Strategies
Sudnow, David, 1
Sugarman, Susan, 105
Summaries
in narratives, 18, 68
in teaching, 17
Switching
code, 2
prosody, 113
style, 4
Syntax, 106, 128, 188
Systems
communication, 103
role, 11, 216
social, 10

T

"Talking funny," 32
Tasks
as content, 184
difficulty of, 197
Teaching, 17, 111-121
orientation in, 116
Teasing, 70, 83-89
sexual, 170-175
Test, role playing, 212
Text structure, 5
Threats, 41-42, 51-52, 77, 86
Tok Pisin, 3
Topic, 3, 4, 136-137, 225, 234-235, 241
comment, 9
continuity, 169-170
shifting, 4, 9, 19
Topicalization, 135-138
Transactional situation, 193-196, 203
Turkish, 21, 171, 174-176, 179
Turner, Roy, 1
Turn filling, 28
taking, 13-16, 20, 86-87, 89-90
Turns, 2, 4, 140, 143
Tying, 14
in narratives, 99

U

Utterances, definition of, 29

V

Variability, 2, 4
Verbal play, 17-47, 67-90
Voice qualities, 198
Volume, 53, 54
Vygotsky, Lev, 13

W

Waletsky, Joshua, 16, 92, 95, 96, 101
Watson-Gegeo, Karen Ann, 14-17, 27, 67-90, 95, 114
Weeks, Thelma, 4, 229
Weir, Ruth, 34, 35, 125
Wells, Gordon, 20
Wright, Herbert, 112

Y

Young, Christine, 188

A
B 7
C 8
D 9
E 0
F 1
G 2
H 3
I 4
J 5

Date Due

AUG 9 '88			
DEC 17 1988			
APR 24 1989			